Tenth Edition

Fred J. Hecklinger

Bernadette M . Black

NATIONAL CERTIFIED CAREER COUNSELORS

TRAINING

for *Life*

A Practical Guide to Career & Life Planning

Kendall Hunt
publishing company
4050 Westmark Drive • P O Box 1840 • Dubuque IA 52004-1840

Book Team

Chairman and Chief Executive Officer   Mark C. Falb
President and Chief Operating Office   Chad M. Chandlee
Vice President, Higher Education   David L. Tart
Director of National Book Program   Paul B. Carty
Editorial Development Manager   Georgia Botsford
Developmental Editor   Denise M. LaBudda
Assistant Vice President, Production Services   Christine E. O'Brien
Senior Production Editor   Charmayne McMurray
Permissions Editor   Elizabeth Roberts
Cover Designer   Jenifer Chapman

Train image on cover © copyright Mikael Damkier, 2009.
Used under license from Shutterstock, Inc.

BRIEF CONTENTS

CONTENTS

PREFACE

After more than 63 combined years in the field of career and life planning, we are committed to the following concepts and values.

1. Adults are fully capable of making career and life decisions for themselves.

2. When adults become actively involved in establishing career and life plans, they are happier, more satisfied, and feel more in control of the direction of their lives.

3. Throughout their lives, adults search for personal and career satisfaction and need to carefully analyze each transition along the way.

4. Adults have the power to change, to grow, and to achieve their own definition of success.

5. Life satisfaction comes from successfully integrating career and lifestyle so that they complement each other.

6. Adults can learn to manage their careers and to maintain fulfilling lifestyles.

7. Adults can progress most effectively by building on their strengths and by seeking to expand the positive options in their lives.

8. The career and life planning process never ends. Planning for retirement is just as important as planning for another career. Planning is important even after retirement in order to maintain a rewarding and fulfilling lifestyle.

We have written *Training for Life: A Practical Guide to Career and Life Planning* to help adults develop their career and life objectives, decide how to achieve these objectives, and take action in making career and life decisions. It is impossible to separate career from lifestyle. Individuals are not one-dimensional. This book deals with career and lifestyle as an integrated whole, taking the reader through more traditional career planning topics of self-awareness, job investigation, and job campaign, while also addressing the equally important topics of change, job enhancement, and healthy lifestyle characteristics.

We believe that adults can grow and flourish by taking an active role in planning their careers and lives. This text can be used as a workbook in classes, in individual counseling, in workshops, and as a self-instructional aid. Use a pencil or a pen as you read this book. Fill in the checklists, answer the questions, and take an active role in shaping and molding your future.

ACKNOWLEDGMENTS

Training for Life was first published by Kendall/Hunt in 1982. Over the past 27 years, our book, through nine revisions, has been read by thousands of adults, used as a resource by hundreds of counselors, and helped job hunters who found it on library shelves. We continue to be pleased by its influence and proud of its use by adults who seek to understand themselves and to grow throughout life's journey.

In the early 1980s, we were motivated to write and publish a career/life planning text because of the absence of adult-focused career resources. It was important to translate existing career and adult development theories for adult community college students with whom we were privileged to work.

While many career and life planning books and resources designed especially for adults are now available in most bookstores, *Training for Life* remains a pioneer in the career/life planning field. The breadth of topics, variety of resources, and self-directed approach speak to adults who are engaged in planning their future. We are proud of the history, longevity, and contents of *Training for Life*.

We are indebted, first and foremost, to our immediate families for their loving support and encouragement:

Margaret C. Hecklinger, who has contributed significantly to many revisions,

John M. Hecklinger, Thomas L. Barnes, Allison A. Curtin, and Kevin R. Curtin.

In addition, we express our appreciation to our colleagues and friends within the Virginia Community College System, especially those at Northern Virginia Community College, Alexandria Campus, and at the University of Virginia. Our special gratitude goes to Nancy Wallace, who updated the resources and references for this edition. A special thank you goes to our colleagues at Kendall/Hunt Publishing Company for their editorial expertise.

Fred Hecklinger

Bernadette Black

ABOUT THE AUTHORS

Fred J. Hecklinger, Ph.D.

Fred J. Hecklinger, retired Professor Emeritus at Northern Virginia Community College, served for 28 years as Coordinator of Counseling Services and Dean of Student Development at the College's Alexandria Campus. Currently, he provides professional counseling services at the Federal Deposit Insurance Corporation, the Transportation Security Administration, and The United States Department of State. In addition, he delivers seminars on the transition to retirement for the National Institute for Transition Planning. He is a guide at Frank Lloyd Wright's Pope-Leighey House, a property of the National Trust for Historic Preservation, and at the National Building Museum. He is a Licensed Professional Counselor in Virginia and a National Certified Career Counselor. He has a bachelor's degree in chemistry, a master's degree in education, and a doctorate in counseling. He is an avid opera fan, golf enthusiast, and welcomes any opportunity to travel.

Bernadette M. Black, Ed.D.

Bernadette M. Black is enjoying the fruits of her labor as *Training for Life* clearly recommends! Her recent retirement has opened new possibilities and adventures for volunteer service, travel, golf, learning, part time work and tending overlooked areas of life. Her goal to expand and nourish individual aspiration for the common good thrives. With 35 years as an educator in higher education, she advised and taught master's and doctoral students as the Director of the Social Foundations of Education program for University of Virginia's Northern Virginia Center in Falls Church. She also served as Director of Professional Development for the Virginia Community College System, where she created and implemented a nationally award winning program for faculty in Virginia's 23 community colleges. At Northern Virginia Community College she directly served a diverse student population as a counselor and professor. Bernadette is a National Certified Career Counselor and her doctorate was earned from UVA in counselor education. She presently resides in Vienna, Virginia, with her husband, Tom, where she continues to cultivate the individual aspirations of their six children, their spouses, and grandchildren.

INTRODUCTION

Training for Life: A Practical Guide to Career and Life Planning can be your ticket to a better, more satisfying future. This book, together with your thoughts, feelings, and experiences, will help you to assess your strengths, interests, and values and to examine your lifestyle. You will be provided with a route to manage your career and to create the lifestyle that is best for you. This book will help you to:

- Develop some short- and long-range goals for your career and lifestyle planning while remaining open to new possibilities along the way

- Gain an appreciation of the transitions in your life

- Make informed decisions and commitments about your career

- Actively plan your future

- Create your own luck

- Develop a lifestyle plan that will extend into retirement

- Revitalize your present job or career

- Look at the big picture rather than at each part of your life as a separate entity

TRAINING FOR LIFE

Compare your journey through life to a train trip. You are constantly moving ahead, with many stops along the way. With every mile and every new passenger, the train changes. Each new person you meet and each new experience changes you. Just as the train will take on new passengers, employees, and supplies, and will eventually let them go, so will you take on new interests, friends, and skills. Some you will choose to keep and others you will let go. But just as the train keeps going, remaining basically the same, so do you keep going. You are changed by your experiences, but you always come back to **you**. **You alone** must make the decisions that significantly alter your journey through life.

As you wait at the train station, you are filled with anticipation and thoughts about the upcoming trip. What new experiences will you encounter? What different people will you meet and get to know along the way? What challenges lie around the corner? The tracks are visible only at the beginning. The end is nowhere in sight. The unknown can be exciting, a knot in your stomach, or a mix of both. As always, the choice is yours. Your trip is uniquely your own.

Just as the train picks up speed, slows down for tunnels and curves, and encounters bumpy tracks, delays, and detours, your journey through life will be marked by fast, slow, smooth, and rough travel. At times the direction in which you are headed may not seem very clear, but it is there, just as the train tracks are there. You may end up going in circles, but you still keep moving, just as time keeps moving. Whenever you come to a junction and have to decide which track to take, you must make a decision. Some of these decisions can significantly alter the direction of your life. **You** run your life, just as the engineer controls the train. You will be responsible for making decisions. You will have to invest time and energy on this journey, but the rewards will be well worth your investment. You will meet many new and interesting people and encounter a wide variety of experiences. Each person that comes into your life, and every unexpected occurrence teaches you something. Be an aware traveler with an eye to adventure and to expanding your experiences.

As you go through your career and life planning process, enlist the help of others who are a part of your life: family, friends, and colleagues. They can provide important advice, encouragement, support, and assistance, but they cannot take over your role as engineer of your trip through life. Listen to others, seek their help, and then make your decisions. This book will help you get the information you need to make critical life decisions and deal successfully with important life transitions. There are many routes to follow. There is no one right route for all people.

You may even need to create your own tracks for your trip. However, by using this book and by getting help from others, you will be better able to choose the route that is best for you.

You are now on your journey and have already traveled a long distance. Do you like the direction that your life is taking? Do you feel that you have control over where you are going? You must decide whether to take charge of your trip and be the engineer or simply be a passenger on your train, letting others make the critical decisions for you. The career and life planning process requires work, just as running a train is more work than being a passenger. However, this work can be rewarding and enjoyable. Put the process to work for you as you begin to establish your life and career goals. Start **now** to plan your trip and make the most of all the sights and experiences along the way.

THE CAREER AND LIFE PLANNING PROCESS

What is career and life planning and how can it help you? It enables you to make decisions about the time you spend in your career and your life. By following an organized approach to career and life decision making, you will be able to make more effective decisions now, and in five years, ten years, or twenty years. You will feel that you have more control over the course of your life. You may not always know exactly where you are headed, but by knowing and using the career and life planning process, you can make better decisions when you come to each junction along the way and have to choose between two or more routes.

The career and life planning process involves gathering information so that you can make realistic decisions based on facts and self-knowledge rather than on your own feelings or the suggestions of others. Think back to your last major purchase, perhaps a home or a car. How much time and energy did you spend researching and uncovering information about this purchase? What did you do to get the information you needed?

Home	Car
Ask neighbors	Research written evaluations
Inspect building	Talk with other owners
Talk with owners	Talk with salesperson
Talk with real estate agent	Talk with a mechanic
Talk with former owners	Test drive and inspect vehicle
Spend time in neighborhood	Go to other showrooms
Research home values	Look at competition
Talk with mortgage officer	Talk with loan officer

If you are employed full-time five days a week, 50 weeks a year, for 40 years, you will spend approximately 10,000 days or 80,000 hours at work. This is a major part of your life, certainly more important than any house or car purchase. Therefore, it is essential for you to take the time and action that are necessary to plan your career. In addition, take time to plan your nonworking hours so that you can create a fulfilling lifestyle. Your career and lifestyle are basic to your achievement of happiness and satisfaction with life. The investment of your time in the career and life planning process can have great rewards.

Richard Nelson Bolles did not define the career and life planning process, but he certainly continues to popularize and advocate the philosophy of self-empowerment. His widely read book, *What Color Is Your*

Parachute? (Bolles, 2008), has encouraged many to define career goals and find jobs with some measure of satisfaction while retaining personal dignity and confidence. Bolles has masterfully translated theory into practice. *Training for Life* also translates theory into practice, not by requiring you to write a detailed autobiography, but by providing exercises and checklists that stimulate self-examination and thought. The process is the same, the means vary, and the results will follow after careful and deliberate assessment of yourself.

The importance of the career and life planning process has been demonstrated by people who have studied the work life, career patterns, and personal needs of adults. For example, Abraham Maslow (1970) classified human needs within a hierarchy. Basic needs such as food, water, and safety are in the lower part of the hierarchy, while other needs such as love, knowledge, self-respect, and self-actualization form the upper part. People work not only to satisfy the more basic needs but also to fulfill their need for a sense of purpose, for self-worth, and for success. It is important to recognize work as an integral part of this sense of fulfillment. Of course, it is difficult to deal with the higher level needs if the lower level needs have not been met. In practical terms, it is difficult to deal with career satisfaction if one has not met basic human needs.

John Holland (1997) noted that people in similar occupations have similar personalities and personal preferences. In making a career decision, therefore, it is helpful for a person to consider careers that attract people with similar interests and personality characteristics. Interest in a career and in the people with whom one works is often the key to motivation. This is the basis of the extensive use of interest inventories in the career planning process. Holland developed six descriptive themes that are simple to explain and simple to understand. Based on the assumption that certain kinds of people tend to go into certain kinds of work, Holland's theory has withstood the test of time and has been accepted by many in the field of career and life planning.

David Tiedeman (1990) provided a model for career decision making that was based on the individual's ability to find answers within him- or herself. Tiedeman's holistic view of the individual was predicated on the belief that the individual has the power to create a career.

Donald Super's evolutionary view of career development illustrated the dynamic nature of this process. Super (1957) identified two major stages in career development: the exploratory stage and the establishment stage. Within these stages, he defined five major tasks:

1. Crystallization—considering career goals and formulating general preferences

2. Specification—investigating career options and ongoing self-examination

3. Implementation—setting out to achieve one's career goals and obtaining a job in the desired field

4. Stabilization—maintaining a position and developing competence in one's career

5. Consolidation—planning ahead for future career growth

Super's framework provided for the interrelatedness of roles—which include child, student, leisurite, citizen, spouse, homemaker, parent, and worker—and theaters—which include home, community, school, and workplace. To Super, career development was an ongoing process, involving continual change and evaluation throughout one's life.

Confirming the ever-changing nature of the adult developmental process is the work of Nancy Schlossberg (1981), Frederic Hudson (1997), William Bridges (1980), Daniel Levinson (1986, 1996) and others who have studied how adults progress through major and minor life transitions. Adults change their personal goals, career goals, and values throughout their lives. It is important to deal positively with change, to reassess one's dreams, and to adjust one's goals at various points in life. This periodic assessment and the action that is taken after the assessment—whether it be to change jobs, find a new career, develop new interests, or set new priorities—is very important in maintaining a positive outlook on life and in avoiding the crises that many adults confront. Erik Erikson (1959) maintained that people go through eight developmental stages. The last stage, integrity versus despair, is particularly crucial in dealing with the life and career planning process in the later years. It is very important to integrate one's life, to adjust one's dreams, and to maintain a positive approach to the years ahead, rather than to despair over lost opportunities and life's failures.

A career theory that holds particular promise is John Krumboltz's (2004) notion of career happenstance. His theory encourages adults to remain open to life's unexpected opportunities that often occur when we are least prepared and when we least expect them. While having a plan of action is important, it is also important sometimes to allow chance happenings to interfere with those plans, as these happenings may hold transformational opportunities. Krumboltz characterizes indecision as a normal part of the career process and maintains that adults need to welcome happenstance into their lives by listening to others, capitalizing on chance occurrences, and making the most of unexpected situations. Krumboltz encourages replacing anxiety about uncertainty with the spirit of adventure and exploration. It can be fulfilling to approach career and life planning with a sense of wonder, exuberance, and trust in the process for one's ability to arrive at the "right" destination.

Career and life planning is an ongoing process that is important for everyone. It does not stop at a specific age or when you enter the career of your choice. It even continues into retirement. For this reason, *Training for Life* provides chapters on dealing with change, making the most of your job, and on maintaining quality and balance in your life. There is no one right way to start the process, as long as you *do start.* You may wish to begin with Section One and work through the sections in order. However, you may want to start elsewhere in *Training for Life,* depending on where you are in the career and life planning process. Here are some suggestions:

- If you are just getting started and are considering a variety of different careers, start with Section One.
- If you need a job immediately and have an idea of what you want to do in the future, start with Section Four.
- If you have a job and feel that you cannot change jobs right now, but would like to investigate ways that you can make your job better and more rewarding, start with Section Five.
- If you are actively considering one or two careers but are not sure what the future holds or what the job market really is like, start with Section Three.
- If you feel that you need some kind of change in your life but are not sure just what to change, start with Section Two.
- If you are primarily concerned with establishing a fulfilling lifestyle, start with Section Six.

Do not feel that you have to make big decisions right away. Start working on this book. Talk with people. Set some short-term goals. Some examples of short-term goals are:

- Learn a new skill or "brush up" on a skill that you need in your job.
- Make one or two changes in your job that may increase your job satisfaction.
- Update your resumé.
- Make a change in your lifestyle, such as beginning an exercise program.
- Set up a few informational interviews.
- Take a course in a school or college.
- Investigate other job opportunities.
- Become involved in a community activity that intrigues you.
- Begin to plan for a second, third, or fourth career.
- Start to develop a viable retirement plan.

Use goals like these to help you get started with your career and life planning. The tracks on the following pages represent your trip through *Training for Life.* Get on the train at the point along the route that is the best for you right now. As you travel, remember that you have control over the direction of your train ride through life. Be the engineer of your personal train and watch the new horizons open up for you as you direct your exciting journey.

References

Bolles, R. N. (2008). *What color is your parachute?* Berkeley, California: Ten Speed Press.

Bridges, W. (2004). *Transitions: Making sense of life's changes*. (2nd ed.) Cambridge, MA: Perseus Books.

Erikson, E. (1959). *Identity and the life cycle*. Psychological Issues I.

Holland, J. L. (1997). *Making vocational choices: A theory of vocational personalities and work environments* (3rd ed.). Odessa, FL: Psychological Assessment Resources.

Hudson, F. M. (1997). *The adult years: Mastering the art of self-renewal*. San Francisco: Jossey-Bass.

Krumboltz, J. D. & Levin, A. S. (2004). *Luck is no accident: Making the most of happenstance in your life and career*. Atascadero, California: Impact Publishers.

Levinson, D. J. (1986). *The seasons of a man's life*. New York: Ballantine Books.

Levinson, D. J. & Levinson, J. D. (1996). *The seasons of a woman's life*. New York: Alfred A Knopf.

Maslow, A. (1970). *Motivation and personality* (2nd ed.). New York: Harper & Row.

Schlossberg, N. (1981). A model for analyzing human adaptation to transition. *The Counseling Psychologist, 9*, 2, 1–18.

Super, D. E. (1957). *The psychology of careers*. New York: Harper-Collins.

Tiedeman, D. V. & Miller-Tiedeman, A. (1990). Career decision-making: An individualistic perspective. In D. Brown and L. Brooks (Eds.) *Career choice and development* (2nd ed., pp 308–337). San Francisco: Jossey-Bass.

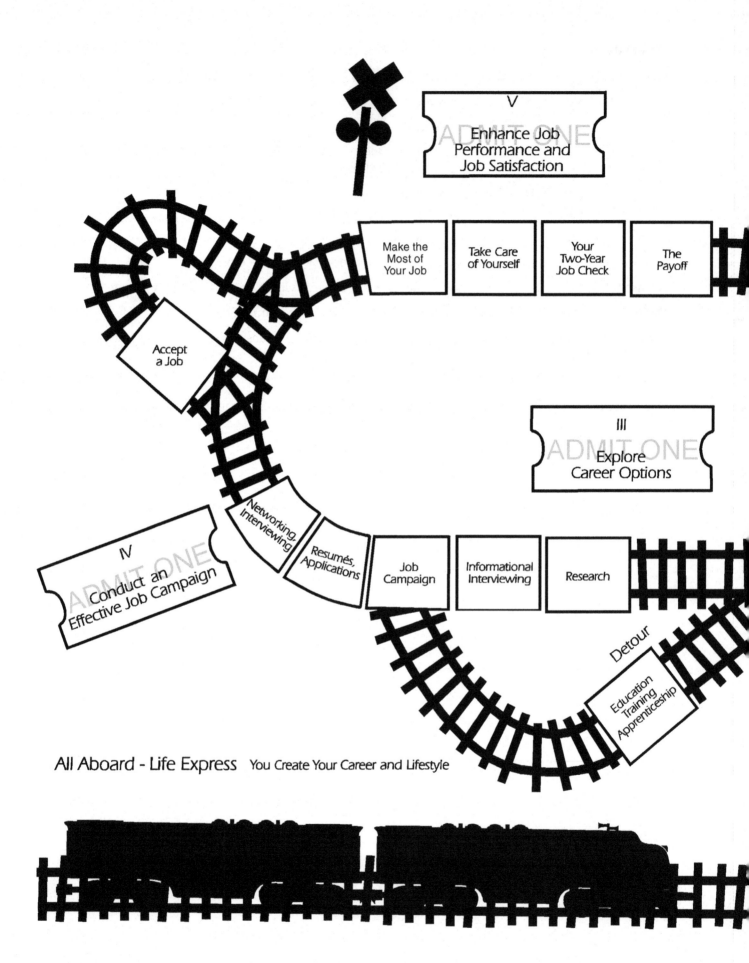

All Aboard - Life Express   You Create Your Career and Lifestyle

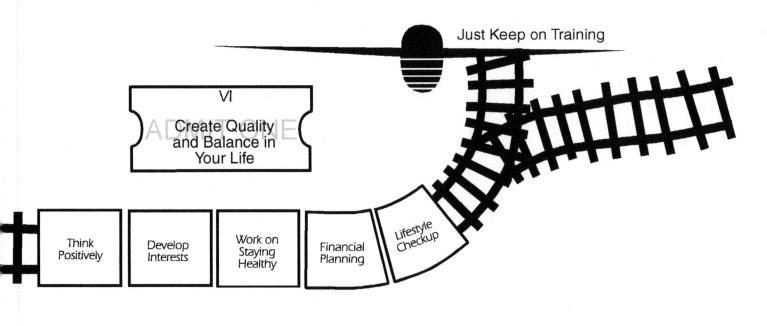

Just Keep on Training

VI

Create Quality
and Balance in
Your Life

ADMIT ONE

Think
Positively

Develop
Interests

Work on
Staying
Healthy

Financial
Planning

Lifestyle
Checkup

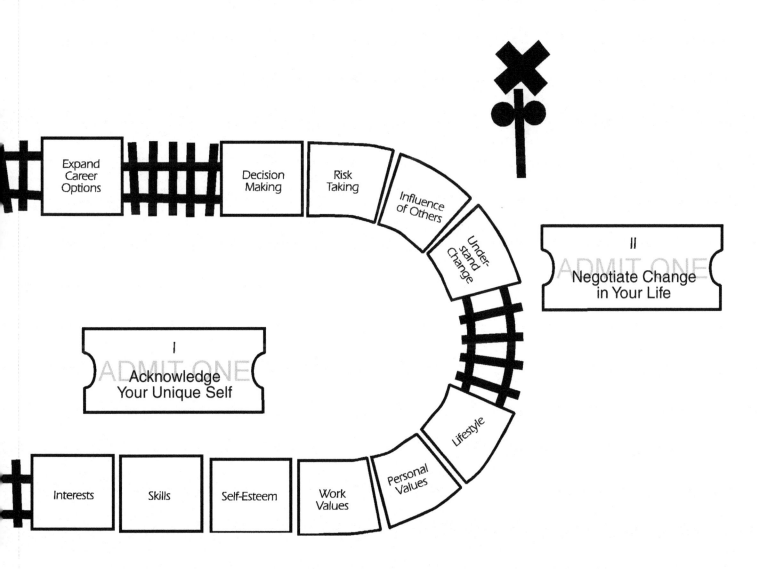

Expand
Career
Options

Decision
Making

Risk
Taking

Influence
of Others

Under-
stand
Change

II

Negotiate Change
in Your Life

ADMIT ONE

I

Acknowledge
Your Unique Self

ADMIT ONE

Interests

Skills

Self-Esteem

Work
Values

Personal
Values

Lifestyle

SECTION *one*

Acknowledge Your Unique Self

This section of *Training for Life* prompts you to evaluate several critical factors about yourself. These factors are significant as you consider creating an effective and meaningful career and life plan. Your life continues to evolve as you mature, develop, and grow. You are a unique combination of characteristics, values, needs, and goals. The lifestyle or career that is meaningful for a friend, parent, and relative may not be meaningful for you. You are the one who needs to make career and lifestyle decisions based on your own evaluation as you consider multiple life directions. To begin the process of career and life planning, ask yourself the following questions:

1. What are my work values? How important are these values in my assessment of a potential position or career?

2. What are my interests? How might I integrate my interests into a potential career?

3. What are my skills and abilities? What new skills would I like to learn? How might I enhance my existing abilities?

4. What are my personal values? How do these values affect my career and my way of life?

5. What confidence do I have in myself and in my ability to navigate life's transitions? How can I enhance my self-esteem?

6. What lifestyle considerations are important to me? How does my lifestyle complement my career and does my career complement my lifestyle?

These questions are important to consider whenever you make life and career decisions. If you are just beginning to decide what career you want, an analysis of these factors can help you to make better choices. If you are thinking about changing careers, it is important to ask yourself these questions before deciding what type of change you want. If you are thinking about starting a new career after having been a homemaker, answering these questions can help you to get started. Use the following information, checklists, and exercises to help you answer these and other questions. Supplement this work with discussions with family, friends, and counselors. There is no one right way to begin the life and career planning process. There are many ways to proceed and you can feel free to jump into this text whenever you want. Allow your curiosity to lead you through the exercises and checklists. The most important thing is to *do* something—don't procrastinate. Take an inventory of your own unique needs and characteristics. This is a good way to start.

> **The journey to authentic power requires that you become conscious of all that you feel.**
>
> —Gary Zukav, *Seat of the Soul*

CHAPTER 1

Work Values

Our first stop on this journey begins with work values. You now have the opportunity to consider what you value most in a current or potential position. This also serves as a logical point to launch your self-assessment since previous work experience will provide valuable information as you seek to discover:

- What is it that makes your work rewarding?

- What kind of physical surroundings are important to your effectiveness?

- What responsibilities do you seek in a position?

- How much contact with other people do you need to feel comfortable?

- What purpose will your work have for you, for your community, for our country, for the world?

These questions are not easily answered. The identification of your unique set of work values holds the potential key. Give serious thought to your priorities as you begin to assess previous working environments. The next few pages are designed to help you to gain some clarity about your work values.

WORK VALUES ASSESSMENT

Consider each of the following work values. Think about what you need for your work to be satisfying. Focus on what is important to you and not someone else. Use the scale to rate each value in terms of its importance to you. Think generally of any career or job that you would like to have and then rate each value as being very important, moderately important, or not important in terms of **your** job satisfaction. Place a check mark (✓) in the column that best represents your choice.

Work Value	Very Important	Moderately Important	Not Important
ENVIRONMENT			
Work in pleasant office surroundings			
Have my own office			
Work alone with minimal outside influences			
Collaborate with my work colleagues			
Work in a trusting environment			
Receive acknowledgement of my efforts at work			
Rely on supportive work colleagues			
Be respected as an authority in my field			
Contribute to my community			
Mentor others at work			
Accept and invite challenges			
Help others to learn and grow			
Be able to share my opinions freely			
Work in a large organization			
Work in an urban setting			
Take public transportation to work			
Work close to home with a short commute			
Work with my hands			
Develop transferable skills to build my credentials			
Use my physical skills in my work			
Use my mental skills in my work			
Use writing skills as a major component of my work			
Analyze and problem solve			
Resolve conflicts and make decisions			
Change laterally from one position to the next			
Advance from one position to the next			
Have social activities outside of work with colleagues			
Free to take risks			
Act without fear of mistakes or reprisal			

Work Value	Very Important	Moderately Important	Not Important
OUTCOMES			
Produce a visible end product most days			
Create something tangible			
Convince others to do something or buy something			
Accept few immediate results but gain long-term results			
Work steadily over time toward the end result			
Contribute in a significant way to a successful team outcome			
Use evaluations to improve my performance			
Correct my course of action based on feedback from others			
CONDITIONS			
Travel frequently			
Have flexible work hours			
Maintain regular work hours			
Telecommute by working at home a day or two a week			
Have access to the latest technology			
Work independently without much feedback			
Work in a large office with many colleagues			
Work in a high-energy, stimulating work setting			
Meet new people almost every day			
Work primarily outside, come rain or shine			
Work indoors			
Work at a desk in an office			
Have opportunities for learning through my work			
Participate in a variety of professional development activities			
Have good job security			
Make a commitment and stick with one organization			
Juggle multiple priorities and responsibilities			
Earn ample sick and vacation leave			
Earn overtime pay or other additional compensation			
Work little or no overtime			
Have a good retirement and benefits package			
Earn a high salary			
Experience minimum interference with home life/lifestyle			
Attend and participate in meetings			
Blend working alone and with colleagues			
Focus attention on making outside contacts			
Initiate a new business			
Be appreciated and respected for my work			

Work Value	Very Important	Moderately Important	Not Important
LEADERSHIP			
Be my own boss			
Supervise and lead others			
Have supervisors and co-workers whom I respect			
Have clear directions for what I need to do			
Create vision and mission statements			
Assume a position of authority			
Create changes based on priorities and analysis			
Listen to colleagues			
Convey understanding and firmness			
Exude trust and confidence in others			
Think and act quickly			
Facilitate learning and growth			
Diagnose problems			
Learn and integrate computer skills			
Mobilize resources			
Articulate plans			
Set the standard			
Observe and investigate issues			
Provide leadership to achieve significant results			
Serve as a catalyst in the organization			
Be effective behind the scene			
Work as a part of a team			
Accept and build on existing talents			
Use poise and skill in making public appearances			
Provide constructive feedback to improve performance			
Recognize and celebrate individual and collective successes			
Move an organization forward despite obstacles			
Nourish and encourage diversity			
Practice diplomacy			

Now look back at your assessment of work values and particularly at those you checked as being very important. List them in the spaces below.

1. _____   11. _____

2. _____   12. _____

3. _____   13. _____

4. _____   14. _____

5. _____   15. _____

6. _____   16. _____

7. _____   17. _____

8. _____   18. _____

9. _____   19. _____

10. _____   20. _____

Look at the above list. Put a check mark (✔) next to those work values that you feel are *most* important for your career and job satisfaction. Check at least five (more if you wish). Think of possible careers that are likely to fulfill your most important work values. Write them in the following spaces.

Possible careers to fulfill my most important work values:

1. _____

2. _____

3. _____

4. _____

5. _____

YOUR IDEAL (AND NOT SO IDEAL) JOB

Think of your ideal workday. Don't think of a specific job as much as the kinds of activities in which you would be involved, the kind of place where you would work, the type of people with whom you would work, what your supervisor (if any) would be like, how you would spend your time, your hours, and the skills you would use. In the following spaces list as many factors as you can that would make up your ideal workday.

1. My ideal work environment would be:

2. The type of responsibilities I would enjoy are:

3. The type of people with whom I would like to work are:

4. The structure of my ideal workday would be:

5. The skills I would most like to use are:

6. Other aspects of my ideal workday are:

Now think of a workday that you absolutely would **not** want. What skills, activities, people, and situations would you want to **avoid**? Write as many of these as you can in the following spaces.

1. Places that I would not want to work are:

2. Types of work I would dislike are:

3. Types of people I want to avoid are:

4. The type of workday I would dislike is:

5. Skills I don't want to use are:

6. Other things I want to avoid are:

Describe the **type** of organization that you would like to work for. What characteristics and what purpose would the organization have? How would it be managed? List your responses in the following spaces.

1. Size and structure of the organization

2. Purpose of the organization

3. Management style of the organization

4. Other characteristics I want to explore

Think of an organization that you would *not* want to work for. What would be some of the characteristics of this organization? List them in the following spaces.

1. Types of organizations I want to avoid

2. Purposes I don't agree with

3. Management styles I don't want

4. Other characteristics I want to avoid

Now look back at your responses to the four previous questions. What conclusions can you draw from your responses? What careers might provide you with your ideal workday? What careers should you avoid? What organizations appeal to you and what organizations turn you off? Write your conclusions in the following spaces.

_____

_____

_____

_____

HOW IMPORTANT IS YOUR WORK?

For many people, work defines much of their basic identity. Everyone works, whether for pay, volunteer, or at home, and for a variety of reasons. Whether work is the most important force in a person's life or just a part of a person's existence, it does play a major role in the lifestyle of most people. Abraham Maslow, a social psychologist, viewed the human personality in light of motivation. His hierarchy depicts individual needs. Maslow (1970) assumed that human nature is good rather than bad and that we move in the direction of growth by fulfillment of our needs. Balancing our needs promotes health and encourages spontaneity, freedom, and creativity. Maslow asserted that if we deny or suppress our needs, we become ill. Creative self-expression is an integral part of the personality and the need to express oneself becomes a force in the personality, which continues to encourage growth and risk-taking. The importance of self-actualization can be seen in Maslow's hierarchy of needs (pp. 35–47):

Most people work to achieve the basic needs in levels one and two. A person must have these needs fulfilled in order to work on achieving the needs at the higher levels. If a person has a sufficient income, physiological and security needs can be satisfied. A person's work enables her or him to associate with other people and to maintain a family, thus contributing to the fulfillment of the needs in level three.

As a person begins to fulfill needs in level four, self-esteem, work takes on even more importance. No longer does work simply provide an income and interpersonal associations. For a person to achieve self-esteem, it is important to develop a sense of confidence, mastery, and achievement in one's life. One gains the respect and appreciation of others for one's accomplishments, and a certain measure of status is achieved. For many people, the primary source of the development and achievement of self-esteem is their work.

If the needs in levels one through four have been substantially fulfilled, a person begins to satisfy the need for self-actualization. This is a difficult need to define, because it varies from person to person and deals with a person's concept of having purpose, or mission, in life. In order to become self-actualized, one must work toward realizing one's potential. Many people begin to reach toward fulfillment of their potential through their work. This need is illustrated by the many thousands of independently wealthy persons who work very hard and are very involved in their work, even though they do not have to work for financial reasons.

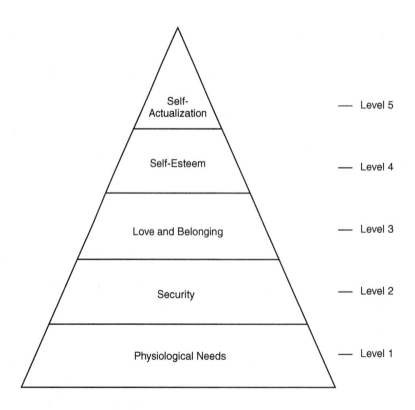

Work is a driving force for many people and a source of fulfillment of many individual needs. The importance of work can be demonstrated by surveys that indicate that most retired persons would still prefer to be involved in some form of work. How important is work to you? Keep in mind that it is essential to develop a comprehensive lifestyle in which you gain fulfillment of your needs through a combination of your relationships, activities, and interests. Try to avoid tying too much of your identity and purpose to your work by maintaining a balanced lifestyle. Remember, however, that work plays an important role in your development of self-esteem and in your progress toward self-actualization.

What If You Didn't Have to Work?

Imagine that you are independently wealthy. You have an after-tax income of $250,000 a year from funds that were left to you by a benefactor. Would you work? If so, what kind of work would you do? If you would not work, how would you spend your time? Write your responses in the following spaces.

_____

_____

_____

_____

_____

Now assume that you don't have an after-tax income of $250,000 a year. What could you do to achieve some of the same things that you said you would do if you had that income? What is stopping you from doing them? Write your responses in the following spaces.

_____

_____

_____

_____

_____

Think back to the times in your life when you felt most satisfied and fulfilled. Have you ever felt that you were achieving a sense of self-actualization? When was it? What were you doing and what skills and abilities were you using? Write your responses in the following spaces.

_____

_____

_____

_____

_____

WORK VALUES

A knowledge of your work values is essential as you plan your life and career. Your work takes up a great deal of the time in your life. What you value about your work may be quite different from what another person values. Analyze your work values before you make career decisions. Look back at your work values inventory and at your responses to the questions on work values. What are your most important work values? What conclusions can you make about the kind of workday you want and about the kind of organization with which you want to work?

CHAPTER 2

Interests

An analysis of your interests offers you insight into potential careers and lifestyles that could be satisfying and fulfilling. If you enter a career that is related to your interests, your chances of being successful in and enjoying that career are enhanced. Your interests are the key to developing a fulfilling lifestyle. It is unreasonable to expect that most of your interests will be fulfilled by a career, so cultivating interests outside of work will enrich and broaden your life. It is important to:

- Recognize and identify your interests.

- Evaluate which interests enhance your life.

- Determine how your interests may relate to a career option.

- Decide how other interests could be fulfilled outside of your work.

- Develop new interests as a source of fulfillment and creativity.

Another step in career and life planning is to acknowledge the value of your interests and their potential relationship to future career options. Your interests may serve as a guide as you assess what is most important to you. What do you really enjoy doing in your leisure time? When is it that you lose track of time and space? What are you engaged in when you feel satisfied with your creativity or production? What interests draw you in and hold the potential for paid employment? The following activities will help you to evaluate your interests.

HOW DO YOU LIKE TO SPEND YOUR TIME?

In the spaces below, list fifteen ways that you like to spend your time. Think of the interests that you really enjoy, things that you would choose to do if you did not have other demands on your time and things that interest you most. Try to fill in all of the spaces.

Ways I like to spend my time	Have I done this in the past two months?
1. _____	_____
2. _____	_____
3. _____	_____
4. _____	_____
5. _____	_____
6. _____	_____
7. _____	_____
8. _____	_____
9. _____	_____
10. _____	_____
11. _____	_____
12. _____	_____
13. _____	_____
14. _____	_____
15. _____	_____
Others _____	

Consider your list. Are there ways that you like to spend your time that you could turn into possible careers? Do you know of other people who have turned their interests into careers? Many courageous individuals have listened to the call of their interests and have pursued creative, nontraditional, and sometimes risky career alternatives. For example, if you really enjoy learning about food and dining out, you could consider becoming a food critic for your local newspaper.

You may wish to keep many interests that you listed as part of your avocation, rather than trying to make a living through them. For example, turning golf, needlepoint, cooking, or weightlifting into career options may alter their value to you. Your interests nourish and fulfill you and add balance and meaning to your life. You are more than the functions that you fulfill at your work. Your interests expand and broaden you as an individual by providing clearer definition to your life. However, one of the best approaches to selecting a satisfying career is to take something that you already do for enjoyment and turn it into your work. Are there any careers that might relate to the ways you like to spend your time? Write a few possible choices in the following spaces.

1. _____   5. _____

2. _____   6. _____

3. _____   7. _____

4. _____   8. _____

Look at your list again. There are probably many ways you like to spend your time that could not be turned into careers, but are still very important for a fulfilling lifestyle. In the following spaces, list those ways you like to spend your time that you really want to make time for in your life.

1. _____   5. _____

2. _____   6. _____

3. _____   7. _____

4. _____   8. _____

In what ways can you structure your lifestyle to make sure that you will have the time, money, and opportunity to pursue these interests?

1. _____

2. _____

3. _____

4. _____

Look at your list again. In the column on the right, make a check mark (✓) after each activity that you have done in the past month.

How many activities did you check? If you did not check many, how can you change your lifestyle **right now** so that you can do more of the things that interest you most? List below some specific changes that you can make **now** so that you can have more time for the things you like to do.

1. _____

2. _____

3. _____

4. _____

For many adults, time seems to be a barrier to fulfilling interests. Remember that the less time that you have, the more important it is for you to make time for your interests. Ignoring your interests over long periods of time can be unhealthy for you and for those who are significant in your life. Attention to your interests leads to self-satisfaction, self-enhancement, and self-empowerment. If you take care of your needs through nurturing your interests, you may well have more to offer your career, your family, your friends, and life in general. Pursuing your interests and developing new interests add to the energy in your life.

DEVELOP A PLAN TO PURSUE YOUR INTERESTS

Once more, look back at your list of ways you like to spend your time. What are five of your most important interests, the things that interest you most and that you definitely want to include as a part of your life either at work or away from work? List them in the following spaces.

1. _____

2. _____

3. _____

4. _____

5. _____

Now try to think of at least four possible ways that you can pursue each of these interests. For example, if you have a major interest in music, you could pursue this interest by being a musician, by working in a music store, by working in administration for a musical organization, by listening to music, by singing in a chorus, by playing in a band on weekends, by attending concerts, by reading about music, by being a music critic, by teaching music, and many others. Creatively expand the possible ways that you might fulfill your major interests.

Interest number one _____

Ways to fulfill this interest.

1. _____

2. _____

3. _____

4. _____

Interest number two _____

Ways to fulfill this interest.

1. _____

2. _____

3. _____

4. _____

Interest number three _____

Ways to fulfill this interest.

1. _____

2. _____

3. _____

4. _____

Interest number four _____

Ways to fulfill this interest.

1. _____

2. _____

3. _____

4. _____

Interest number five _____

Ways to fulfill this interest.

1. _____

2. _____

3. _____

4. _____

OCCUPATIONAL ENVIRONMENTS

Do certain types of people go into certain kinds of work? If they do, where would you fit in? It can be help-ful to look at your interests and preferences and then compare them with the interests of people in various kinds of work. Some research has shown that your chances of success and happiness in a career are improved if you share similar interests and preferences with others in that career. According to John Holland (1997), the world of work can be divided into six categories. People with certain personality characteristics do tend to go into certain types of work. These categories can be called **occupational environments**.

Holland's theory is one of the most widely accepted approaches to understanding career choice. Research has generally supported Holland's basic contention that personality type and occupational choice are related. Holland's theory forms the basis for a categorization of occupations and for a meaningful way to look at the world of work.

The four assumptions of Holland's theory are:

1. There are six personality types. These types are made up of attitudes, skills, preferences for vocational and leisure activities, life goals, values, and problem-solving skills.

2. Work environments can be categorized into six types.

3. People search for appropriate environments that are consistent with their skills, abilities, attitudes, and values.

4. There is a reciprocal relationship between people and environments. Personality and environment in-teract to affect a person's behavior.

Holland encourages individuals to use this structure as a basis for greater in-depth research. It is a beginning, rather than a completion of the information-gathering stage of career exploration. It is very helpful to consider Holland's six occupational themes as you expand and then narrow possible career options. Holland's occupational environments are as follows.

Realistic

People in this category tend to be interested in mechanical things and to have mechanical abilities. Many like to work with objects, tools, and machines. Many tend to be athletic and are interested in activities where they can use their physical abilities. They tend to enjoy working with their hands. They are very practical in their outlook on life and often enjoy working outdoors. They prefer an active life rather than a sedentary lifestyle.

Some examples of jobs in this category are construction worker, carpenter, mechanic, skilled trades, police officer, dental technician, forester, farmer, military officer, and air traffic controller.

Investigative

People in this category are interested in observing and analyzing situations before they act. They like to investigate situations and solve problems. They are very interested in learning and are likely to continue their education. They like to evaluate possibilities and are task oriented. They tend to enjoy dealing with abstract problems and have a need to understand how things work and why things are the way they are. They like to design equipment and develop solutions to problems.

Some examples of jobs in this category are engineer, chemist, computer programmer, biologist, economist, social scientist, physician, research worker, physicist, systems analyst, meteorologist, mathematician, dental hygienist, tool designer, optometrist, and x-ray technician.

Artistic

People in this category like to use their imagination in dealing with situations and tend to be quite independent. They prefer an unstructured environment where they can create and use their artistic abilities. They like to innovate. They express themselves in artistic ways and could often be described as being unconventional. They are independent and need room to express themselves and their creativity.

Some examples of jobs in this category are singer, actor, fashion model, actress, musician, interior decorator, reporter, artist, public relations person, author, advertising manager, composer, technical writer, photographer, and music teacher.

Social

People in this category like to work with other people in a helpful and supportive way. They like to inform, teach, enlighten, and train others. They like to help others solve problems and develop their potential. They tend to be concerned with the welfare of others and are very humanistic in their approach to dealing with others. They are often skilled with words and like to be with other people. They tend to be quite sociable and feel responsible for helping others who need assistance.

Some examples of jobs in this category are clinical psychologist, waiter or waitress, minister, teacher, marriage counselor, speech therapist, nurse, personnel director, dietitian, child care director, social worker, bartender, and ticket agent.

Enterprising

People in this category are energetic and like to assume leadership roles. They enjoy being in charge of other people, and persuading others to do something or to buy something. They often work hard to achieve power and status, and financial gain is an important goal. They enjoy material wealth and will work hard to achieve it. They like to manage and influence other people. They tend to be goal directed and welcome the opportunity to advance in an organization or in their own enterprises.

Some examples of jobs in this category are realtor, lawyer, buyer, farm manager, business executive, salesperson, marketing director, bank manager, recruiter, sales manager, insurance investigator, and florist.

Conventional

People in this category like well-ordered activities, and usually enjoy office work. They like to know what is expected of them and appreciate a system in which there are well-defined tasks. They tend to like to work with data and to use numerical and clerical skills. They are interested in following things through in detail and they also like to follow the instructions of others.

Some examples of jobs in this category are bank examiner, bookkeeper, court reporter, computer operator, credit manager, secretary, accountant, and telephone operator.

Where Do You Fit In?

Now look back over the six occupational environments. In which environment would you feel most comfortable? Does one stand out as your clear choice or is it difficult to choose? In the following spaces, write three choices, in order, of the occupational environments in which you would feel most comfortable.

First choice _____

Second choice _____

Third choice _____

Many career resource centers are organized using these six occupational environments. For example, you can go to a resource center and investigate all of the possible careers in the realistic category. It is also interesting to combine categories, since most careers involve a variety of interests and skills. For example, some engineering careers involve both realistic and investigative interests. Some social service careers involve both social and enterprising interests. Use these occupational environments to expand your investigation of possible careers. In the following spaces, write as many careers as you can that would fit into the occupational environments that you chose.

1. _____   6. _____

2. _____   7. _____

3. _____   8. _____

4. _____   9. _____

5. _____   10. _____

INVENTORIES AND INTERACTIVE CAREER EXPLORATION PROGRAMS

You may also wish to further explore your interests by taking one or more interest inventories. These will not necessarily tell you what you do well, but they will help you to categorize your interests and to compare them with those of people who are working in various careers. Some of the more widely available interest inventories are described here.

Strong Interest Inventory

The *Strong Interest Inventory* (SII) is the most widely used interest inventory today, having received several major updates over the years. Considerable research supports the relationship between a high score on one of the SII's occupational scales and satisfaction in that occupation. The individual who completes the SII is able to compare interests to the interests of people who are happy and successful in specific occupations. In this way, the individual is able to determine trends in the type of occupations that correspond with interests.

Self-Directed Search

This inventory was developed by John Holland to determine which of Holland's six occupational categories a person prefers. The responses on activities, competencies, occupations, and self-estimates provide a rank order of choices for three of the six categories. The *Self-Directed Search* is self-scored and is complemented by the *Occupations Finder* and *Educational Opportunities Finder*, reference booklets of hundreds of occupations that are organized according to Holland's six categories.

Campbell Interest and Skill Survey

The *Campbell Interest and Skill Inventory* provides an integrated view of your interests and skills. It measures your degree of interest in seven broad occupational areas and estimates your confidence level in your ability to perform in the same occupational areas.

Kuder Career Search with Its Person Match

The *Kuder Career Search with Person Match* shows the relationship between a person's interest profile and those of people in various college majors and occupational groups. Its approach of comparing people on the basis of interests is similar to that of the SII. It provides occupational biographies for the 14 closest matches to an individual's interest profile.

Myers-Briggs Type Indicator

This assessment is based on the assumption that individuals have specific preferences in their personality that determine the way they deal with personal relationships, with information, with work environments, with problem solving, with decision making, and with many other aspects of life. The *Myers-Briggs Type Indicator* is designed to evaluate preferences in four different areas, from which a type is derived. The four areas are preferences for introversion and extroversion, sensing and intuition, thinking and feeling, and judging and perceiving.

Interactive Career Choice Programs

Advances in information technology have resulted in the development of a variety of computerized and self-instructional programs that provide help in career decision making. Some programs are highly interactive and help the user to assess interests, values, skills, and other factors before obtaining career information. Others primarily offer an efficient method of obtaining educational and career information. Three of the more popular programs are SIGI, DISCOVER, and CHOICES. For information on these organizations you can call or visit the following Web sites:

SIGI 3
www.sigi3.org
1-800-633-3321

DISCOVER
www.act.org/discover
1-800-498-6068

CHOICES
www.bridges.com
1-800-281-1168

Many states have special programs, established through Vocational Information and Occupational Coordinating Committees (VOICC), that distribute information about employment projections and salaries within the individual states. Many resources for career planning are available through the World Wide Web. See chapter 15 for information.

Some of the inventories and programs mentioned should be used with the assistance of a professional counselor. Consider your objectives, your current progress in career decision making, and the career and life planning options available before you decide to take any of these inventories. Share your career concerns with a counselor. Together you can decide which, if any, of these inventories are appropriate for your needs. The results of your assessments can be interpreted by your counselor.

If you would like to locate a certified career counselor, a listing has been developed by the National Board for Certified Counselors. You can obtain the listing of certified career counselors in your state, a consumer guide to counseling, and a brochure describing client rights and responsibilities by contacting:

National Board for Certified Counselors, Inc.
3 Terrace Way, Suite D
Greensboro, North Carolina 27403-3660
Tel. 336-547-0607
FAX 336-547-0017
Website: http://www.nbcc.org
Email: nbcc@nbcc.org

Following are suggestions for places to obtain these inventories, computerized guidance programs, and related counseling assistance. Call to check the type of services, cost, eligibility, location, and hours of operation.

- Community colleges

- Libraries

- Career counselors

- Four-year colleges and universities

- Human resource development departments in companies

- High schools

- Adult education programs

- Women's centers

- Private counseling centers

- State employment commissions
- County agencies
- Local chamber of commerce
- Career resource centers

Inventories and career guidance packages will not provide you with quick and easy answers to your career and life questions. As always, those answers lie within you. However, these inventories and interactive career exploration programs can be valuable tools that you can use in the career and life planning process.

INTERESTS

Your interests hold the key to a rewarding and satisfying life. Any career that is based on your interests may be very rewarding for you. A variety of interests is needed to maintain a well-rounded lifestyle. This becomes particularly important in your later years when work may take on a less important place in your life. Pursue your interests on and off the job, and *develop new interests as you go through life.* It is never too late to develop interests. The time to start is now!

> *Today, I understand vocation quite differently—not as a goal to be achieved but as a gift to be received.*
>
> —Parker Palmer, *Now I Become Myself*

CHAPTER 3

Skills and Abilities

Consider your unique combination of skills and abilities. You normally feel satisfied performing tasks that you do well using the personal characteristics that come naturally to you. This circular process of continuing to do what you do well builds your self-confidence and adds to your self-esteem because you become more proficient and comfortable. However, you should stretch your skills and abilities with every opportunity that presents itself, creating opportunities to reach beyond your comfort zone and develop new and potentially rewarding skills. This is one way to expand your potential and explore other career areas.

Each of us has a unique combination of skills and abilities. According to Richard Bolles, the author of *What Color is Your Parachute* (2008) and the reigning career and life planning guru, we have at least 200 to 300 skills and abilities in our repertoire. A skill is an expertise that is developed through attention, practice, and study. An ability, on the other hand, is defined as innate, or as a special talent that you possess and use automatically. You are most likely to list your skills quickly because you have spent time, energy, and perhaps money to develop them. Some examples might be tennis, golf, technical writing, computer work, or public speaking. Abilities are often more difficult to pinpoint because you may overlook or underestimate their value in work and in play. You may think that everyone has the same athletic coordination that you have or the same way of handling difficult customers. You may be shortchanging yourself! Your assets, both skills and abilities, may serve to illuminate your journey as you seek fulfillment in your job and in your life. Learn how to capitalize on your own unique combination of skills and abilities.

This chapter will help you consider your skills and abilities by examining the components of three recent successes. You will then select and review a combination of self-management skills that serve you well in your life and in your career. This will be followed by a self-evaluation of your skills and abilities. Remember, only you can improve and enhance your skills and abilities to meet the challenges in your life. This adventure awaits you!

When assessing your skills and abilities, avoid these common pitfalls:

- Don't undervalue your own unique set of skills and abilities. Take a positive approach toward assessing what you can do.

- Don't limit yourself to just your major skills. You may overlook many small but important skills that you use every day.

- Don't dwell on your weaknesses. Too much emphasis on weaknesses or on skills that you do not have can turn into excuses for not doing something with your career or life. Remember that you are paid in a job for what you *can* do, not for what you *cannot* do.

In our society, it has traditionally been more acceptable to acknowledge negative qualities rather than to emphasize positive characteristics. However, it is important for you to recognize and acknowledge your strengths. Your skills and abilities help you achieve your goals. They are the key to:

- Knowing yourself better

- Making positive career decisions

- Conducting a successful job campaign

- Building a learning plan

Discover what skills and abilities you possess. Be able to acknowledge them and articulate them to colleagues and friends. Finally, expand your skills and abilities by developing them to the best of your potential. In *The Three Boxes of Life*, Richard Bolles organized skills in three distinct categories (1981, p. 142):

- Self-management skills

- Functional skills

- Work content skills

The following exercises will help you identify and understand your unique combination of skills and abilities. You will first analyze some of your past successes and then identify the self-management skills, functional skills, and work content skills that you possess and those skills that you would like to develop.

THREE SUCCESSES

Before you categorize your own unique set of skills and abilities, think back over the past two years and identify at least three successes that you have enjoyed. They can be great or small. The only requirement is that they gave you a measure of satisfaction with yourself. Your successes can be drawn from any area of your life. Take some extra time to review some of the highlights from your most recent past. If you have more than three successes, choose the ones that gave you the most satisfaction. If you are having difficulty thinking of more than one or two successes, look over your personal calendar and take note of the special events you have experienced. That may jog your memory about successes that have given you satisfaction.

As an example, look at Ruth J.'s successes from the past two years. They may give you some ideas about your own recent successes.

Example: Ruth J

Successes

Number 1 Success

With little advance notice and little preparation, substituted for son's soccer coach. The team won the game.

Number 2 Success

Earned 15 college credits at Capital Community College, which helped me get a promotion to assistant manager of my division.

Number 3 Success

Trained my dog, P.J., to become an effective watch and house dog.

Now write three of your successes in the spaces below.

My Successes

Number 1 Success _____

_____

_____

Number 2 Success _____

_____

_____

Number 3 Success _____

_____

_____

You have chosen these three successes for a reason. Now you will analyze and identify what it was in these successes that helped you feel good about yourself. By exploring your successes you will uncover some interesting information about yourself, and that is what this exercise is all about. First, let's take Ruth's number one success and analyze it. Then, analyze your own successes.

Example : Ruth J

Number 1 Success

With little advance notice and little preparation, substituted for son's soccer coach. The team won the game.

    a.   What motivated you to do this?

        Challenge of doing something new, help the coach, help the team

    b.   What abilities or skills did it take for you to accomplish this?

        Organization, fast thinking, encouragement of others, enthusiasm conveyed to the team, work with team parents

    c.   Who is responsible for this success?

        Fourteen little boys, the coach, and son who gave me his permission to coach.

    d.   Did you accomplish this alone or with others? Who?

        With others—the team members

    e.   What were the circumstances surrounding this success?

        Outside, soccer field filled with cheering parents and children

    f.   What was the payoff (reward) for this success?

        Working with eager eight-year-old boys, had the opportunity to contribute to their first win of the season, helped the coach

    g.   How did you feel about this success?

        Scared at first when I agreed to coach but thrilled with the results. My risk paid off!

Now that you see how this analysis is done, think about your own successes by answering the same questions.

My Analysis of Success #1

I succeeded in:

_____

_____

a. What motivated me was:

_____

_____

b. I used the following skills or abilities in this success:

_____

_____

c. Who was responsible for this success?

_____

_____

d. Did I accomplish this alone or with others? Who?

_____

_____

e. What were the external circumstances surrounding this success?

_____

_____

f. What was my payoff or reward for this success?

_____

_____

g. How did I feel about this success?

_____

_____

My Analysis of Success #2

I succeeded in:

_____

_____

a. What motivated me was:

_____

_____

b. I used the following skills or abilities in this success:

_____

_____

c. Who was responsible for this success?

_____

_____

d. Did I accomplish this alone or with others? Who?

_____

_____

e. What were the external circumstances surrounding this success?

_____

_____

f. What was my payoff or reward for this success?

_____

_____

g. How did I feel about this success?

_____

_____

My Analysis of Success #3

I succeeded in:

_____

_____

a. What motivated me was:

_____

_____

b. I used the following skills or abilities in this success:

_____

_____

c. Who was responsible for this success?

_____

_____

d. Did I accomplish this alone or with others? Who?

_____

_____

e. What were the external circumstances surrounding this success?

_____

_____

f. What was my payoff or reward for this success?

_____

_____

g. How did I feel about this success?

_____

_____

Evaluation of Your Analysis of Your Successes

You can now evaluate your three successes by looking for a pattern in your three sets of answers. Is there a common thread that links your successes? For example, in answer to your first question, are you motivated to help others, overcome great odds, or take risks? Are there similar skills and abilities that keep appearing in each of your highlights? Do you continually attribute your successes to someone else? Are you achieving your significant events alone, as part of a team, or as a leader? Are there certain circumstances that encourage you to succeed such as stress, pressure, competition, projects, or structure? What are your intrinsic or extrinsic payoffs for your success? Consider your own special needs, and look for patterns. These may be significant as you shape your career and life goals. You may want to discuss your responses with someone who can provide quality feedback and insight.

a. What motivates me?

_____

_____

b. What skills and abilities do I like to use?

_____

_____

c. Responsibility for my success lies with:

_____

_____

d. I have accomplished my successes with the help of:

_____

_____

e. Circumstances that motivate me are:

_____

_____

f. The payoffs or rewards I want are:

_____

_____

g. My successes make me feel:

_____

_____

SELF-MANAGEMENT SKILLS

How do you relate to other people? Are you punctual? Are you organized? How do you perform under stress? Are you enthusiastic? These are all self-management skills. One might call these personality or character traits, because they are a basic part of your nature. However, they actually are skills that are specific to you and do not depend on any particular job or career. They can be enhanced, developed, and controlled, if you wish to do so. For example, you can learn to be more punctual if it is important to you. You can learn to be more organized. You can work to improve your performance in stressful situations.

It is important to consider your self-management skills when planning a career or job change. Try to match your career or job to your skills or to those skills that you plan to develop. If you are a very enthusiastic person, try to find a job in a setting where your enthusiasm will be an asset. If you are attentive to detail, this can be an asset in many job settings. On the other hand, if you know that you do not have a certain self-management skill and do not intend to develop it, try to avoid choosing a job that requires the skill. If you have difficulty getting going in the morning and being punctual, and do not wish to change, avoid taking a job that requires you to show up at 7:30 A.M. sharp. If you have difficulty concentrating, try not to choose a job that requires you to concentrate amid many distractions.

In some cases, a self-management skill that is a disadvantage in one job may be an asset in a different job. For example, flexibility may be detrimental in certain jobs requiring strict accounting practices such as auditing, but flexibility can be a positive skill when working with a community recreation program. If you are adventuresome, you could be an asset to an organization that needs people who are willing to take risks and try something new, but you may feel stifled and out of place in a highly structured organization. If you can identify a career that complements your self-management skills, your chances for happiness and success in the career are enhanced.

As you complete the following exercise, include all of your experience in your past and present work, education, home, volunteer, and other activities. You do not need a certificate or a degree hanging on your wall before you acknowledge that you possess certain skills. The following is a listing of some self-management skills. Go through the list, *circle* those skills that you possess, and **check** five or more self-management skills that you would like to develop in the near future.

Self-Management Skills

Academic	Dominant	Intuitive	Risk taker
Adventurous	Daring	Kind	Realistic
Alert	Discreet	Likeable	Rational
Active	Dignified	Light-hearted	Responsible
Adaptable	Energetic	Logical	Reflective
Accurate	Enjoyable	Loving	Resourceful
Aggressive	Efficient	Loyal	Reserved
Assertive	Enthusiastic	Modest	Serious
Attractive	Empathetic	Motivated	Sensitive
Adaptable	Extroverted	Meticulous	Successful
Analytical	Eager	Moderate	Secure
Affectionate	Easygoing	Mature	Spontaneous
Ambitious	Forgiving	Methodological	Supportive
Broadminded	Farsighted	Natural	Serene
Calm	Fair-minded	Organized	Strong-minded
Creative	Firm	Original	Sincere
Curious	Flexible	Open-minded	Sensible
Courageous	Forceful	Obliging	Self-controlled
Competitive	Formal	Outgoing	Self-confident
Clever	Frank	Optimistic	Strong
Competent	Friendly	Opportunistic	Stable
Cheerful	Goal-oriented	Organized	Tactful
Clear-headed	Genuine	Painstaking	Tough
Curious	Good-natured	Persevering	Tolerant
Cautious	Gentle	Prudent	Thoughtful
Conservative	Generous	Positive	Thorough
Charming	Honest	Patient	Teachable
Cooperative	Healthy	Poised	Tenacious
Caring	Hard working	Purposeful	Trusting
Cool	Helpful	Practical	Trustworthy
Considerate	Hopeful	Polite	Theoretical
Charitable	Inventive	Pleasant	Unassuming
Confident	Individualistic	Progressive	Understanding
Capable	Informal	Precise	Unaffected
Conscientious	Industrious	Quick	Unexcitable
Careful	Introspective	Quiet	Versatile
Consistent	Imaginative	Reflective	Warm
Deliberate	Intellectual	Relaxed	Wise
Determined	Independent	Reliable	

Now look at your list and at those skills that you circled. In the following spaces, write at least five (and as many as ten) of your top self-management skills that you would like to use in a career.

1. _____   6. _____

2. _____   7. _____

3. _____   8. _____

4. _____   9. _____

5. _____   10. _____

Now list at least five (and as many as ten) self-management skills that you would like to develop.

1. _____   6. _____

2. _____   7. _____

3. _____   8. _____

4. _____   9. _____

5. _____   10. _____

FUNCTIONAL SKILLS

Functional skills cover the basic tangibles of work. They can be broken down into three basic areas: people, and things. These skills involve doing something to something, acting on something, or doing something with someone. They can be thought of as action verbs such as computing, teaching, or operating. These skills are generally transferable from one job to another. Once you have learned a functional skill, you take it with you and can apply it in a different setting. For example, if you are good at analyzing data in one job, you will probably be good at analyzing data in another job.

The following diagram, adapted from the *Dictionary of Occupational Titles* (Fine, 1991, p. 1005), illustrates the three general categories of functional skills. Note that the more elementary skills are at the bottom and increase in complexity toward the top. Each skill usually involves all of those below it. For example, if you want to be involved with people, you can do it at a relatively basic level (helping, serving) or at a much higher level (mentoring, negotiating).

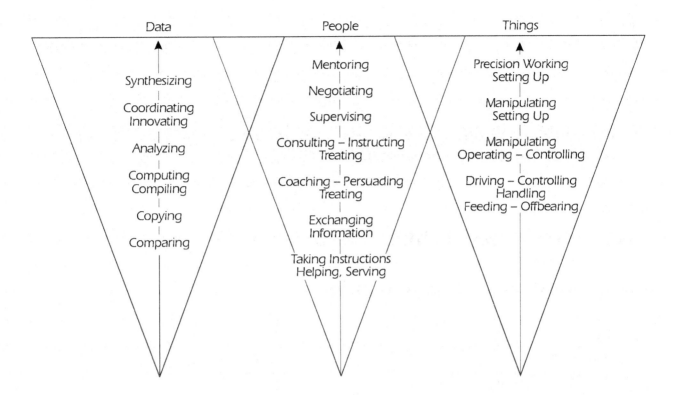

	Data		People		Things

Data: Synthesizing, Coordinating, Innovating, Analyzing, Computing, Compiling, Copying, Comparing

People: Mentoring, Negotiating, Supervising, Consulting – Instructing, Treating, Coaching – Persuading, Treating, Exchanging Information, Taking Instructions, Helping, Serving

Things: Precision Working, Setting Up, Manipulating, Setting Up, Manipulating, Operating – Controlling, Driving – Controlling, Handling, Feeding – Offbearing

Functional skills and abilities serve as the foundation of your expertise as you journey from one point to another. You present your unique combination of these skills and abilities to a potential employer by demonstrating your effectiveness in your current position, building a solid reputation, networking with others, developing a well-designed resume, and conducting positive job interviews. Capitalizing on your unique combination of skills and abilities is critical as you define potential options. Recognize your gifts in a multitude of areas as you distinguish yourself from other applicants.

How can you focus on your combination of functional skills? First, think about what skills you have used in your career and personal life. Have you continued to use and develop those functional skills in different areas of your life? Are you incorporating your functional skills now?

Our American culture does not encourage boasting about our unique combination of skills and abilities. However, when you are seeking a new job or a new career, this is exactly what you need to do in an effective job search. Don't think of yourself as boasting. Your primary goal is to educate potential employers about your talents and strengths as you position yourself to contribute to an organization. Your job is to explain and "sell" your skills and abilities in an authentic way, so that an employer will see the value you will add to the organization. If you are not seeking employment by others but plan to start your own company, you will have to "sell" your unique combination of skills and abilities as you obtain investors or customers for your business. Functional skills and abilities are critical to your success in every case.

You may have some questions that include:

How can I develop skills and abilities?
What are those strengths that I can capitalize on to move forward in my career?
Can I be empowered by using these strengths as I consider my options?

To answer these questions, it may be helpful to think of specific individuals whom you respect and admire. What qualities have you observed in them? Do you admire them for possessing these gifts or for using their talents wisely? This distinction is an important one as you determine your unique combination of functional skills and abilities. How will you use your own talents wisely?

Begin now to identify your functional skills and your abilities. In the following listing of skills and abilities, **circle** the skills and abilities that you **possess** and **check** (✓) the skills and abilities that you would like to **develop**.

Remember that certification is not necessary. Acknowledge your strengths with confidence! Be generous to yourself.

SELF-EVALUATION OF SKILLS AND ABILITIES

Communication Skills and Abilities

Writing

_____ Inform others

_____ Edit my own and others' work

_____ Summarize

_____ Research online

_____ Format documents

_____ Type accurately

_____ Read for content

_____ Use technical writing skills

_____ Speak and use other languages

_____ Be persuasive on paper

_____ Compose letters and email

_____ Synthesize several sources

_____ Write speeches

_____ Keep meticulous records

_____ Take accurate notes

_____ Proofread

_____ Analyze critically

_____ Conduct academic research

_____ Know several computer software packages

_____ Organize using PowerPoint

_____ Publish own work in newsletters or online

_____ Keep a diary

_____ Track own accomplishments weekly, monthly

_____ Convey enthusiasm

_____ Write with conviction and power

_____ Cite references using appropriate style

Helping

_____ Advise individuals

_____ Coach a team or individual

_____ Lead with authority

_____ Mentor individuals

_____ Negotiate with difficult people

_____ Interpret assessments or reality

_____ Influence colleagues

_____ Persuade others

_____ Articulate your position

_____ Empathize with others

_____ Speak publicly

_____ Conduct training

_____ Teach something difficult to others

_____ Convince through argument

_____ Counsel others

_____ Disaster relief counseling

_____ Listen attentatively

_____ Motivate others to reach their goals

_____ Support individuals to achieve

_____ Perceive needs of others

_____ Understand different perspectives

_____ Capitalize on diversity

_____ Arbitrate difficult situations

_____ Provide solace to others

_____ Problem solve with others

_____ Develop a team or a community of learners

_____ Communicate warmth

_____ Become certified to assist others

_____ Develop interpersonal/human relations skills

_____ Become adept at conflict resolution

_____ Empower others to believe in themselves

_____ Host and welcome individuals graciously

_____ Facilitate personal or professional growth

Creating

_____ Compose a song, poem, or jingle

_____ Design a house or room

_____ Illustrate a book or magazine

_____ Paint a room or portrait

_____ Sculpt a figure

_____ Draw a landscape or cartoon

_____ Write a short story or novel

_____ Sing in a choir or in the shower

_____ Invent solutions

_____ Observe problems differently

_____ Imagine possibilities

_____ Demonstrate with showmanship

_____ Develop aesthetic sense

_____ Act in a play or movie

_____ Display flowers beautifully

_____ Landscape gardens or parks

_____ Decorate interior spaces

_____ Create visual displays

_____ Design structures

_____ Weave, knit, cross-stitch

_____ Organize meaningful social events

_____ Use software to create cover page

_____ Layout for a magazine or newsletter

_____ Transform a house into a home

_____ Dance for fun and release

_____ Chart choreography

_____ Compose the perfect picture

_____ Photograph groups and individuals

_____ Build furniture or cabinets

_____ Engage in home improvement projects

_____ Move into a totally new situation

_____ Play an instrument

_____ Conduct the orchestra for fun

_____ Attend and enjoy a play, ballet, opera, concert

_____ Support arts financially

_____ Engage in one artistic endeavor

_____ Expand perspectives of others

_____ Think and see the world differently

_____ Lose track of time and space when engaged

_____ Become enthralled with your creative process

Organizational Skills and Abilities

Managing

_____ Build trust

_____ Empower colleagues to get the job done

_____ Classify tasks and people

_____ Systematize duties to be performed

_____ Like routines and processes

_____ Track and follow data

_____ Prioritize tasks for self and others

_____ Handle details

_____ Solve day to day problems

_____ Make routine decisions

_____ Keep order

_____ Supervise people

_____ Recruit talent

_____ Keep records

_____ Build outside contacts effectively

_____ Handle many tasks simultaneously

_____ Remember details

_____ Establish the organizational culture

_____ Develop and administer budgets

_____ Interpret policy

_____ Invest in team building

_____ Inform and include colleagues

_____ Capitalize on team diversity

_____ Be sensitive to human relationships

_____ Benchmark standards

_____ Chair purposeful meetings

_____ Work well under stress

_____ Design projects

_____ Implement other's decisions

_____ Develop precise and measurable outcomes

_____ Follow-though on details

_____ Set goals systematically

_____ Welcome details

_____ Follow directions

_____ Accomplish tasks one step at a time

_____ Seek set schedule

_____ Like control and seek to control

_____ Get job done effectively

_____ Appreciate colleagues in the organization

_____ Assert preferences and ideas

_____ Confront others on difficult matters

_____ Make the organization run smoothly

_____ Delegate work without hesitancy

_____ Help leader to succeed

_____ Know computer software

_____ Chart patterns and changes

_____ Responsible for other's effectiveness

_____ Account for outcomes

_____ Demonstrate straightforward style

Analyzing

_____ Think ahead with an eye on the present

_____ Manage and develop a budget

_____ Use mathematical ability

_____ Integrate accounting skills

_____ Plan for company investments

_____ Use financial savvy

_____ Know appropriate computer software packages

_____ Review financial goals and compare to outcomes

_____ Think abstractly

_____ Lead colleagues

_____ Evaluate current realty

_____ Analyze critically

_____ Demonstrate business ethics

_____ Demonstrate facility with numbers

_____ Calculate with ease

_____ Conduct analyses with statistics

_____ Use scientific methods and practice

_____ Investigate inconsistencies

_____ Ask the hard questions

_____ Accept responsibility for the good of the whole

_____ Observe industry standards

_____ Serve as a catalyst for change

_____ Demonstrate leadership qualities

_____ Invite perspectives of others

_____ Read the numbers accurately

_____ Interpret the facts for others

_____ Inspire trust

_____ Write and articulate persuasively

Technical and Physical Skills and Abilities

Technical

_____ Repair computer glitches

_____ Understand and build own computer

_____ Troubleshoot auto problems

_____ Forecast challenges

_____ Test air or water—quality control

_____ Engage in auto maintenance

_____ Construct a deck or addition

_____ Design and estimate kitchen overhaul

_____ Use computer to draft (AutoCAD)

_____ Survey county projects

_____ Learn mechanical drawing for fun

_____ Like using tools of any kind

_____ Enjoy laboratory work

_____ Translate measurements to materials

_____ Read blueprints accurately

_____ Sophisticated mathematical ability

_____ Manipulate numbers rapidly

_____ Utilize medical skills

_____ Diagnose problems

_____ Use laboratory skills

_____ Agile in motor and physical coordination

_____ Measure accurately

_____ Teach others to operate software

_____ Use engineering skills

_____ Work confidently with machinery

_____ Use hands with speed and precision

_____ Learn about electronics and gadgets

_____ Own and utilize current technology

_____ Experiment with the power of technology

_____ Integrate current technology

Physical

_____ Use athletic ability

_____ Demonstrate coordination

_____ Require an active lifestyle

_____ Exercise routinely

_____ Walk, bike, run, swim for a clear mind

_____ Develop or use dexterity

_____ Enjoy physical endeavors

_____ Keep stress at manageable levels

_____ Stretch the mind on a regular basis

_____ Avoid monotonous routines

_____ Hike for pleasure

_____ Stretch sometimes beyond comfort zone

_____ Engage in yoga for mind-body benefits

_____ Maintain a healthy diet

_____ Seek balance between work and play

_____ Listen to body for symptoms

_____ Travel to learn and extend perspectives

_____ Attune to nature and bodily rhythms

_____ Learn to golf

_____ Attend to pains and aches

_____ Project positive body image

_____ Walk with confidence

_____ Visit the doctor for regular checkups

_____ Care for self and others

_____ Walk or tend to pet's needs

_____ Seek outdoor activities

_____ Stretch muscles daily

_____ Plan for financial independence

_____ Play ping pong

_____ Compete in softball, bowling, or volleyball

_____ Play cards: bridge, canasta, poker

_____ Use weights to enhance strength and stamina

_____ Follow doctor's orders for health

_____ Avoid self-defeating addictions

_____ Seek natural sunlight

_____ Keep physically strong

_____ Avoid unnecessary injurious behavior

_____ Plan work around physical activity

_____ Feel healthy and generally happy

_____ Tend to negative self-talk

_____ Cultivate a circle of confidants

_____ Love your life

Look back at your list and write those skills and abilities that you have **circled** in the following spaces.

Skills and abilities that I possess

1. _____

2. _____

3. _____

4. _____

5. _____

6. _____

7. _____

8. _____

9. _____

10. _____

11. _____

12. _____

13. _____

14. _____

15. _____

16. _____

17. _____

18. _____

19. _____

20. _____

Now look back at your list and write in the following spaces those skills and abilities that you have **checked**.

Skills and abilities that I would like to develop

1. _____   6. _____

2. _____   7. _____

3. _____   8. _____

4. _____   9. _____

5. _____   10. _____

WORK CONTENT SKILLS

The third type of skills, according to Bolles (1981), are work content skills. These skills relate to a specific job and are normally very specialized. Work content skills usually require you to remember something very specific in order to do a job. They tend to be less transferable from one job to another than are functional skills. You develop these skills as you move from job to job. Some you may retain; others you may lose.

Examples of work content skills are knowing how to fill out a particular set of government forms, knowing how to take apart a specific brand of refrigerator, knowing the sales patterns of a department store, knowing the steps to take when inspecting a building, knowing how to operate a printing press, and knowing the names of all the customers on a sales route. You may use functional skills in developing work content skills. For example, a good memory will help you to remember the names of the customers on a sales route that you have taken over.

It is important to be aware of your work content skills, particularly those that you can use in other settings. In addition, when you apply for a job, beware of job descriptions that list many specific work content skills that are really transferable functional skills. Many employers describe jobs in terms of much more specific skills than are in fact required. You may actually have the skills that are necessary for the job.

Now think of some of your work content skills and list them in the following spaces.

1. _____   6. _____

2. _____   7. _____

3. _____   8. _____

4. _____   9. _____

5. _____   10. _____

SKILLS AND ABILITIES

You now have a listing of your skills in the three areas. It is not essential that you know all of your skills, but it is important to acknowledge that you do have all three types of skills and that you can describe major examples of each. Of the three types of skills, functional skills are probably the most important to articulate, because they are very transferable from one experience to another. There is a tendency in describing a job to list the job requirements in work content terms when actually most of the skills required are functional. Try to analyze any job or new experience for the actual skills required and avoid going for new training to obtain skills that you already may possess.

In evaluating a job for the skills required, ask yourself the following three questions.

1. **Self-management skills.** What types of personal characteristics do I need for this job?

2. **Functional skills.** What kind of actions do I need to do this job well?

3. **Work content skills.** What kind of special knowledge do I need to do this job well?

> *The whole secret of a successful life is to find out what it is one's destiny to do and then do it.*
>
> —Henry Ford

CHAPTER 4

Personal Values

What matters most to you in your life? In Chapter 1, you assessed your work values in order to determine the types of work and working conditions that would be best suited to your needs and goals. In this chapter, you will assess your personal values. These values relate to all parts of your life and form the basis of your decision making. Values can be abstract or specific as illustrated by the following examples:

- family
- friendships
- helping others
- religious commitment
- creativity
- security

- honesty
- pleasure
- financial achievement
- material possessions
- a satisfying career
- good health

Whether you realize it or not, every time you make a choice about doing one thing as opposed to another, you make a value decision. Most major decisions involve value conflicts. If you get a job offer in another town, you have to move. Career values may conflict with family and friendship values. When you have a decision that involves two or more conflicting values that are of major importance to you, the decision can be extremely difficult to make. You can, however, make these decisions more effectively if you know **what your most important values are and the priority that you give to each**.

The following exercises will help you to understand what personal values are, which personal values are important to you, and how you rank them. Your values are expressed through your actions. If you can bring your actions and life choices into harmony with your values, you will feel more in control of your life and more satisfied with the decisions you make. Your personal values can also play an important role in the type of career that you choose and in the career decisions that you make throughout your life.

PERSONAL VALUES AND ACTION

The following is a list of personal values that are important to many people. Read them briefly. Are some more important to you than others?

- justice
- family
- leisure
- friendships
- social consciousness

- independence
- healthy life
- personal appearance
- recognition
- innovation

- honesty
- environment
- work
- financial security
- intimacy

The following is a list of ways that you might actually put these values into action. Taking the values just given, match them with the appropriate action. Write the value in the space provided.

Action	Values Represented
You do volunteer work to help others less fortunate than you.	_____
You spend a good deal of time getting yourself ready to go to work in the morning.	_____
You get upset when one person takes credit for what another has done.	_____
You like having your own home and living by your own resources.	_____
You enjoy doing new things and like to encourage others to try something new.	_____
You carefully schedule time to do things with your children and your spouse.	_____
You work to become an authority in your field and you enjoy this status.	_____
You demonstrate an interest in others and actively maintain personal contacts.	_____
You exercise, watch your diet, and don't smoke.	_____
You have several activities outside of your job that you do for your enjoyment.	_____
You volunteer at the wildlife organization and nature center.	_____
You are preparing for a comfortable retirement.	_____
You refuse to cheat on your income tax.	_____
You renew your wedding vows with your spouse of 25 years.	_____
You take pride in the service that you provide your customers.	_____

The answers are probably quite apparent, but it is important to note that the values indicated are fulfilled by action, not by feelings or general statements. It is one thing to say that you value something, but it does not become a real value until it becomes translated into **action**.

PERSONAL VALUES ASSESSMENT

The following is a list of personal values. Go through this list and rate the personal values in terms of their importance to **you**. Place a check mark (✔) in the category that best represents your feelings about how important each value is to you.

Personal Value	Very Important	Moderately Important	Somewhat Important	Not Important
Good health				
Many close friendships				
Having a large family				
A fulfilling career				
A long life				
A stable marriage				
A financially comfortable life				
Independence				
Being creative				
Intimacy with another				
Having children				
A variety of interests and activities				
Freedom to create my own lifestyle				
Having a house				
A happy love relationship				
Fulfilling careers for me and my spouse				
Contributing to my community				
Abundance of leisure time				
Happiness				
Ability to move from place to place				
A life without stress				
Strong religious involvement				
A chance to make social changes				
To be remembered for my accomplishments				
Helping those in distress				
Freedom to live where I wish				
A stable life				
Time to myself				
Enjoyment of arts, entertainment, and cultural activities				
Enjoyment of arts, entertainment, and cultural activities				
A life without children				

Personal Value	Very *Important*	Moderately *Important*	Somewhat *Important*	Not *Important*
A life with many challenges				
A life with many changes				
Opportunity to be a leader				
Opportunity to fight for my country				
A chance to make a major discovery that would save lives				
A good physical appearance				
Opportunity to establish roots in one place				
To write something memorable				
A chance to become famous				
To help others solve problems				
To make lots of money				
A stable environment for my children				
Other:				

Whenever you make an important or difficult decision, it usually involves choosing between conflicting values. In order to help you make career and life decisions, it is necessary that you have some idea not only of your most important personal values, but also of the priority that you give them. In the following spaces, list at least ten of your most important personal values from your personal values assessment.

1. A stable marriage
2. Financially comfortable
3. Fulfilling careers for spouse & I
4. Help others solve problems
5. Stable environment for children
6. Having children
7. establish roots
8. intimacy w/ another
9. Good health
10. a house

Now look at your list. In the space below, list your top *five* personal values **in order of priority**, with number one as the most important.

1. _Stable enviranment for children_ first priority
2. _Stable marriage_ second priority
3. _fulfilling careers_ third priority
4. _Financially comfortable_ fourth priority
5. _establish roots_ fifth priority

You have assigned priorities to your most important personal values. Now ask yourself the following questions and write your answers in the spaces provided.

1. Does your life right now reflect your values? Is the time you spend consistent with your priorities?

   Yes, it does, for the most part

2. If the time you spend in your life right now does not reflect your personal values, how can you change your life so that the time you spend is more in keeping with your values?

3. Are there some parts of your life that you would like to change but that you cannot right now? If so, what is your timetable for bringing your lifestyle more into harmony with your values?

   A fulfilling career for spouse & I. We are both struggling

4. What kind of career or career change would be most in keeping with your personal values?

   One where I am able to leave work at work for the most part

5. Think about someone whom you have known and respected, someone who may have served as a role model for you. What special personal qualities did that person have?

   I honestly can't think about anyone being a true role model for.

6. Which of these special qualities would you like to develop?

   Not having a true role model, I guess
   I would like to develop a way to balance a fulfilling career w/ my person values bk they mean so much to me

PERSONAL VALUES DECISIONS

Values can be discussed and considered from a theoretical point of view. However, you really make a value decision whenever you take action. The following questions illustrate decisions that must be made. These decisions involve value conflicts. There is no right or wrong answer. Answer them from your own perspective, using your own personal values.

1. You and your spouse are employed. You enjoy your work very much and are heavily involved with it. You have no children. Your spouse received a job offer in a city 300 miles away. It is an excellent job and your spouse really wants to take it. You don't want to leave your job. What would you do?

   Move

   List the values involved in this decision.

   Marriage, financial, fulfilling, no children

2. Your son has a basketball game at 7:00 P.M. It is the last game of the year and you have promised your son that you will be there. At 5:00 P.M. your boss comes to your office and says that there is a project that must be done right away. You know it will take 3 to 4 hours to complete. What would you do?

   Work on it until 6:30, go to the game, & finish after the game

   List the values involved in this decision.

   Children, happiness, stable environment for children, stress

3. You have worked hard all week. You haven't had much time to spend with your family. You love golf and your friends ask you to play golf on Saturday. Although you do not have anything specific scheduled for Saturday, you know that the golf game will take up most of the day. What would you do?

   Maybe ask to play 1/2 course

   List the values involved in this decision.

   happiness, time to self, stress

4. You are working with records. Your supervisor comes to your desk and tells you to destroy certain records because it will be in the company's best interests to do so. You know that it is illegal to destroy these records. What would you do?

   Not destroy it, ask him to do it

   List the values involved in this decision.

   stress, honesty

5. Your child is sick and has a fever. You have a very important meeting at work and there is no one who can take your place. Your spouse is out of town. You might be able to get a sitter, but it would be difficult to do so and you are worried about your child's condition. What would you do?

   Try to get a sitter for the meeting only otherwise cancel

List the values involved in this decision.

children, Stable life for children, family values

6. You are happy in your work and you have children. You like to spend time with them. A promotion has been offered to you, but it would involve your working most Saturdays. What would you do?

Not take it

List the values involved in this decision.

Children, Stable life for children, time to self

7. You have just come into a certain amount of money. Your present car is sufficient to meet your needs, but you would like to get a new one. Your family would like to take a trip to Europe. There are not sufficient funds to do both. What would you do?

Trip to Europe

List the values involved in this decision.

experiences, cultural, family time,

8. You have just completed college and have accepted your first job. You are living with your parents but you want to move out to a place of your own. Your parents really want you to stay at home for a while longer. You would save money by staying at home. What would you do?

Stay for a few months & move

List the values involved in this decision.

Financial stability

9. You have worked hard all week and it is now Friday afternoon. You and your spouse have three separate social engagements to attend over the weekend. It is important to your spouse that you attend. You would really prefer to stay at home and relax. What would you do?

Attend events

List the values involved in this decision.

Stable marriage, happy relationship

10. You have been working at the same job for twenty years and you're very tired of it. You make a good salary and have family responsibilities. You would really like to change careers but you feel that it would call for substantial sacrifices for members of your family. What would you do?

Discuss w/ my spouse to see if there could be an opportunity to change, but stay if needed

List the values involved in this decision.

Stable environment, financial, house, happiness, fulfilling career

PERSONAL VALUES

You are constantly making value decisions, whether you are aware of it or not. If you assess your most important personal values and prioritize them, you will be better able to make decisions and will feel more in control of your life. You will also feel more comfortable with your decisions after you have made them. If you are not now living your life according to your values, it will be helpful to consider changing the way you spend your time so that your lifestyle can become more consistent with your values. As you go through life, your values may change and your priorities may change. Take time every so often to assess your lifestyle to see if it is in keeping with the personal values that are currently a priority in your life.

CHAPTER 5

Self-Esteem

WHAT IS SELF-ESTEEM?

Your self-esteem is based on how you feel about and value yourself. Do you appreciate all the facets of yourself? Self-esteem means different things to different people. If you feel good about yourself and feel comfortable about where you are in life and where you are going, you probably have developed positive self-esteem. Self-esteem may be related to appreciating your physical appearance, contributing through work, achieving a title of influence, helping others, growing as a person, enjoying interpersonal relationships, and earning money. Your self-esteem is your evaluation of these and other areas of your life.

It is important to feel positive about yourself. Developing self-esteem provides you with a strong foundation for the development of healthy relationships, contributions through work, balance in life, risk taking, satisfactory decisions, and self-acceptance. Remember that self-esteem is related to your values and is therefore very personal. The following are some basic concepts about self-esteem.

1. It is important for you to develop self-esteem because it will help you in all areas of your life.

2. Develop **your own** mechanisms for maintaining self-esteem. Learn to "pat yourself on the back" for an achievement rather than depending on others for that reward.

3. Although developing self-esteem from within is important, you can also derive it from others. It is nice to hear others compliment you on your appearance, your job, your beliefs, and your decisions. Positive comments from others can add to your self-esteem.

4. You can take specific action to enhance your self-esteem. Locating supportive friends, going on a diet, trying something new, obtaining positive feedback on the job, or just smiling more often so that others smile back at you are all actions that you can take to increase your self-esteem.

WHERE DOES YOUR SELF-ESTEEM COME FROM?

The following activities are designed to help you assess the sources of your self-esteem.

When Do You Feel Positive about Yourself?

Think about the times that you feel positive about yourself and about what you have done. What are the sources of those positive feelings? What are you saying to yourself when you are feeling positive? How are you perceived by others when you are feeling positive? In the following spaces, describe activities and occasions in which you feel positive about yourself. This can be in the present or in the past and the categories are provided as a guideline. Don't be limited by them.

Your physical appearance

_____

_____

_____

Relationships with others

_____

_____

_____

Your work

_____

_____

_____

Involvement with organizations

_____

_____

_____

Learning experiences

_____

_____

_____

Sports and physical activities

_____

_____

_____

Use of knowledge and skills in different ways

_____

_____

_____

Other sources of positive feelings

_____

_____

_____

When Do You Feel Negative about Yourself?

Now think about the times when you have experienced negative feelings or disappointments. What are the sources of these negative feelings? What are you saying to yourself when you are feeling negative? How do others respond to you when you are feeling negative about yourself? Write your thoughts in the following spaces.

Your physical appearance

_____

_____

_____

Relationships with others

_____

_____

_____

Your work

_____

_____

_____

Involvement in organizations

_____

_____

Learning experiences

_____

_____

Sports and physical activities

_____

_____

Use of knowledge and skills in different ways

_____

_____

Other sources of negative feelings

_____

_____

Feeling some fear about this process of evaluating yourself is normal. Keep going. Be brave.

Now review your responses to compare the positive and the negative feelings that you have listed. When do you feel positive about yourself? What factors are present when your self-esteem is high? Write several of them in the following spaces.

_____

_____

_____

_____

_____

Look back over your negative feelings and experiences and consider the factors that tend to undermine your self-esteem. What conditions are present when you feel negative about yourself? Write them in the following spaces.

_____

_____

_____

_____

_____

What can you do to increase the positive factors that enhance your self-esteem and decrease the negative factors that undermine your self-esteem? Developing your self-esteem is a lifelong process that is well worth the effort. Now, look at self-esteem in another way.

What Is Your Perception of Self-Esteem?

The messages you received about yourself as you grew up helped to determine your adult self-image. As an infant, you were egocentric and totally absorbed in yourself. You were not born with beliefs about yourself, but rather, you were born with a *clean slate* and developed your self-esteem through interaction with others. In this section, you will be asked to consider how you perceive self-esteem in others. By doing this, you will learn more about your personal definition of self-esteem.

What is self-esteem on a practical level, and how does it show up in your everyday life? Consider what low self-esteem looks like to you and then consider the same questions for high self-esteem.

How does someone reveal low self-esteem? In the space below, list some of the characteristics of a person with low self-esteem.

_____

_____

_____

What does a person with low self-esteem say? In the space below, describe what this person sounds like.

_____

_____

_____

In your opinion, how does a person with low self-esteem feel?

_____

_____

_____

Think of a person, real or fictitious, whom you consider to have low self-esteem. How does that low self-esteem manifest itself in the person's daily life?

_____

_____

_____

Now think of a person whom you know that you feel has high self-esteem. In the space below, describe that person.

_____

_____

_____

What does the person with high self-esteem look like? What characteristics does the person with high self-esteem possess?

_____

_____

_____

What does the person with high self-esteem say? What does the person sound like?

_____

_____

_____

In your opinion, how does the person with high self-esteem feel?

_____

_____

_____

How does the person's high self-esteem manifest itself in the person's daily life?

_____

_____

_____

Self-esteem is often overlooked in the process of considering career and life options. Researchers have repeatedly confirmed that the way you feel about yourself is linked to career and life satisfaction. It is important to understand the concept of self-esteem and how it relates to your life. Your behavior is affected by your self-esteem.

Lack of time, constant noise, and plain, everyday life may obscure your inner feelings and thoughts. The radio in the car, the television at home, the needs of others, the demands of work, the push and pull of finances, and unceasing chores fill our lives with duties, responsibilities, and often pandemonium. Yet it's important to free up time to explore your values and evaluate your self-esteem. This review can benefit all the areas of your life.

YOUR SELF-ESTEEM TREE

First, consider your uniqueness by completing the following sentences on the Self-Esteem "I" Tree. The branches of your tree bear many buds. Imagine that it is spring and the buds are about to bloom. Each blossom is unique and beautiful, just as your thoughts and feelings are special. A single bud is special, but when you step back and notice the entire tree full of buds, the view is breathtaking. Your uniqueness is similar to the tree's beauty.

Create some quiet space and time in your life to really explore your uniqueness by completing the following Self-Esteem "I" Tree. Listen to your inner self and respond with the first idea or words that come into your mind. Those first reactions are the correct ones for you.

Consider the individual branches of your tree one at a time and then step back and admire the entire tree, complete with the buds. Just as the buds are fragile, your self-esteem is very delicate and vulnerable to outside forces. The harsh, cold wind and elements can damage the blooms on the tree. Criticism, negative joking, constant comparisons, embarrassments, rejections, and negative labels damage your self-esteem until you begin to question yourself, believe the negativity, and even incorporate the negative thinking into your behavior. Then the negative on the outside becomes part of you.

You can become your worst critic, ignoring your needs, feelings, and goals. Care of yourself becomes secondary or even last on the long list of things to do. A tree requires watering, sun, pruning, and fertilizing in order to thrive, bloom, and grow. Similarly, your self-esteem requires even more tender and loving care. Why is it that caring for other living things is natural, but caring for self-esteem is so overlooked? Your self-esteem requires at least as much if not more care from the primary caretaker—you.

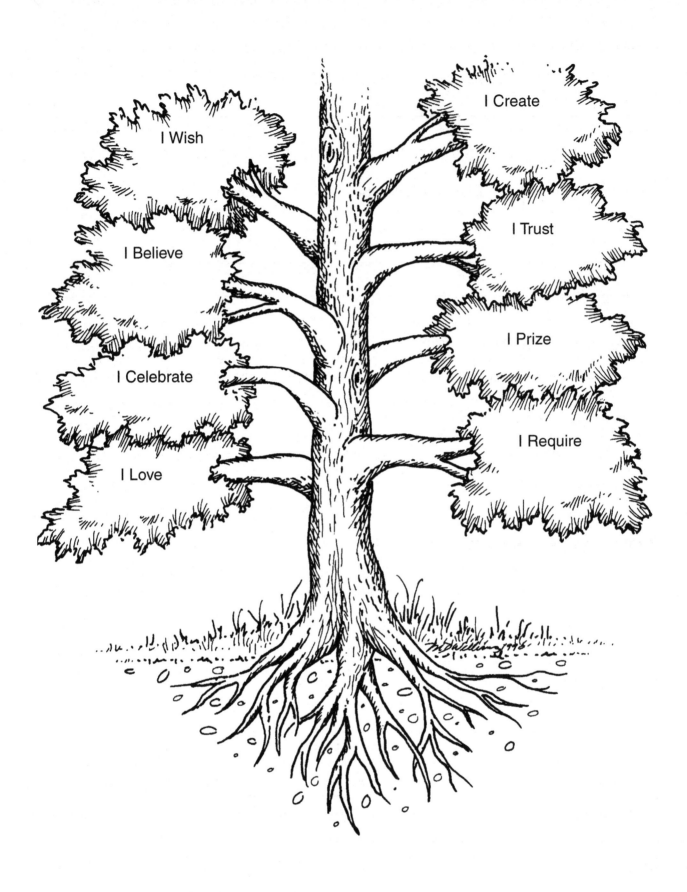

I Wish

I Create

I Believe

I Trust

I Celebrate

I Prize

I Love

I Require

LABELS, POISONERS, AND CULTIVATORS OF SELF-ESTEEM

Sometimes feelings keep you from accomplishing a desired task or goal. An appropriate analogy to the theme of self-esteem is the flight of the honeybee. The honeybee is a curious insect. Aerodynamically, the honeybee is not supposed to fly, because the weight of its body is greater than the wings should be able to carry. The bee does not know this, and no one has successfully informed the bee. It flies and completes its mission by pollinating blossoms, never knowing that technically it should not be able to fly. What may be holding you back from accomplishing your mission? Are any negative labels, thoughts, fears, or criticisms sticking with you and keeping you from accomplishing your goals?

Carrying around old labels can be a heavy burden. Sometimes, you confirm that these labels are correct by creating circumstances that support your belief in them. Labels can limit you if you stop short of achieving your goals.

What are some of the positive labels that you had growing up? Some examples are pretty, cute, handsome, fun, sweet, helpful, smart, popular, leader, sharp, cool, neat, coordinated, quick, mature, mannerly, well-behaved, good, thoughtful. Write some of the positive labels that you heard about yourself.

_____

_____

_____

What are some of the positive labels you choose to describe yourself now?

_____

_____

_____

What are some of the negative labels that you endured as you grew up? Some examples are four-eyes, smart aleck, slow, selfish, homely, shy, loud, bad, dummy, stupid, lazy, too tall ("too" anything), goody-two-shoes, wise guy, clumsy, weak, nerd, geek, and metal mouth. Write some of the negative labels that you heard about yourself.

_____

_____

_____

What are some of the negative labels that you choose to describe yourself now?

_____

_____

_____

Just as you would not consider poisoning a growing, healthy tree, it would be a sheer waste to poison flourishing self-esteem. Consider the following obstacles to self-esteem that poison the spirit and kill creativity. This list has been adapted from the work of Sidney Simon, a noted author and authority on the issues of self-esteem (1989, pp. 51–119).

Self-Esteem Poisoners

- Underestimating your abilities as a reason not to try
- Believing that you do not deserve better
- Magnifying every setback as proof of failure
- Expecting perfection immediately
- Creating a self-fulfilling prophecy of unworthiness
- Engaging in addictions that eventually control everything
- Moving in a self-destructive pattern that spirals downward
- Passivity to decisions and events
- Guilt and shame
- Derogatory thinking about yourself and allowing others to confirm these negative thoughts

Do you find yourself engaging in any one of these behaviors? If so, place a check mark next to each poisoner that seems to block you. The poisoners and the negative labels that you have identified may be held over from childhood and adolescence or may have been acquired in your adult years.

What can you do to reverse the effects of these self-esteem poisoners and labels? Developing and nurturing your self-esteem is important, just as you would care for your trees or plants. Make your self-esteem work for you and not against you in the career and life planning process. The following suggestions may help you to plan a strategy for growing and nurturing your self-esteem. This list has also been adapted from the work of Sidney Simon. Check those that you would like to encourage in your own life.

I know there are aspects about myself that puzzle me, and other aspects that I do not know. But as long as I am friendly and loving to myself, I can courageously and hopefully look for the solutions to the puzzles and for the ways to find out more about me.

—Virginia Satir, *Self Esteem*

Self-Esteem Cultivators

- Find positive mentors and role models.
- Risk by expanding horizons—learn something new.
- Seek and build emotional supports.
- Reclaim lost power—make the difficult decision.
- Stop blaming others, anyone, anything, everyone, the world.

- Recognize individual uniqueness in yourself and in others.
- Create human warmth by joining.
- Acknowledge your values and allocate your time accordingly.
- Be productive. Start by achieving the little goals.
- Write your goals and fulfill them—start small and work up.
- Visualize a path clear of obstacles.
- Visualize high self-esteem, and feeling positive.
- Keep a journal in which you explore your present dilemmas, feelings, and thoughts.
- Give positive feedback to significant others in your life.
- Use the following sentence starters:
  - I appreciate your . . .
  - I value your . . .
  - I respect your . . .
  - I prize your . . .
  - I admire your . . .
- Request positive feedback from significant others.
- Reprogram your negative thoughts with positive ones.
- Replace your old "shoulds" with "wants."

YOUR ACTION PLAN TO ENHANCE YOUR SELF-ESTEEM

Review your plans for improving your self-esteem and make a commitment to yourself and at least one other person that you will address one or more of the sixteen self-esteem cultivators. Write those that you have selected and list several specific actions that you can take to increase your self-esteem.

_____

_____

_____

_____

_____

_____

The purpose of life is undoubtedly to know oneself.

—Mohandas K. Gandi

CHAPTER 6

Lifestyle Considerations

What kind of life do you want to live? Do you want to live in a specific part of the country? Do you want to live in a rural setting or in a metropolitan area? Do you want to be involved in community activities, or do you want to be left to yourself? Do you want to live near your relatives? Do you want to have cultural activities available to you, or would you rather live where you have ready access to the outdoors without many people around?

In considering any career or life decisions, it is very useful to evaluate what lifestyle considerations are important to you. If access to entertainment and cultural opportunities is important, you probably want to live in a metropolitan area. This may affect the type of career decision you make. If you wish to live in a rural area, then you should choose a career that will allow you to locate there. If you want to travel often, you may wish to choose a career that involves frequent travel.

LIFESTYLE ASSESSMENT

The following listing of lifestyle considerations will help you assess which are most important to you. Go through the list and place a check mark (✓) in the appropriate category, indicating how important that lifestyle consideration is to you. There may be only a few that are very important. If so, you have more flexibility in forming a lifestyle that is compatible with the considerations. If, however, certain lifestyle considerations are very important to you, these may have a very significant influence on your career and life planning.

Lifestyle Considerations	Very *Important*	Moderately *Important*	Not *Important*
WORK RELATED LIFESTYLE CONSIDERATIONS			
Spend no more than 15 minutes commuting to work			
Live close to work			
Be able to walk to work			
Live where my significant other can have a job			
Travel for my job			
Have little or no travel for my job			
Move frequently for my company			
Settle into one community and stay there			
Develop a secure financial future			
Have a good retirement system			
Work part time			
Telecommute part of the week			
Use flextime for scheduling hours			
Work on weekends and nights			
Enjoy social contacts with my work colleagues			
Own my own business			
Have my own office			
Drive from place to place for my job			
Schedule my own work day			
Try to make a difference			
Commit to a larger vision			
Engage in public service			
Be a part of a team			
Love my work			
Receive reimbursement for credit classes			
Have computer access			
PERSONAL CONSIDERATIONS			
Own my own home			
Live in an apartment			
Live in a rural setting			
Live in a suburban community			
Live in or near a city			
Live in a stable community			

Lifestyle Considerations	Very Important	Moderately Important	Not Important
Live in a moderate climate			
Enjoy the change of seasons			
Live in a warm climate			
Have time to develop my interests			
Have time to attend children's activities			
Be active in my community			
Spend time with arts and crafts			
Seek adventure trips on weekends			
Engage in volunteer work			
Run for political office			
Eat out often			
Cultivate my own garden			
Build/create things with my hands			
Live where people share my values			
Live near the water			
Be close to cultural opportunities			
Grow plants and flowers			
Travel for adventure			
Have a second home			
Live close to stores			
Live near quality health care services			
Care for grandchildren			
Learn formally and informally			
Be active in my church or synagogue			
Take in a movie			
Attend plays and concerts			
Integrate physical activity easily			
Live near a park			
Have access to cable television			
Be able to enjoy a pet			
Live near clear cell phone reception			
Be near entertainment			
Live where children can walk to school			
Live near relatives			
Be able to develop new friends			
Have a yard and house chores			
Play organized sports			
Develop new sport interests			
Be able to obtain wireless Internet			
Enjoy organized activities			
Engage in activities with my significant other			
Spend time with neighbors			
Enjoy time alone			

Now review your list. In the following spaces, write five to ten of the lifestyle considerations that are most important to you.

1. _____   6. _____

2. _____   7. _____

3. _____   8. _____

4. _____   9. _____

5. _____   10. _____

How can you structure your life and career in the future so that you can fulfill these lifestyle priorities? What influence would they have over your choice of a career or over your choice of where and how you want to live? Write your responses in the following spaces.

_____

_____

_____

_____

_____

_____

_____

_____

In summary, your total lifestyle is very important to your life satisfaction and to your general mental and physical well-being. It is important to maintain a variety of interests and activities outside of your work that can form the basis of a well-rounded lifestyle. Make specific plans for achieving not only your career goals but also the lifestyle of your choice. In future years, it may be difficult for many people to fulfill their needs for self-esteem and self-actualization primarily through their work. A well-developed, balanced lifestyle may hold the key to future success, happiness, and fulfillment.

> ***Try to realize, and truly realize, that what stands between you and a different life are matters of responsible choice.***
>
> —Gary Zukav, *Seat of the Soul*

Acknowledge Your Unique Self

You have now evaluated your work values, interests, skills, personal values, and lifestyle preferences. This knowledge can help you to make life and career decisions based on what you need and what you want. Knowing yourself is the essential first step in effective career and life planning. To summarize what you have found out about yourself in Section I, it may be helpful to return to the questions asked at the beginning. Review your original responses throughout the section as you complete this summary.

WHAT ARE MY WORK VALUES?

In the following spaces write at least five of your most important work values.

Work values   Others

1. _____   _____
2. _____   _____
3. _____   _____
4. _____   _____
5. _____   _____

How do your work values relate to a career or lifestyle you might choose? Write your answer in this space.

What are my interests?

In the following spaces write at least five of your major interests.

Major interests	Others
1. _____	_____
2. _____	_____
3. _____	_____
4. _____	_____
5. _____	_____

How do these interests relate to a career or lifestyle you might choose? Write your answer in this space.

What are my skills and abilities?

In the following spaces write at least five self-management skills and at least five functional skills that you have or would like to develop.

Self-management skills	Others
1. _____	_____
2. _____	_____
3. _____	_____
4. _____	_____
5. _____	_____

Functional skills and abilities	Others
1. _____	_____
2. _____	_____
3. _____	_____
4. _____	_____
5. _____	_____

How do your skills relate to a career or lifestyle you might choose? Write your answer in this space.

What are my personal values?

In the following spaces write at least five of your most important personal values, in order of priority.

Personal values	Others
1. _____	_____
2. _____	_____
3. _____	_____
4. _____	_____
5. _____	_____

How do your personal values affect your choice of a career or lifestyle?

What are my five top self-esteem cultivators, and what action can I take to build my self-esteem?

Self-esteem cultivators	Actions I can take to build my self-esteem
1. _____	_____
2. _____	_____
3. _____	_____
4. _____	_____
5. _____	_____

What lifestyle considerations are important to me?

In the following spaces write at least five of your most important lifestyle considerations.

Lifestyle considerations	Others
1. _____	_____
2. _____	_____
3. _____	_____
4. _____	_____
5. _____	_____

In order to achieve this lifestyle, what type of career do you need? What other actions must you take? Write your answer in this space.

Now proceed to Section two, Manage Change in Your Life, where you will explore how to use the information about yourself from this chapter as you begin to consider the changes that are before you.

ADDITIONAL RESOURCES

General Resources for Career and Life Planning

Albion, M. & Kang, L. (2006). *Passion at work: How to find work you love and live the time of your life.* Upper Saddle River, NJ: Prentice Hall.

Bernstein, A. B. (2004). *Guide to your career.* NY: The Princeton Review.

Boldt, L. (2004). *How to find the work you love.* NY: Penguin Books.

Bolles, R. N. (2005). *How to find your mission in life.* Berkeley, CA: Ten Speed Press.

Bolles, R. N. & Bolles M. E. (2008). *What color is your parachute? 2009: A practical manual for job-hunters and career-changers.* Berkeley, CA: Ten Speed Press.

Borchard, D., Bonner, C. & Musich, S. (2008). *Your career planner.* Dubuque, Iowa: Kendall/ Hunt Publishing Company.

Bronson, P. (2005). *What should I do with my life?* NY: Random House.

Cannon, J. (2005). *Now what do I do? The woman's guide to a new career.* Herndon, Virginia: Capital Books.

Eikleberry, C. & Bolles, R. N. (2007). *The career guide for creative and unconventional people.* Berkeley, CA: Ten Speed Press.

Everett, M. (1999). *Making a living while making a difference: The expanded guide to creating careers with a conscience.* Canada: New Society Publishers.

Griffiths, B. (2003). *Do what you love for the rest of your life: A practical guide to career change and personal renewal.* NY: Random House Publishing.

Krumboltz, J. D. & Levin, A. S. (2004). *Luck is no accident: Making the most of happenstance in your life and career.* Manassas Park, VA: Impact Publishers.

Leider, R. J. (2005). *The power of purpose: Creating meaning in your life and work.* San Francisco: Berrett-Koehler Publishers, Inc.

Lore, N. (1998). *The pathfinder.* NY: Simon & Schuster.

Lore, N. & Spadafore, A. (2008). *Now what?* NY: Simon & Schuster Adult Publishing Group.

Maslow, A. (1970). *Motivation and personality* (2nd ed.). NY: Harper and Row.

Merrill, M. A. (2007). *Live the life you love: Discover your purpose and live it with intention.* Garden City, NY: Morgan James Publishing, LLC.

Michelozzi, B. N., Surrell, L. J. & Corbez, R. I. (2003). *Coming alive from nine to five in a 24/7 world: A career search handbook for the 21st century.* NY: McGraw-Hill Companies.

Mitchell, K. (2003). *The unplanned career: How to turn curiosity into opportunity.* San Francisco, CA: Chronicle Books.

Persona, M. (2007). *Moving on: Out-of-the-box wisdom for your career in this ever changing world.* CreateSpace (Self Publishing).

Ryan, R. (2002). *What to do with the rest of your life: America's top career coach shows you how to find or create the job you'll love.* NY: Simon & Schuster.

Sanborn, K. & Ricci, W. R. (2003). *Seasons of your career: How to master the cycles of career change.* NY: McGraw-Hill Companies.

Schein, E. (2006). *Career anchors: Discovering your real values.* San Francisco: Jossey-Bass Publishing.

Shambaugh, R. (2008). *It's not a glass ceiling, it's a sticky floor: Free yourself from the hidden behaviors sabotaging your career success.* NY: McGraw Hill.

Simon, S., Kirschenbaum, H. & Howe, L.W. (1995). *Values clarification: The classic guide to discovering your truest feelings.* NY: Warner Books, Incorporated.

Snodgrass, J. (1996). *Follow your career star: A career quest based on inner values.* NY: Kensington Publishing Corporation.

Snyder, K. (2003). *Lavender road to success: The career guide for the gay community.* Berkeley, CA: Ten Speed Press.

Career Interests and Personality Type Resources

Dunning, D. (2001). *What's your type of career?* Palo Alto, CA: Davies-Black Publishing.

Holland, J. (1997). *Making vocational choices: A theory of vocational personalities and work environments.* Odessa, FL: Psychology Assessment Resources.

Huszczo, G. E. (2008). *Making a difference by being yourself: Using your personality type at work and in relationships.* Palo Alto, CA: Davies-Black Publishing.

Kiersey, D. & Bates, M. (1998). *Please understand me II: Temperament character intelligence.* Amherst, NY: Prometheus Books.

Kroeger, O., Thuesen, J. M. & Rutledge, H. (2002). *Type talk at work: How the 16 personality types determine your success on the job.* NY: Dell Publishing.

Laney, M. O. (2002). *The introvert advantage: How to thrive in an extrovert world.* NY: Workman's Publishing Co.

Tieger, P. D. & Barron-Tieger, B. (2001). *Do what you are* (3rd ed.). Boston: Little, Brown.

Wier, M. (2007). *Confessions of an introvert: The shy girl's guide to career, networking and getting the most out of life.* Lincoln, NB: iUniverse.

Zichy, S. & Bidou, A. (2007). *Career match: Connecting who you are with what you'll love to do.* NY: AMACOM.

Self-Esteem Resources

Branden, N. (2001). *The power of self-esteem.* NY: Barnes & Noble Books.

Branden, N. (1995). *Six pillars of self-esteem.* NY: Bantam Books.

Bums, D. D. (1999). *Feeling good: The new mood therapy.* NY: Harper.

Bums, D. D. (1999). *Ten days to self-esteem.* Newport Beach, CA: Quill Publishing.

Covey, S. R. (2005). *The 8th habit.* NY: Free Press.

Covey, S. R. (2004). *The seven habits of highly effective people.* Updated. NY: Free Press.

Jeffers, S. (2006). *Feel the fear and do it anyway.* NY: Columbine Books.

Jeffers, S. (2005). *The little book of confidence.* Santa Monica, CA: Jeffers Press.

McKay, M. & Fanning, P. (2002). *Self-esteem.* CA: New Harbinger Publishing.

McKay, M., Fanning, P., Honeychurch, C. & Sutker, C. (2005). *Self-esteem companion.* CA: New Harbinger Publishing.

Menter, M. (2004). *Office sutras: Exercises for your soul at work.* York Beach, ME: Red Wheel/Weiser, LLC.

Minchinton, J. (2001). *52 things you can do to raise your self-esteem.* Vanzant, MO: Arnford House Publishers.

Sherfield, R. M. (2004). *The everything self-esteem book: Boost your confidence, achieve inner strength, and learn to love yourself.* Cincinnati, OH: Adams Media.

Shiraldi, G. R. (2001). *The self-esteem workbook.* CA: New Harbinger Publishing.

Vanzant, I. (2008). *Tapping the power within: A path to self-empowerment for women.* NY: Smiley Books.

SECTION *two*

Negotiate Change in Your Life

What would life be like without any changes? Pretty dull, wouldn't you think? It is hard to imagine a life without change, but sometimes too much change, or change that is totally out of your control, can be very stressful. In addition, it is important to be able to initiate changes when you are ready for the next phase in your life. This section will provide a few theories that will assist you to understand the value of change and the process of transition throughout your life. You will appreciate that:

- Change is a normal part of life and is to be welcomed, not avoided.

- Your needs and expectations change as you go through life.

- You can accept responsibility for negotiating change in your life.

- Change means taking risks.

- You can anticipate certain changes, but others can take you totally by surprise.

- It is not the change that you resist, but the difficult process of transition.

- It takes time and energy to accept and integrate major life transitions.

In your career and in other areas of your life, it is important to be able to anticipate potential changes. The four "Ds"—disengagement, disidentification, disenchantment, and disorientation—are internal clues and may alert you to an oncoming change. As the engineer of your train trip throughout life, you have the necessary skills and knowledge to guide your train safely through the rough terrain and conditions that confront you on your journey. The first step is to learn the differences between change and transition. Change, a fact of life in this century, can be described as permanent white water bubbling around us. This section on the negotiation of change begins with an investigation of career and life planning issues for the future and then moves to an overview of meaningful theories that provide valuable insights about change and the process of renewal and life transitions.

CHAPTER 7

Work in the Future

- How will work be defined throughout the twenty-first century?

- What changes will continue to occur technologically and how will these innovations affect your work and your career/life choices?

- What organizational shifts will impact your current and future planning?

- How will the supply and demand of work locally, nationally, and internationally affect work options?

This chapter promises to explore some of these challenges as described by scholars who observe and study economic, sociological, historical, and cultural trends in the world of work. Seven practical recommendations are also offered to maximize the benefit of changes and challenges yet to come.

Three authors have been selected to add to our global understanding of work. Thomas Friedman is a noted *New York Times* columnist, Pulitzer Prize winner, and author of *From Beirut to Jerusalem* (1995), *The Lexus and the Olive Tree* (1999), and *The World Is Flat: A Brief History of the 21st Century* (2007). He describes how competition, specifically free-market capitalism, fuels international economies which in turn affect the nature, the quantity, and the quality of work locally and nationally. Friedman's flat world perspective impacts the future of work.

Daniel Pink, an editor and former White House speech writer, describes the expanded role and importance of right right-brained, creative thinking in *A Whole New Mind* (2006). He asserts that the nature of work is shifting from an information-focused age to a conceptual-focused age where reliance on six human abilities defines future success and satisfaction. These abilities are described later in this chapter. His meaningful commentary about social, economic, and cultural trends provides a similar road map for work in the future.

The third noted author, William Bridges, provides a framework to better appreciate the complex nature of change and transition in our personal lives and in the workplace. His prolific writings include *Transitions: Making Sense of Life's Changes* (2004), *The Way of Transition* (2001), *Job Shift* (1994), and *Surviving Corporate Transition* (1993). A fuller explanation of Bridges' approach to dealing with transitions, along with helpful exercises, is addressed in the next chapter. Bridges describes one notable shift in the world of work that he terms "dejobbing," which moves workers from standard jobs to contract work for limited timeframes.

Together these noted authors encourage us to capitalize on our uncharted journey into the future. On a train trip, we cannot clearly see around each bend of the track or through upcoming darkened tunnels. What we can do is prepare by packing wisely and studying the terrain maps, which may help us to anticipate a multitude of personal and professional challenges, not just now but throughout life. The unknown bumps or crossings need not derail our unique and individual train trip as we navigate our way to a fulfilling future.

> *Nothing can stop the man with the right mental attitude from achieving his goal; nothing on Earth can help the man with the wrong mental attitude.*
>
> —Thomas Jefferson

PREDICTIONS OF EXPERTS

Our first author, Thomas Friedman, asserts that the speed and accessibility of the Internet levels the playing field of work as these factors promote globalization in countries that are prepared to integrate technology and collaborate using free market capitalism. He writes that our world is shrinking because of three reasons:

1. Accessibility of the Internet to promote innovation, collaboration, competition, and creativity anywhere, anytime.

2. Demand for lower costs and greater choices drives developed nations to outsource routine jobs (e.g., call centers) to selected developing nations with qualified workers.

3. Developing nations, specifically China and India, are poised and ready to benefit from the "flat" world with their homegrown workforces who have earned educational credentials in engineering and science.

Friedman (2007) strongly recommends that the United States take immediate action as he predicts an overwhelming shortage of trained engineers and scientists. He states that the United States, in particular its educational system, is not currently anticipating nor addressing the overwhelming demand for technical expertise in engineering and science. On a positive note, Friedman asserts that Americans are well-positioned to tap into their individual and collective creativity, inventiveness, and entrepreneurial capabilities. Small business ownership has tripled in the past decade and is expected to be one of the highest growth areas in the United States. American ingenuity, determination, and persistence can be counted on in tough economic times to spark the next trend or discover the next opportunity. What is significant for us to consider about what Friedman writes?

1. Choose to enroll or major in math, science, and/or technology related courses in high school and college, even if this is a stretch for you.

2. Be prepared for jobs that are not yet invented. Since our technical knowledge doubles every two years, work opportunities will continue to evolve.

3. Increase your knowledge about the nature and culture of work in other countries.

4. Consider entrepreneurship because this is one of the fastest growing options.

5. Learn a language (any language) to enhance your skill set as we act locally and think globally.

6. Nurture your passion and curiosity for a broad range of topics and become a multidisciplinary thinker, combining and overlapping your expertise.

7. Develop and rely on communication and interpersonal skills because the value of one-on-one relationships can never be outsourced.

8. Embrace lifelong learning, either informally (by talking to individuals you meet or reading expansively) or formally (by taking classes, seminars, or engaging in professional development in your field and in other fields). Learning of any kind is here to stay!

> *The most important things you'll ever learn in life are the things you learn after you think you know it all.*
>
> —Harry S Truman

The second noted author important to acknowledge as we consider work in the future is Daniel Pink (2006), who writes persuasively about the value of right-brained, creative thinking. His thesis provides a novel way of considering work as he focuses on our need to seek fun, play, inventiveness, and happiness. He describes a work shift from the information age to what he calls the conceptual age. The conceptual age calls for a new skill set because workers will be asked to move from left-brained thinking, which demands facts, data, and a structured work environment to a more right-brained approach, which joyfully embraces creativity, participative teamwork, humor, and work that has meaning.

Pink states that corporate America is moving from a traditional left-brained work ethic to a more nonconformist, right-brained focus because workers of the future need to think holistically and creatively. Computers now have the capacity to perform left-brained work. We can choose to look at this as a blessing or a curse. Pink contends that this transition, and the resulting freedom from routine work, validates the necessity of American workers learning to rely more fully on the right side of their brains. This shift to the conceptual age of work promises to tap into the wellspring of a new generation of workers. What are Pink's primary lessons for us as we move into the conceptual age of work? Pink wants us to complement our current skill set with six right-brained senses by:

1. Evolving into someone who infuses an aesthetic sense into everyday life through the power of design where utility and significance is valued—a designer. Pink encourages us to live simply and beautifully. He recommends that we create our home, work, and community spaces in a way that will enhance productivity and beauty in our lives.

2. Evolving into someone who captures the essence and spirit of events, places, and things to clarify understanding and appreciation—a storyteller. Pink asserts that stories are the intersection of high touch and high tech as we seek to contextualize situations and events. Narratives are more necessary in the conceptual age because vast amounts of information are accessible. One example relates directly to the medical profession and the training of doctors. Medical students are now introduced to the notion of active listening—paying attention to patients and their symptoms rather than relying on mere diagnostic questions.

3. Evolving into someone who thinks about the entire symphony rather than focusing on one or two instruments in the orchestra—a synthesizer. We should be noticing interconnections and patterns that enable leaps of imagination across narrow discipline boundaries. (Thomas Friedman's books use metaphors to the utmost and serve as a good example of a synthesizer mentality given that he integrates history, economics, and current political and cultural realities to assert that the world is indeed flat. Pink and Friedman encourage us to cross over artificial learning boundaries and apply a multidisciplinary approach to life and work.)

4. Evolving into someone who experiences the world through someone else's eyes and who will be a bridge builder from person to person, business to business, culture to culture, etc.—an empathizer. Computers will never demonstrate genuine empathy so there is no worry about this asset being outsourced! Pink asserts that empathy is more than a skill. It is an ethic for living an authentic and

meaningful life. Human understanding and relationships transcend individuals, families, cultures, and nations. Our world needs empathy now more than ever. Based on Daniel Goleman's (2006) book on emotional intelligence, you can measure your empathy quotient (EQ) with sixty questions provided at the following Web site: http://www.tinyurl.com/dbsd8.

5. Evolving into someone who can enthusiastically laugh, enjoy humor, and play games—a player. Pink validates the importance of childlike fun in our daily lives for health benefits, improved morale, enhanced connectivity with others, and spiritual well being. The value of laughter cannot be overstated. Pink asserts that business cultures that honor joyful and productive interactions leading to greater creativity and collaboration are well-positioned for the conceptual age. Check your own humor quotient through this enlightening humor scale developed by Dr. James Thorson and found at this site: http://www.tinyurl.com/6t7ff/.

6. Evolving into someone who tries to answer deeper and more significant questions in life by focusing on the "why"—a meaning maker. Connecting life work, purpose, and existence to a higher calling empowers and enables mighty contributions to family, community, country, and the world. Thinking and acting beyond individual benefit and stretching to act for the common good, or collective benefit, is noble. Finding meaning in life is a lifelong quest. The following books and authors inspire us with their quest for meaning. Researcher and Tufts University Dean, Robert Sternberg, asserts that thinking beyond oneself for the common good defines wisdom as meaningful. Pulitzer Prize winner psychiatrist Robert Coles wrote *The Call of Service: Witness to Idealism* (1993) in which he explored the resiliency of children who lived in dire circumstances and found meaning in service. Concentration camp survivor Viktor Frankl wrote the classic *Man's Search for Meaning* (1946). He shared the loss of his loved ones along with his dignity but he reclaimed meaning for his life. Computer science professor Randy Pausch wrote and performed *The Last Lecture* (2008) for his three young children. His inspirational lecture, which took place at Carnegie Mellon University, is available for viewing at this site: www.cmu.edu/randyslecture/. Millions of people have found his poignant message a lesson for living life fully. He found meaning in his childhood dreams and he made each one happen, for himself and his family, before his death at age 47 from pancreatic cancer in July 2008.

Reading and learning about these and other journeys provides valuable insights and perspectives. We become richer for their experiences.

Ideas are for everybody . . . if you don't act on your idea, it pops out of your head and jumps into someone else's.

—Stephen Spielberg

Our third author also enriches our understanding of the future of work. William Bridges writes about shifts in the world of work from historical and futuristic perspectives. A shift in the early twentieth century started with the move from rural, farm-oriented labor to jobs in factories and large corporations that led to the growth of cities and fundamental societal changes. The agrarian age, which blended farm work and home life with high individual control about the workday, was replaced with the industrial age, where acceptance of a "job" with high structure, regulation, and repetition became the norm. In the twentieth century, another job shift occurred with the general acceptance of organizations that provide a salary, benefits, security, colleagues, and a sense of identity closely tied to the job title. Now with technological advancements, the elimination of traditional job functions has led to another shift in the way work is performed. Bridges asserts that many factors forced organizations to "downshift" or "dejob" workers. Organizations are less likely to make long term commitments to individuals, especially when contracts for short term work will get the job done cheaper and with less initial investment. Employees are valued based on what they contribute to organizations, their flexibility in accepting new approaches to achieve organizational goals, and their ability to create and work collaboratively in teams to complete projects. Productivity rises while routine jobs are reduced.

Ron and Carol Krannich, in *The Best Jobs for the 21st Century* (1998), emphasize the need for people to prepare for high levels of uncertainty in the future. Their prediction of a slower rate of economic growth, fewer high-paying jobs, more low-paying service jobs, less loyalty to employers and organizations, and a greater need for workers to learn new skills, acquire new experiences, and to be job mobile, is our reality. This husband and wife team stresses the importance of hard work and education as they make the following predictions about the future which remain true today:

> *The best jobs of the future will go to those who empower themselves with a capacity to shape their future. They take responsibility for their employability. They dream possible dreams because they are well-educated, work hard, and know they must be prepared for constant change in the economy, the job market, and their work life.*
>
> (Krannich & Krannich, 1998, p. 2–3)

Tom Gorman (1996) coined the term "multipreneuring" to describe a free agent information age system where employees are continually asked to prove or demonstrate their economic value to organizations. He, along with William Bridges, predicted that business interactions would become more transactional rather than relationship based. Workers are viewed as service providers whose economic value must be obvious.

These authorities help us name and identify trends about the future of work in the twenty-first century, but do not provide comfort or security as we attempt to overcome our worst fears about the future. Their predictions and perspectives provide us with a rationale for what we experience and witness. How shall we anticipate our uncertain future and plan accordingly? It is our belief that those who engage in career and life planning, learn about future trends, and integrate self- and work knowledge will be better positioned to adapt and capitalize on an uncertain future. A summary of these trends is provided to give you a head start on your own future! Check the ones that you believe will have the most impact on you and your career and life plans for the future.

A SUMMARY OF WORKPLACE TRENDS

1. Understand that career change or re-careering is the norm for the majority of workers who can expect to enjoy three to six careers throughout their lives.

2. Recognize that there are significant opportunities for entrepreneurs to develop new services and new ways to approach traditional functions.

3. Be aware that organizations have the ability to track productivity and efficiency precisely and to monitor individual and collective work performance.

4. Assume responsibility for benefits, retirement, and health/life insurance.

5. Realize that fewer long term job opportunities may be available through organizations.

6. Integrate multidisciplinary approaches to solve complex challenges.

7. Emphasize the value of liberal arts or humanities disciplines as well as a multitude of internships to broaden perspectives.

8. Know that work involving information retrieval or repetitive tasks is subject to being outsourced to countries with less expensive labor costs. Workers in those countries will perform this type of work cheaper, quicker, and without complex labor laws (e.g., call centers in India).

9. Choose math and science courses or majors because scientists and mathematicians are in high demand to satisfy technological needs.

10. Prepare for future work by gaining all types of experience, even if that means working two jobs—one to earn a living and another to gain necessary experience.

11. Capitalize on the competencies of a diverse, high functioning team to accomplish work projects both in person and electronically.

12. Focus on the desirability and necessity of multilingual communication and interpersonal skills which are highly valued in the global workforce.

SEVEN TRENDS THAT AFFECT YOU AND YOUR WORK

The fundamental changes that are taking place in the world of work are already causing great upheaval in the workforce, as traditional jobs are eliminated and organizations seek to operate more efficiently. Long-held values of commitment to employees, manifested in secure jobs and benefits, are being challenged. Technological developments will continue to bring about profound change. How will the workplace trends affect you personally and professionally? The following seven trends may provide some insight as you explore your options.

1. **You change careers several times throughout your lifetime.** Changing careers has become the norm rather than the exception. Research indicates that you may work in several career fields, building a series of valuable, transferable skills. The increased likelihood of career change is the result of the changing values of workers, rapid changes in job expectations, and the culture of work in our society. You may not fully appreciate the twists and turns of your career until late in life. **Can you overcome your need for security and move toward desired career paths?**

2. **You are open to the potential of career surprises.** Pay attention to the possibilities and opportunities that exist even in seemingly negative events. A rejection letter or phone call could be turned into a positive experience if you are prepared to discuss other options within the company or to ask for valuable feedback about your interview. There are no disappointments in life, only opportunities if you choose to see the potential that awaits you. **Are you willing to remain open (look, see, and listen) to the potential of career surprises?**

3. **You and your "job" are defined differently.** Organizations increasingly seek individuals who perform specific kinds of work for a specific period of time. This makes jobs, job descriptions, and position titles less important. If you think of yourself as a self-motivated worker with an ownership stake in your career, you will picture yourself as the CEO of your career. This involves your thinking of yourself as an entrepreneur who contributes your unique talents and expertise for a time-limited project. You may work for several organizations simultaneously. Rather than being a jobholder, you have the potential of evolving into an opportunity-seeker. **What talents and expertise are you anxious to contribute to the world of work?**

4. **You develop more adaptive skills for the workplace.** Sophisticated technologies, just-in-time delivery, scarcity of natural resources, lower profit margins, and societal pressures require organizations and individuals to restructure work in more efficient and productive ways. Transferable skills such as teamwork, oral communication, effective writing, problem-solving, critical-thinking, and computational abilities are valuable and marketable. Rotation of responsibilities among team members, flat-

tening of hierarchical structures, and active participation from all organizational levels means that everyone is responsible for productivity and quality. You have the opportunity to contribute to the mission of your organization in very significant ways. **What adaptive skills do you need to learn and develop for the workplace?**

5. **You continue to learn throughout your life.** Postsecondary education adds to your lifetime earning potential. Research indicates that your opportunities and salary increase if you obtain a two- or a four-year degree. Successful completion of college pays big dividends over the course of a lifetime. Even a few college courses increase your marketability and your earnings. Committing yourself to lifelong learning means recognizing that you have something to learn. Consider what skills you may need in order to grow into the next position, and acquire them through professional development both inside and outside the workplace. You must grow to remain competitive and proficient. Your investment in your own learning is a necessity and not a luxury. **What are three things that you wish to learn to maintain your competitive edge?**

6. **You define yourself in broad terms as you seek balance.** Throughout this book you are encouraged to consider plans for your career and your life. This is increasingly important as you develop your own identity outside of a traditional job. In past generations, many tied too much of their identities to THE job. It defined and limited them. You are free to define yourself in a broader way to include the contributions you make to your workplace, but also your interests, your family and friends, your volunteer work, your faith, and many other components of your lifestyle. **How can you expand your identity and move toward balance in your life?**

7. **You have the option of alternative work patterns.** Telecommuting, flextime, compressed work schedules, job sharing, part-time work, and other creative alternatives are more accepted by organizations as they seek to meet the needs of workers and to remain sensitive to the environment by reducing traffic and pollutants. These flexible work patterns continue to expand as organizations receive incentives to promote worker flexibility. Alternative work patterns are quickly becoming the norm and not the exception. This is good news because you become responsible for your productivity and efficiency. You decide how to allocate your time and how to work most effectively. Recognize the benefits of alternative work patterns along with the potential drawback of isolation. A place of work provides a venue for valuable interpersonal relationships. You may need to replace this support if it is not available where you work. **What work pattern will you choose at this stage of your life to contribute effectively to the world of work?**

WORK IN THE FUTURE

The importance of playing an active role in your career and life planning has never been greater than it is today, and it will become even more important in the future. You are less likely to find a "job" providing benefits that you can stay with throughout your work life. It is necessary for you to articulate your skills, abilities, values, and goals and to relate these to a rapidly changing workplace. It is increasingly important to embrace change and to take risks in order to grow in your career.

Pay attention to the emergence of these seven trends in your life. Take full advantage of professional development programs, tuition assistance, or other individualized benefit plans as you continue to learn to maintain your competitive edge. Remain aware of the impact of new workplace trends as you consider opportunities. The world of work continues to change dramatically and requires sophisticated skills, the ability to adapt, and a willingness to view the big picture instead of a narrow specialty. Thriving on a sea of change is a critical asset as you consider emerging opportunities and seek to achieve a desired balance between your career and your life.

CHAPTER 8

The Process of Transition and Renewal

In 1908, the Dutch anthropologist, Arnold Van Gennep (1960), published a book entitled *The Rites of Passage*. He described how traditional societies structured life transitions. Rituals dealing with birth, puberty, separation from a group or society, marriage, incorporation back into a group with new roles and functions, and death were seen by Van Gennep as important ceremonies marking significant occasions in life. He saw these occasions as being made up of three phases: separation, transition, and incorporation.

CHANGE AND TRANSITIONS

The study of adult life transitions has expanded over the years to include age, stage, and phase theories. Some adult researchers deny that any patterns exist in adult development and instead focus primarily on how adults adapt to life. One of the most compelling theories that has emerged from this group is that of William Bridges (2004), who, in the book *Transitions*, described the process of transition.

Bridges (2004) has conceived a valuable framework that provides insight about what happens throughout our lives. He makes a clear distinction between a change and a transition. He defines change as a shift in an exterior situation, such as a move, the loss of a job, a marriage, or a death in a family. He defines transition as the internal shift (p. 97), which occurs in response to the external change. This internal shift could result in greater capacity to understand others, an expanded perspective about the world, a decision to return to school, or a withdrawal from life for a time. The transition is the psychological response or process that is made to accommodate the change that has occurred in life. Bridges believes that there is a distinct transition process characterized by three sequential phases (p. 84).

- **The ending** is experienced by loss and letting go of something, combined with appropriate feelings of grief. This could be the loss of a pattern of behavior, a loved one, a position or status, or an ineffective way of thinking. Bridges considers the ending phase the most significant because it is critical to recognize the necessity of letting go before you can be open to a new beginning.

- **The neutral zone** is an in-between, an insecure, an uneasy time, described as moving into an abyss or experiencing chaos. This phase may be accompanied by feelings of being lost, because not knowing the future is difficult. However, the neutral zone holds great potential for creativity, experimentation, and a clearer world view.

- **The new beginning** is signaled by a sense of being renewed and entering a new chapter of life. One develops new plans and establishes new goals with a sense of anticipation and an enhanced view of self. A new reality emerges. One's ability to accept and adapt to change, gain new world perspectives, and enhance relationships with others, is enlarged.

Bridges's framework is a paradox because it begins with endings. The actions you take to accept the endings enable you to begin anew. He believes that endings are foreshadowed by five "Ds" that include disengagement, dismantling, disidentification, disenchantment, and disorientation (pp. 107–132). These internal signals often begin years before an actual change takes place in your life. Recognizing these signals can make a difference in anticipating change in your life. Be alert to any or all of the following internal signals.

- **Feelings of disengagement**, which involve recognition of the fact that something is not working, a pulling away of the old ways. You are not as committed as before, which is discomforting and disconcerting.

- **Feelings of dismantling**, which involve taking apart some of the structure of your former life and your identity, similar to tearing apart some sections of a house in order to remodel it.

- **Feelings of disidentification**, which involve recognition of the external change together with a questioning of who you are. Your very authenticity as an individual is challenged. Now, whether you are divorced, jobless, or a millionaire, the question emerges: Who are you amidst this change? You are working through the process of transition.

- **Feelings of disenchantment**, which involve questioning of purpose, values, and life in general. What used to work in your favor does not fit any more. This "D" calls into question your long-held belief system. The bottom dropping out may be your signal that an ending has begun.

- **Feelings of disorientation**, which involve dismantling of the old way of being, the old self, the old belief system, and the old reality. You lose your sense of what is real because you have lost the way and the reason you were going there.

How does this apply to you as you negotiate the changes you experience in your life? Remember that you cannot always anticipate or control what life has waiting for you. The unpredictability of life can take your breath away. As the saying goes, "life happens when we least expect it." The focus then becomes your reaction to the change. You may or may not have control over the change, but you do have the opportunity to control your response to the change. You can assume responsibility for negotiating the change and grow through the transition process, even though you may feel disoriented. These feelings go hand in hand with the transition process. This is a normal part of growth. It is the good news and the bad news!

Every phase of the transition process offers great potential for growth. Confronting life's endings offers the possibility of closure through grieving. Wandering in the neutral zone offers great potential for creativity and growth. The new beginning can bring hope and excitement about the future and what is possible. Regardless of our awareness, Bridges believes that this transition cycle recurs in life. He also believes that it is critical to listen to and recognize the discomfort of the five "Ds" as you approach the transition process of endings, neutral zone, and new beginnings. Knowing that these phases are a normal part of the transition process offers some comfort, especially if you happen to be wandering in the neutral zone.

Take time now to consider your life changes and your transitions and anticipate the changes of the future.

List two changes (shifts in **external** situations) that you experienced in the past two years.

   1. _____

   2. _____

In a few words, describe the accompanying transitions (**internal** shifts) for each change.

Which one or more of the five Ds signaled the change that you were about to experience? (disengagement, dismantling, disidentification, disenchantment, and disorientation)

In order to plan to deal with future changes and transitions, how could you have better handled these changes?

What are two changes that you can anticipate in the next year or two?

   1. _____

   2. _____

How do you assess these potential changes in your life? Are the changes you anticipate age-related, stage-related, or phase-related? Are they coming from your need to grow? Are you experiencing one or more of the five Ds?

What are the risks that may be involved with these changes?

What are the risks if the changes do NOT happen?

As you work through this process of anticipating change, consider the following questions:

1. How can I best negotiate the necessary ending(s)? How can I let go and say good-bye appropriately?

2. Can I negotiate the neutral zone by allowing my creativity and inspiration to emerge? Can I tolerate not knowing the answer for an extended period of time?

3. How will I recognize the new beginnings in my life?

    What will that feel like?

    What do I anticipate?

    How can I hold out for the new beginning to occur and **not** rush, but accept the process of transitioning?

    Can I accept **not** knowing the next steps for a period of time?

Ten Qualities of the Self-Renewing Adult

Frederic Hudson (1999), in his book *The Adult Years: Mastering the Art of Self Renewal,* describes a cycle of change that continues throughout our lives. He makes a distinction between "mini-transitions," which deal with minor restructuring of one's life, such as a move or job change, and a "life transition," which involves a major disengagement from most aspects of a person's lifestyle and a reevaluation of goals, relationships, work values, and relationship with the world (pp. 53–74).

Hudson outlines ten essential qualities for adults to be self-renewing (pp. 234–252) and able to deal effectively with change. He believes that, by acknowledging the importance of and the improving of these qualities, a person can prepare to become self-renewing. The qualities that he identified are:

1. **Value driven.** You organize your priorities and allocate the precious resource of time according to what is most important to you. Values are your core, as they provide purpose to your life.

2. **Connected to the world.** You recognize that the relationships in your life are worth the investment of your time and energy. You value others and are willing to work at staying connected. You also remain aware of the world around you and realize that what happens in other parts of the world affects you.

3. **Require quiet and solitude.** You practice the discipline of self-reflection by honoring your private inner life. You recognize when it is time to retreat and focus on your inner self.

4. **Pace yourself.** You take the occasional breaks that are necessary to keep you fresh and on top of your game. You look for quality time to integrate what is really important to you.

5. **Make contact with nature.** You stop to smell the roses, touch the green grass, feel the woods, and see the beauty of the world around you, and do not take any of it for granted. You notice, enjoy, and value the calming and renewing beauty of nature.

6. **Tap into creativity and playfulness.** You laugh often and heartily, food for your soul. You risk creating without concern about quality or perfectionism. The sheer joy of creating leads you to an inner world that you appreciate and celebrate.

7. **Adapt to change.** You feel loss, recognize endings, and seek to understand life as you look for congruence between your private self and your public self. You are willing to accept the short-term pain for the long-term gain as you adjust and modify your life.

8. **Learn from the down times.** You trust the process of transition and tolerate ambiguity as you move through the neutral zones. You endure the disorientation and recognize it as an opportunity to reconfigure your life. You accept responsibility for your life.

9. **Always in training.** You love to learn and adopt learning as an attitude. You desire to build mastery. You invest time and energy in learning, trusting that the payoff will exist personally if not professionally. Your investment is a leap of faith. No learning is wasted on you, since you consider yourself a work in progress. Learning is considered a construction project, accomplished deliberately, one step at a time.

10. **Future oriented.** You create your future by being one step ahead. You honor and appreciate your past while you live consciously in the present and face the future with intention and purpose. You live honorably, consciously, and intentionally. The future concerns you, and you act responsibly to preserve the resources of our world for those who are to come.

Analyze Your Self-Renewing Qualities

Look at the ten qualities on the following rating sheet. Use the rating sheet to analyze your expenditure of resources and your personal satisfaction with your investment. First, consider each of the qualities and assess your **investment** of time, energy, and effort in relationship to each of them. Then, rate your level of **satisfaction with your investment** of time, energy, and effort in relation to each quality. Feel free to add other qualities to the list.

List Self-Renewing Qualities in Priority Order	Investment of your resources of time, energy, and effort					Satisfaction with the expenditure of your resources				
	Rating scale					Rating Scale				
	High				Low	High				Low
1. Value driven	5	4	3	2	1	5	4	3	2	1
2. Connected to the world	5	4	3	2	1	5	4	3	2	1
3. Require quiet and solitude	5	4	3	2	1	5	4	3	2	1
4. Pace yourself	5	4	3	2	1	5	4	3	2	1
5. Make contact with nature	5	4	3	2	1	5	4	3	2	1
6. Tap into creativity and playfulness	5	4	3	2	1	5	4	3	2	1
7. Adapt to change	5	4	3	2	1	5	4	3	2	1
8. Learn from the down times	5	4	3	2	1	5	4	3	2	1
9. Always in training	5	4	3	2	1	5	4	3	2	1
10. Future oriented	5	4	3	2	1	5	4	3	2	1
11. Other Self-Renewing Qualities:	5	4	3	2	1	5	4	3	2	1

Your expenditure of resources may be low, but you may be satisfied with your investment at this time in your life. On the other hand, your expenditure of resources may be high, and you may still not be satisfied with your investment. You may want to invest additional time and energy in this area as you emerge as a self-renewing adult.

NEGOTIATING TRANSITIONS EFFECTIVELY

According to Dr. Nancy Schlossberg (1981) of the University of Maryland, a *transition* is any event or time passage that results in a change in how you see yourself, the world around you, and your relationships with others. You cannot always predict the sequence in which transitions occur, but you can expect many to take place in your lifetime. There are some transitions that you can anticipate because they take place slowly and involve some planning. Some examples of this type of transition are marriage, the birth of a child, and earning a college degree. Other transitions may be unexpected, such as the death of someone close to you or the sudden loss of a job.

Some transitions are easy to deal with; others are much more difficult. How *you* react and how successful you are in dealing with a transition depend on three basic factors.

1.   Your perception of the transition

2.   Your personal characteristics

3.   Your support systems

It is important to learn how you can deal more effectively with the transitions in your life. The following outline is based on work done by Dr. Nancy Schlossberg (1981, pp. 1–18).

YOUR PERCEPTION OF THE TRANSITION

How do you look at a particular transition? When you are faced with a change in your life, it is important to evaluate how you feel about the change and how it affects you. Your attitude about a transition makes a big difference in how successful you are in dealing with it. Some of the factors to consider are:

- **Do you see the transition as a gain or as a loss?** Every change in your life involves some gain *and* loss. Do you approach change with eager anticipation or with great reluctance? A change that at first seems to be a major loss may, in the long run, turn into a major gain. For example, if your job is unrewarding, but you are reluctant to leave, and the organization for which you work goes out of business, you may eventually end up with a job that is much more rewarding. Try to look at the positive aspects of each transition you face.

- **Do you have control over the transition?** Did you cause the transition to happen or did it happen to you? You will react differently if you feel that you have some control over what is happening to you. Examples of transitions you control are choosing to change jobs, choosing to marry someone, and choosing where to live. Examples of transitions over which you have little control are serious family illness, your child's choice of a spouse, and the loss of financial aid due to a change in government policies. Often, you may in fact have more control than you think. When dealing with a transition over which you feel you have little or no control, try to identify those factors over which you do have some control and work on them.

- **Is the source of the transition internal or external?** Does the transition come from you or from others and conditions around you? Internal sources can be such factors as changes in your health, in your values, or in your career goals. External sources might be an imposed change in job responsibilities, children leaving home, or the loss of a close friend. You may feel more in control if the source of the transition is internal. However, it is also important to evaluate how you can control and respond to a transition when the source is external.

- **Is the timing of the transition on-time or off-time?** You expect certain changes in your life to take place at certain times. Examples of this would be retirement in the early or mid sixties and children going to college after graduation from high school. These are usually anticipated and planned for. On the other hand, there are changes that may be off-time. Examples of this would be forced early retirement or the loss of your spouse through separation or early death. Off-time transitions can be more difficult to deal with, especially if you have a strong feeling that certain changes should take place at certain times in your life.

- **Does the transition come suddenly or gradually?** You can plan for a gradual transition, such as children leaving home, a coming marriage, or the birth of a child. It is more difficult to plan for a transition such as a heart attack, an accident, or a sudden loss of financial resources. Also, a promotion or inheritance may present the need to make difficult decisions immediately.

- **Is the transition permanent, temporary, or uncertain?** If you and your spouse have a newborn child and it is your first, you can expect the transition in your lives to be quite permanent. If you move from one city to another, the loss you feel and the strangeness of being in a new place will most likely be temporary. If you have an accident or health problem and the prognosis is uncertain, it is more difficult to plan ahead. This type of transition may be much more difficult to deal with.

- **What is the degree of stress involved?** If you feel that you have no control over a change in your life, it is likely to be more stressful to you. Also, sudden change creates more stress than gradual change. If you have people who can provide help and support as you work through a transition, you can reduce the amount of stress you feel. Anything you can do to gain some control of your situation will also reduce stress.

YOUR PERSONAL CHARACTERISTICS

How do your own personal characteristics affect the way you deal with transitions in your life? In evaluating how you can more effectively manage change, it is important to consider several factors that relate specifically to you.

- **Your sex and sex-role identification.** Generally, women are better able than men to tolerate stress, and women have fewer stress-related illnesses. If you are a man and see yourself as the primary breadwinner for your family, the loss of your job may hit you harder than if you see your role of provider as a shared responsibility with your wife.

- **Your health.** If you are not physically or mentally well, it will be more difficult for you to deal with a major transition. For this and other reasons, it is important to stay physically active and to obtain assistance, if necessary, to work through any emotional concerns that you may have.

- **Your age and life stage.** If your organization makes you retire early, it is an unexpected transition to make in your life stage. If you are in your forties, you may be reluctant to make a career change because you feel that you should be more "stable" at your age. If you are a woman reaching 40 and want to have your first child, you may have misgivings because you feel that you are "too old." This type of age-referenced behavior can often be very self-defeating and restricting.

- **Your mental approach.** Do you look at a glass of water and see it as half full or half empty? You can take a negative, even catastrophic, view and look on the dark side of most changes. However, you can look at change as a new opportunity and concentrate on the positive aspects of any transition.

- **Your values orientation.** If you intensely value work as the number one priority in your life and then lose your job or don't receive an expected promotion, it will hit you much harder than if you have a more balanced set of family, work, and leisure values. If you have strong ties to your extended family and to your community, it may be very difficult for you to accept a job in another part of the country.

- **Previous experience with a transition of a similar nature.** If you have already had one child, the process of pregnancy, birth, and early childcare is usually easier the second time. If you have been out of work and have had to conduct a job campaign, it is usually easier if you have to do it again. If you have dealt successfully with a crisis in your life, you can probably handle another crisis more effectively.

YOUR SUPPORT SYSTEMS

What kind of support is available to you when you are dealing with a transition? It is important to obtain the help that you need and not always try to "go it alone." It is also important to have your support systems established *before* you really need them. Possible sources of support are as follows.

- **Interpersonal support systems.** If you have family support, a network of friends, or some intimate relationships, you have good sources of support for dealing with a transition. It is important to develop and maintain your interpersonal support systems as a normal part of your lifestyle. Remember that this support system does not have to involve a lot of people. Even one close friend, your spouse, or a family member who can help you through some difficult transitions can make a world of difference.

- **Institutional and community support systems.** In addition to your own interpersonal support systems, it may help to use some of the services available in the community. Examples of these services are community agencies, workshops, counseling and mental health services, special-interest groups such as AA, the Widow-to-Widow Program, and Parents Without Partners, college and adult education courses, and church groups. Do not be reluctant to ask for help. The assistance and support can be critical to your successful progress through a difficult transition.

TRANSITIONS

In the following chapters you will investigate other topics related to the transitions that you may face at various stages in your life. Before you read on, however, let's summarize some of the major considerations when you face change.

1. You need to be aware of three basic factors.

   - Your perception of the transition

   - Your personal characteristics

   - Your support systems

2. You need to realize that it may take a long time to adapt to a loss or to a major transition.

3. You need to make use of the resources available to you and to set up support systems ahead of time.

4. Your attitude is important as you integrate a transition in your life. It is helpful to look at the positive aspects of a transition and to work on them.

5. There are different types of transitions. Some can be completed easily. Others may take much more time and effort.

CHAPTER 9

Understanding Change

What changes have you experienced in the past ten years? It's natural for adults to have changing needs and changing roles. This has increasingly become a matter for study by psychologists and others. In the past, most of the emphasis in studying human developmental needs was placed on young children and teenagers. Adults were considered to be relatively stable unless some serious change, such as mental illness, arose. This attitude was consistent with the relatively stable lifestyle that was promoted and perceived as "healthy" for most adults—a stable job with the same organization over a number of years, a family, house, car, and all the trappings of a consistent, successful lifestyle.

Many people, however, are reluctant to accept a societal definition of what a good adult lifestyle should be. People do change and often need something different, or something more. It is important for you to evaluate where you are in your development and to analyze some of the forces within you that may be calling for change. Also, since the economic environment and the world of work are changing, you will need to change in response to these forces.

It is important to note that many of the adult development theories have a limited research base and have narrowly focused on white, middle-class adults in Western cultures. This means that wide applicability of adult theories to women and other cultures may pose some questions, but we can still learn from the meaningful data that exist.

While some theorists accept the notion of age and stages in adult development, others do not segment adult behavior or awareness. One such theory is that of Perun and Bielby (1980), which focuses on the uniqueness of individual development by considering the timing of experiences and internal changes. The rate of change and the timetable of changes vary with each individual and are affected by culture, gender, race, and other factors. With these limitations in mind, the following is a summary of the adult developmental tasks and behaviors that most adults go through to some extent. Remember that the descriptions and time periods are very general.

THE EARLY ADULT YEARS (AGES 20–40)

The early part of this period involves much testing of skills and establishment of the individual's independence and identity. Parents play a less important role in influencing an individual's decisions or lifestyle than they did before. Peer groups are more important as the individual searches for personal identity. There is a tendency to reach out toward others in an attempt to develop intimacy in relationships. In some cases this is fulfilled by marriage. In other cases, close friendships meet this need. This period is usually marked by the end of full-time education and the beginning of full-time work. The individual may hold a variety of jobs, because working environments and job skills are tested. The need to start at the bottom of the ladder in many organizations and the often slow movement into areas of increased responsibility can be a source of frustration. Many individuals have a need to move quickly and may not be accepting of older people and "the establishment." Another potential source of frustration can come from the scarcity of career-oriented jobs due to economic downturns and organizational downsizing. Some young people may feel that they must accept jobs they consider to be unfulfilling or beneath their skills and education.

This period is marked by the dreams and possibilities that go with a feeling of an unlimited future. So many opportunities exist that there is often little concern with long-range planning. There is usually a desire to create an independent life structure and an identity separate from parents and previous family associations. Often during this period, an individual benefits from having a "mentor," who provides acceptance, support, and assistance in the individual's development.

Although many individuals set up housekeeping on their own well before the age of 20, this period marks a time when possessions of significance may be acquired as the individual moves into a home of her own. There may well be limited financial resources, which sometimes can lead to impatience in achieving tangible goals, such as a home. An individual may be tempted to remain at home with parents in order to stretch financial resources, and this can delay the establishment of independence that is one of the major life tasks of this period.

Family skills are often tested during this time, most frequently through a marriage relationship and by the effort it takes to make such a relationship work. In contrast to earlier generations, individuals may choose a wide variety of relationships and lifestyles. Single-parent homes are more common, as are long-term relationships that do not necessarily involve marriage. Blended families with children from previous marriages and adoptions by couples or by single individuals are examples of the variety of relationships that are generally perceived as acceptable by society. Perhaps one of the most significant developments in recent years has been the crumbling of the stereotypes about what a "typical" family or relationship should be like. Individuals feel more free to develop lifestyles based on their own needs and values, rather than on what they think they "should" do.

In summary, the early part of this period can be one of rapid growth and development, a period in which opportunities seem great—so great that there may be frustration over the rate with which some goals are achieved. This is a period of testing, learning, and developing skills and identity as an adult.

As one enters the thirties, there may be a reevaluation of life's purpose, and an individual may question early decisions that were made regarding self, career, and family. It is important to sit back, evaluate, and consider changes that can be made. An individual's values may change considerably from the twenties to the thirties, and these should be taken into account in considering change. For many individuals, progress in their careers and in other life endeavors has brought a greater degree of self-confidence and self-worth. Recognition has been gained for accomplishments on and off the job, and the individual has the satisfaction of making more of an impact. There may well be more payoffs from work in terms of higher status, prestige, pay, and a feeling of success. Others may just be starting their careers or changing to new careers. Some may not like the work they are doing but may be reluctant to initiate a change. Some may look to outlets other than work for fulfillment. In many cases, workers in this period of life spend a lot of time on the job.

Family responsibilities can consume a lot of time and energy during this period. Given the need to juggle work, family, and other responsibilities, there may not be much time for an individual to pursue personal interests or for a couple to spend time together or to develop and maintain relationships with friends and extended family members. If there are children in the household, there are constant challenges of all kinds, from getting them to soccer games on time to dealing with moodiness during the teenage years. If one is involved in a marital or other relationship, it is very important to save some time for the relationship and to maintain effective communication. There may be changing roles as both partners in a relationship pursue their career and life goals. No longer is it expected that the female partner will stay home with the children and defer to the male partner's career needs. The resulting integration of roles can enhance communication.

Physical changes begin to take on a greater significance during this period. It is easier to put on weight. Hair may begin to disappear or turn gray. Physical strength and capabilities may not be quite the same as before. For the first time, the individual is reminded that there is an aging process. There is a tendency to compare progress in career, family, and status with that of friends and relatives, and of others one's age. This age-referenced behavior can be overcome by concentrating on one's own needs, goals, and values. Many individuals need to have some evidence of success, whether it be through job status, acquisition of material goods, accomplishments of children, or through other means. As one approaches the late thirties, there may be a feeling that it is important to make things happen now.

This may be the most dynamic of all life periods. It begins with relative youth and ends with middle age. More issues are confronted during this period than during any other, and the decisions that are made can determine an individual's lifestyle for years to come.

THE MIDDLE ADULT YEARS (AGES 40–60)

This period could be characterized as the "half-empty or half-full" period, meaning that one's outlook toward life can make a huge difference in the way that one progresses during this time. Researchers have determined that at some point in their forties, individuals tend to begin thinking in terms of time they have left rather than time from birth. Others have emphasized the need to reevaluate one's dreams and life goals, to integrate one's successes and disappointments, and to establish new goals and dreams. As the general population ages, whole sections of gift shops displaying "over 40" items have appeared. Most of the items contain a lot of black and humorously reflect the stereotypes of aging. There is no problem with having fun during this transition. The problem comes when the individual begins to believe the stereotypes. This is often associated with the so-called "midlife crisis," in which an individual has great difficulty integrating his progress through life and may act out in unproductive or self-defeating ways.

Some people may experience rich career growth during this period, while others are able to relax and help others to grow, drawing on the depth and richness of their experience. Still others may be frustrated by the lack of career growth potential and may seek a change in their jobs or careers. There may be fewer opportunities for change, but it is important to deal realistically with the opportunities that are available, rather than falling into a pattern of job dissatisfaction or lethargy. There is the opportunity to establish new career goals, which may involve being a mentor to others, using skills outside of one's job, or becoming involved in new directions within one's profession.

Changes outside of one's career may include the growing independence of children and the opportunities to reach out to others and to cultivate new friendships. As one's responsibilities with work and family diminish, there can be more time to devote to outside activities and relationships. More time can be devoted to the relationship with one's partner or friends. Although researchers once thought that the transition of children moving away from home would be very difficult for many people, this is not the case. There is much more of a problem when children do not move out and establish their independence or when they return after having been on their own.

Although the early forties can be a time of upheaval, the mid to late forties can be a period of settling down. If the individual can come to a realistic reassessment of dreams and goals and can make decisions and modifications to career and lifestyle, there is the opportunity for increased self-acceptance and greater enjoyment of life. The individual may be more willing to settle down, may be less driven, and may be more able to relax. There may be less perceived pressure to achieve, less of a rush to reach major goals, but instead a desire to enjoy life. Leisure time becomes more important. There may be fewer family responsibilities and possibly more friends. There is a reaching out for new friendships and for new ways to achieve satisfaction in life. This is an opportunity to develop new paths and new dreams, to adjust to them and to set a new life structure. By dealing positively with midlife, an individual can find new ways for life to become more enjoyable and rewarding. Hobbies and other interests can take on a whole new meaning and importance in life.

The latter part of this period is marked by a mellowing process, in which there can be softening of feelings and relationships, with more emphasis on everyday joys, minor achievements, and irritations. Some individuals attempt to deal with the aging process by returning to some of the things they feel symbolized the happiness of their youth. This denial of reality can often bring frustrating and unhappy results. Other individuals, having dealt with midlife changes and having gone through the settling down of the late forties, enter this period with few regrets. New experiences, friendships, and activities are tried with varying results. The individual is now definitely a member of the "older" generation and may have difficulty accepting this fact. Some approach advancing years with a sense of discouragement and withdrawal, whereas others see this as an opportunity for new freedoms, with fewer family responsibilities.

An individual's career may have reached a plateau by this period. There may continue to be challenges, but they may be of a more modest nature. Some deal with this by entering second careers where the challenges of starting something new provide stimulation. A realistic evaluation of alternatives is necessary during this period.

Although there may be fewer family responsibilities, with children grown and independent, the new role of grandparent can be a comfort and provide new opportunities for family involvement. There may be concern over the care for aging parents and for finding facilities to meet their needs. For those who have partners, the new role that developed in the forties and fifties continues in this period, with more opportunities to do things together and to share activities and interests with friends. The woman may now have the need to expand her world by finding individual fulfillment through work and independent activities, while the man may be more content to take an active role in family affairs. This expansion of roles in the later years is common to many cultures. As the individual goes through the fifties, there can be two distinct approaches. One is to view the period with resignation, withdrawal, and discouragement, and to face the aging process with negativity and fear. The other approach is to see this period as an opportunity to try new things and to make new friendships, unencumbered by some of the responsibilities and demands of earlier years. It is the time to ask "what is the quality of life I want in this phase of my life?"

THE LATE ADULT YEARS (AGES 60–75)

Census statistics estimate that by 2020, 18 percent of the total population will be over the age of 65, which is a sharp increase from 11.5 percent in the early 1990s. This increase in life expectancy is worldwide and not just in the United States. Due to improved health care and utilization of good health practices, individuals are better able to approach this phase of life with great anticipation and renewed vim and vigor.

Many people face retirement during this period, but the concept that people retire at age 65 and take it easy is a misleading stereotype. In most jobs, there is no longer a mandatory retirement age. Even though people can work as long as they wish, the average age at which people retire has not risen significantly. Individuals simply have more options and now have the opportunity to exercise those options regarding retirement or career change. Many retire much earlier than age 60 in order to change their lifestyle or to enter a new career. It is possible to enter retirement with a sense of loss of self-worth if an individual defines too much of herself in terms of career role, but there are many opportunities, with or without paid work, to maintain a rich and varied lifestyle in the sixties and beyond.

Some of the major developmental tasks during this period are to decide when and whether to leave one's career, what kind of lifestyle to pursue, how to deal with the aging process, maintaining relationships with one's partner and others, and planning for the future. As in the transition of the forties, it is possible to fall into a negative pattern of dwelling on lost opportunities and longing for the return to the "good old days." One of the most important tasks is to integrate one's life experiences and to move on to new experiences and new opportunities.

As the population changes, there are increasing work opportunities for people in their sixties. Many gain fulfillment from part-time work, because it allows more flexibility in a weekly schedule. Others use the extra time as an opportunity to help others or to use their skills in a variety of volunteer activities. It is important to assess what needs are fulfilled by an individual's work and to develop a plan to fulfill those needs through a variety of activities. A diversity of interests can help to fulfill very important needs.

The most common concern of people over 60 is whether they will be able to remain financially secure in their later years. This is certainly important, given the fact that people are living longer than in past generations. Issues such as health care, housing, safety, long-term care, and inflation take on an added degree of importance when an individual considers a lifestyle based on a retirement income. Long-term planning is essential. Health factors become much more important during this period of life. Individuals must realize that they can play an active role in maintaining good health practices and can actually increase their chances of living longer. (See Section Six.) One of the most important needs of this period is to be prepared for change. A flexible, positive attitude, good health practices, and good support systems can help an individual to deal with the changes and losses that can mark this period.

THE OLDER ADULT YEARS (AGE 75 AND ABOVE)

The older adult years could be characterized by losses: loss of friendships or spouse through death, loss of physical stamina, loss of hearing. However, since life expectancy is on the rise in the number and percentages of older adults, the loss of interpersonal relationships may be minimized. By the year 2020, census statistics estimate that there will be 6.7 million Americans age 85 and older.

Many older adults continue to contribute their gifts and expertise to the workforce or as volunteers. Opportunities to mentor and share wisdom gained through life experience abound and one only needs to look for them. Studies show that mental abilities are preserved in healthy older adults and that there is superior social reasoning in this age group compared with younger adults. While work productivity declines, it is important to note that one study of 172 composers, which considered the quality and quantity of work produced in the later years, discovered that the masterpieces were judged to be created late in life. Expertise, experience, and wisdom can enable the older adult to contribute to the greater good in creative and outstanding ways.

During this phase the older adult is cognizant of the impact of physical changes. This phase brings a loss of height and skin elasticity and a diminishment of the senses, most notably smell and hearing. The slower rate of reaction time and the loss of strength varies greatly from person to person but becomes more of a factor. An older adult should not engage in timed work functions that would prove to be frustrating and self-defeating. However, the "use it or lose it" caution is one to heed during this phase. Studies indicate that physical activity and exercise as well as mental stimulation have a profound effect on the individual's capacity to function effectively into the eighties and beyond.

YOUR OWN LIFE STAGE, AGE, AND PHASE

As you consider the characteristics of the various life stages, you may see certain ones that apply to you in your own age, stage, or phase. Life is complex and we do not move through stages and phases at the same time and in the same way with the same perspectives. What may be an especially critical or stressful time for one at a particular stage may be an easy time for another at the same stage. Why consider ages, stages, and phases at all? They provide a framework and a very loose timetable to give an understanding and an appreciation of life's developmental tasks and challenges, those that are past accomplishments and those yet to come.

Identify three developmental tasks and challenges that you are experiencing related to your current age, stage, or phase. These life transitions provide great opportunity to redefine and re-strategize your approach to living with zest and vigor.

First developmental task or challenge:

Second developmental task or challenge:

Third developmental task or challenge:

In this phase of my life, what do I want to learn?

1.

2.

3.

In this phase of my life, how do I want to contribute my gifts and talents?

1.

2.

3.

Now consider your **next age, stage, or phase** and select one developmental task or challenge that you are looking forward to.

I am looking forward to this developmental task or challenge:

In this next phase of my life, what do I want to learn?

1.

2.

3.

In this next phase of my life, how do I want to contribute my gifts and talents?

1.

2.

3.

Is there a developmental task or challenge that you see in your future that you are **not looking forward** to facing?

In what ways can I plan to more effectively negotiate this challenge?

1.

2.

3.

UNDERSTANDING CHANGE

Each age, stage, and phase has its rewards, drawbacks, and distinct challenges. Some challenges may be extrinsic or very visible as significant points in life, such as a graduation, a marriage, a death, or a promotion. But, there are other, more subtle challenges constantly occurring inside you, such as gaining insight and greater understanding, or forgiving someone who hurt you. Another intrinsic challenge may be a nonevent or not getting something that you expected, such as giving birth to a child or gaining a certain status in the military or in business. These internal or nonevents also have a profound impact on life because they are for the most part hidden to others, so the support for these challenges is not as available.

What are the developmental tasks or challenges that are in your age range, stage, or phase? Acknowledging these encourages you to address rather than deny existing realities of your life. Anticipating the next age or phase enables you to prepare for the next developmental tasks. If you can successfully anticipate and prepare for what is to come, you may be able to minimize the potential negative effects, appreciate the benefits, and create positive adjustments. Your capacity to learn and contribute your gifts and talents at each age and stage provides you with a gateway to growth, acceptance, and wisdom. Keep asking these last two questions:

In this phase of my life, what am I anxious to learn?

In this phase of my life, how do I want to contribute my gifts and talents?

Since change is constant, life transitions and developmental tasks are a natural part of your existence. Living life with purpose and intention is a choice. Each age and stage brings opportunity to grow, understand, and appreciate life in a more meaningful way. You can choose negativity or you can see opportunity at each stage of your development. The next chapter provides you with a framework to analyze the influence of others in your life. A big part of how you view your world can be found in your choice of friends and confidants. They can affect your view of yourself, your world, and your perception of others.

> *Only in growth, reform and change, paradoxically enough, is true security to be found.*
>
> —Anne Morrow Lindberg, *The Wave of the Future*

CHAPTER 10

Influence of Others

- How could you extend the benefit from your interaction with others throughout your life?

- How might others help you to navigate and capitalize on life's challenges and joys?

Because change is a given commodity in life, are we expected to go it alone or to enhance our support systems and demonstrate resilience?

This chapter identifies and explains four potential groups of people who may serve your interpersonal needs as you look for meaning and insight throughout your personal and professional journey.

- Your personal board of directors

- Your support groups

- Your interpersonal network of contacts

- Your mentors

IDENTIFY YOUR PERSONAL BOARD OF DIRECTORS

As you evaluate the influence of others over your ability to make decisions, consider which people to include on your personal board of directors. These are the special people to whom you can most easily and most productively turn when you need help in making decisions. You depend on these people to really listen to you and to understand your needs—you know them well and trust them. They can focus on helping you consider what is best for you. They are the people whose opinions you respect, to whom you can turn for advice, steady counsel, insight, and an honest assessment of your options. They are people who will set aside their own agendas and concentrate on *your* needs.

Your personal board of directors may include selected family members, but you should think carefully about which family members you wish to include. Remember the requirement that they be able to concentrate on your needs in making a decision. Your personal board of directors may include some of your closest friends. It may include a professional career counselor or therapist, someone who has served as your mentor, or someone to whom you can turn for counsel, support, and advice at your place of work. Your personal board of directors are those people who provide an anchor for you and whom you can depend on and trust to be there when you need them. You may call on certain members of your board for certain kinds of decisions—you don't have to convene the whole board for every matter that comes up. Some may help with decisions regarding your career, some with family issues, and some with personal decisions. It is important to include several people on your board but to choose them carefully. They can be a tremendous resource as you make decisions and negotiate change.

This diagram represents your personal boardroom. Write on the chairs the names of the people who sit on your personal board of directors. Don't be concerned if you have some empty chairs. Take special note of who sits to the immediate right and left of you. These members of your board have significant impact. Also take special note of all those at the table. Is there someone who should sit closer to you, whose help you wish to enlist more than you have so far?

Are there others whom you would like to include on your personal board of directors? Are there areas in your life where you need someone to fill an empty place on your board? If so, make an effort to identify people who can serve on your board in the future. Evaluate the effectiveness of your board frequently, because you never know when new challenges will require special assistance. Remember that counseling professionals can help to fill gaps that may exist. Unlike a corporation, you do not have to publish the names of the members of your board. Individuals may not even know that you consider them to be members of your board. What is critical is that you identify specific individuals on whom you can count for quality advice, support, and assistance in time of need.

CONSIDER THE VALUE OF SUPPORT GROUPS

Support groups are different from your personal board of directors. While support groups also help you with life transitions, they offer greater opportunities to share your thoughts or ideas about a particular matter as well as provide potential sources of research or current information on specific issues. In addition, support groups can help you to grow with others, to provide or receive encouragement, and possibly to develop friendships with those with whom you share a common bond. While your board of directors is focused on your individual needs, support groups hold the potential of fulfilling your need for targeted support around one or more issues.

There are many types of support groups. Here are some examples:

- Classmates or alumni
- Neighbors or civic association members
- Church members
- Gym members
- Book club members
- Teams and sport groups
- Travel clubs
- Hospice grief groups

- Career growth and financial planning groups
- Weight control groups
- Service or volunteer organizations (e.g., Lions, Rotary, or Kiwanis Clubs, American Red Cross)
- Political action groups
- Personal growth groups
- Alcoholics Anonymous or Adult Children of Alcoholic groups

- Cancer survivor groups
- Veterans groups for women and men
- Health related groups
- Parents without partners groups
- Bible study groups
- Chamber of Commerce groups
- Ecology groups

Support groups inform us, create bonds, provide outlets, and help us make a difference and find meaning as we seek to understand our own experiences by sharing them with others. Often, it is a serious situation, such as the death of a family member or a life threatening diagnosis, that propels us to seek out necessary support from established groups. If you are currently reluctant to join a support group, know that this opportunity is available to you when and if the time calls for such an intervention. Research indicates that participating in support groups and remaining open to a variety of relationships with others helps us to live happier and longer lives. Belonging to a support group that shares your passion for the environment, health, spiritual growth, or our country's welfare can be a splendid investment of your time, talent, energy, and resources. In the following spaces, on the left side, list your current support groups where you have been an active and contributing member. On the right side, identify those support groups that might hold potential for you to grow, either personally or professionally. Do not add any more than three and if you do not have any listed for the near future, that is just fine. Do not be concerned if you do not fill in any of these blanks.

Current Active Support Group Membership

1. _____

2. _____

3. _____

Potential Support Group Membership

1. _____

2. _____

3. _____

EXPAND YOUR INTERPERSONAL NETWORK OF CONTACTS

Remaining open to interactions with others is very important. One excellent way to meet others is through networking. Networking can often be misunderstood and trivialized in the workplace culture. Developing a network of associates and colleagues requires interpersonal skills beyond "meet and greet." Networking holds the potential of enhancing your future prospects and expanding your knowledge base but that is NOT the primary reason for networking which, first and foremost, is to build RELATIONSHIPS with others who share similar interests or goals. Being honestly and authentically willing to exchange information, ideas, and services is a benefit of networking with others. Your indicaton of a desire to re-connect with others after your first meeting, by sending them informative articles, Web sites, data, or names of individuals who might be of assistance, builds relationships and extends the value of your own network. If you can go an extra mile by remembering others' interests or their children's names, you have related in a positive and memorable way. Connecting with individuals in a deeper and meaningful way helps them to remember you when you are in need. If you are thinking about starting your own business, networking is a critical tool to build your clientele. Start and maintain this practice today!

Where do you network? Just about anywhere!

- Conferences
- Meetings
- Social gatherings
- Friends of friends
- Volunteering
- Interest sessions
- Associations
- Informational interviewing

- Families of friends
- Contacts with the public
- Online interest groups through the Internet

- Seminars
- Classes
- Email

Some questions you might want to consider are

1. How can you expand and capitalize on your existing networks?
2. What type of contact is appropriate and acceptable if you are starting to build your own network?
3. Where do you begin to network?

In answer to these and other questions, here are a few networking protocol strategies.

- **Get email addresses** and other contact information as you remain open to meeting new and unfamiliar people so that you can listen and learn.

- **Be prepared** because everywhere you go is a potential networking opportunity—meetings, gym, walking in your neighborhood, social gathering, a vacation, or a support group meeting.

- **Be interested** as you focus on the other person in a genuine and authentic way. It is not about you but about them!

- **Connect** by asking open ended, deeper questions rather than closed questions that require "yes" and "no" answers (e.g. **Not:** Did you like this lecture? **But:** What lessons from this lecture will you share with colleagues?).

- **Follow-up** via email or post in a few days, but no more than a week after, by sending requested information or helpful articles or Web sites that tap into your previous conversation with the person.

- **Remember** details about each individual by keeping track of names and unique identifiers, and review them before you expect to see the same person again. (**Helpful hint:** write the information you want to remember and then review before you revisit the same meeting or group.)

- **Establish** a relationship with each person in your network of contacts, not through group emails, but with a phone call, lunch, or meeting to discover mutual interests, challenges, opportunities, or options.

Networking provides an opportunity to expand your thinking as you consider life and career decisions. You discover how others approached similar decisions and you meet those who will provide you with valuable information about your field, the job market, and/or future prospects. You may even network with a potential employer. Perhaps the greatest value of networking is that your life is enriched as you expand your personal contacts and you are exposed to new ideas and relationships. Your ability to incorporate creative and innovative networking strategies is a critical skill you will develop as you maintain contact with people who you will serve and who will serve you as well. Learn through networking and integrate the lessons learned into your work and lifestyle. Answer the following questions in the following box to identify a potential action plan for networking:

How might you implement some network protocol strategies immediately?

_____

_____

How can you expand your current network of contacts; what actions can you take now to ensure that you develop or enhance this skill?

_____

_____

Reflect on these questions and write a few action steps that you are willing to take now and in the future.

_____

_____

> *I find that the harder I work the more luck I seem to have.*
>
> —Thomas Jefferson

FIND A MENTOR

Many people who have studied adult development have emphasized the importance of a mentor as a positive factor in dealing with career and life decisions. A mentor is someone who can provide you with insight, support, reflection, and sound advice. You may even wish to consider having more than one mentor. While your career growth can benefit from your having a mentor, it may be possible to have a mentor for other areas of your life, such as your creative self or religious self. How do you choose a mentor? Here is a list of qualities to look for in a mentor. However, do not expect your mentor to possess all of these qualities.

Qualities of a Good Mentor

Consider the following when you look for someone to be a mentor.

1. **A mentor is someone who listens.** A mentor can give advice, but also *listens to you* and tries to understand what *you* want and need.

2. **A mentor is secure.** A good mentor has most likely reached a level of comfort in her life and career. This allows the mentor to give more to you without being overly concerned about her own position. This is especially important if you and your mentor work for the same organization.

3. **A mentor is not self-referent.** Many people respond to an idea or to a question by describing what they did or what happened to them. While this can sometimes be very helpful, a good mentor will try to understand what is going on in *your* life and career and will center on *your* needs.

4. **A mentor will make time to see you.** Although you will not be talking with your mentor every day, you should be able to have regular access to your mentor, in person or by telephone. However, be careful not to become overly dependent on your mentor.

5. **A mentor has a genuine interest in you** and a desire to help you grow.

6. **A mentor should be a moderate risk taker.** A mentor who values the status quo above all may not be able to provide the support you need when you are thinking about making a change or taking a risk.

7. **A mentor should be politically astute.** A mentor who knows the ins and outs of an organization or a professional field is a valuable resource. By sharing how to accomplish things in an organization, the mentor can provide thoughtful and useful assistance.

8. **A mentor should be able to grasp the big picture.** A mentor should be able to look at the total organization or situation and at your relationship to it. A mentor who has a very narrow focus may not have the perspective you need.

9. **A mentor should be someone who shares your values.** Look for a mentor whose ideas are compatible with yours. You do not have to think alike, but it is preferable that you both be comfortable with the basic concepts such as the relationship between work and your private life and the qualities needed for a successful career.

10. **A mentor should be someone who is flexible in dealing with people and ideas.** A mentor should not be someone who applies rigid standards and who feels that there is only one right way to do something.

Where to Find a Mentor

You can find a mentor just about anywhere, but here are some suggestions.

1. **On your job.** Your mentor could be your supervisor, if your supervisor has many of the qualities of a good mentor.

2. **On your job, but not your supervisor.** Often, someone who is not in the immediate chain of command that affects you may be able to be a good mentor, since the person would be familiar with the organization but would have some distance from your immediate work situation.

3. **A friend.** Any friend who has the qualities of a mentor can act as your mentor.

4. **A colleague in a similar organization.** Sometimes, a good mentor can be someone who works in a job situation that is similar to yours so that she can better understand the dynamics of your work environment.

5. **A family member.** A family member who has the qualities of a good mentor could easily be your mentor. However, remember that family members often tend to favor stability in decision making and often find it difficult to be objective in providing help.

6. **A colleague in a professional organization.** A good way to find a mentor is to go to professional meetings and develop a network of colleagues. Through this network, you may find a person to be a mentor.

7. **A teacher.** A former or current teacher can often provide the perspective and support that you need from a mentor.

8. **A former colleague.** A good way to find a mentor is to keep in touch with someone with whom you have worked in the past. This person will have the benefit of having known you in the workplace but will have a different perspective from someone with whom you presently work.

A good mentor can be someone of either sex and any age. A mentor does not have to be older, although often an older person would have been able to develop more of the qualities of a good mentor. It is important to remember that there is a limit to the time that you can expect a mentor to give and to the type of issues that you ask a mentor to help you address. Try to be sensitive to the number of times you contact your mentor.

Don't endanger your relationship by making too many demands on your mentor's time. In addition, there are some issues with which you may need additional help. When you are experiencing significant personal, emotional, or career problems, you may wish to seek professional counseling. Your mentor can provide valuable support during such times, but only as a part of your overall support system.

INFLUENCE OF OTHERS

It is important to seek the support of others as you make decisions throughout life. Some people may have a very large personal board of directors, many support groups, and a large network. Others may choose to have a much smaller board and fewer support groups. It is not important whether you have a huge network of support. What matters is that you have some people to whom you can turn to for support in making decisions and in dealing with a variety of life issues.

If you find at a certain point in your personal or professional life that you are "stuck in a rut" without the necessary interpersonal resources to guide or encourage you, consider employing the services of a life or career coach. Coaching has evolved into a very valuable support for individuals and for business entities. Many businesses and educational systems hire executive coaches for their upper management staff or administrators. The service of a coach could help you break free of indecision or confusion since there is great value in obtaining an outside opinion or impartial advice. Coaches are readily available in most cities or through the Internet. Be sure to check coaching credentials and ask for the names of previous clients before you move forward with a coaching arrangement. It will be important for you to ascertain if there is a match between what you expect and your coach's ability to deliver.

It is also important to remember that you are your number one supporter and that you have the ultimate responsibility for making a decision. It is important to control the influence that others have in your life and to choose your sources of support wisely. In the end, you must listen to your inner self and make your decision based on your own needs, the information you have obtained, and the help you have received from others. Do not expect others to make decisions for you. That is unfair to them and to you. Be your own best friend when it comes to making your final decision. You will find that your confidence will grow, spurred on by the support that you receive from others and by the decisions that you make for yourself.

> *Superior performance depends on superior learning. People's natural impulse to learn is unleashed when they are engaged in an endeavor they consider worthy of their fullest commitment.*
>
> —Peter Senge, *The Fifth Discipline*

CHAPTER *11*

Taking Risks

As you go through life, it is important to continually evaluate your options and to explore alternatives. It may take you a long time to get the information you need. However, there will come a time when you have to make a choice, and this may involve some risk.

Life demands that we continually evaluate options and explore alternatives. It may take considerable time to secure necessary facts, data, and information that will move the process along. We try to diminish stress by researching facts and filling in knowledge gaps. Finally, a choice is necessary. This leap into the unknown usually involves some risk.

- Are you risk averse?
- Do you welcome the thought of the unknown and are you willing to make the leap of faith without much angst?
- How risky is the current decision you are facing?

This chapter helps you consider the notion of risk from an intellectual perspective. The emotional aspect of risk will continue to be an area to wrestle with in your own space and time.

This point, where you must make a decision about your direction, can be compared to a junction in the route of your train trip through life. You have to choose which track to follow. This is a place where many people stop the career and life planning process. Unable to choose, they wait at the junction, unwilling to risk going in the wrong direction. They would like to know exactly what lies ahead in both directions, but they cannot see that far. They would like to experience the trip without making the commitment to get on the train. They may believe that there will be too much risk involved in making a choice. But is there also risk in remaining at the junction? To take no action is to make a decision by default, and, indeed, there is risk in doing nothing.

HOW WILLING ARE YOU TO TAKE RISKS?

In order to make a decision about your future, it is important to evaluate the risk that *you* are willing to take. Some people are much more able than others to take risks involving their careers, due to fewer family responsibilities, financial situation, skills to fall back on, and other factors. Other people are simply more willing to risk, to take a chance, and to take action without knowing fully what the outcome will be. In fact, it is impossible to know completely the future outcome of major decisions.

In all growth, there is usually some risk. Taking risks does create stress, but what would a life without stress be like? It would probably be very dull and would not involve much growth. In order to grow, we often must put ourselves in stressful positions by taking risks. The potential for change is in all of us, but it is up to each individual to decide how much risk to take for each change. We can do excellent research before making a major decision in order to decrease the unknown factors and reduce the amount of risk. But the final decision must be made, and it will usually be impossible to eliminate all risk. After all, as Helen Keller wrote: "Life is either a daring adventure or nothing."

If you are thinking of evolving into an entrepreneur, the following Web site will help you assess your readiness to take certain risks and will provide you with valuable feedback. See the Risk Assessment Quiz for Starting Your Own Business developed by Georgia State University Small Business Development Center (2007) at: www.gsu.edu/~wwwsbp/entrepre.htm. These 35 questions enable you to self-assess and evaluate your readiness for this learning adventure.

Following are questions to help you evaluate the results of the many risks that you have already taken in your life as an adult. The goal is for you to gain insight into the effectiveness of your past decision making. Your ability to take risks in the future may be impacted by the quality of your decisions and past results.

1. What are two of the greatest risks that you have taken in your life?

    _____

    _____

2. Why were these risks? What did you stand to gain? What did you stand to lose?

    _____

    _____

    _____

    _____

    _____

3. What happened as a result of your taking these risks?

    _____

    _____

    _____

    _____

    _____

4. What responses did you encounter from others before, during, and after you took these risks?

_____

_____

_____

_____

_____

5. How did you feel after you took these risks? Did it affect your self-confidence in any way?

_____

_____

_____

_____

_____

TEN GUIDELINES FOR TAKING RISKS

It is important to remember that change will occur whether we like it or not. At times it may be worth taking a risk to maintain control over the direction of your life. It is important to develop possibilities and a perspective on the future so that you can determine the value of taking risks to achieve personal goals. The following are some factors to consider in taking risks.

Ten Guidelines

1. Be informed. Obtain the information you need.

2. Estimate loss. What is the worst thing that could happen?

3. Consider your motivation. Why are you taking the risk?

4. Evaluate the pros and cons.

5. Act deliberately.

6. Make an action plan.

7. Be committed to your action plan.

8. Be prepared to make adjustments, if necessary.

9. Take responsibility for your actions.

10. Be realistic in your expectations.

RISK ASSESSMENT

Now think about *one* risk that you may want to take in the near future. Ask yourself the following questions.

1. What is the risk that I may want to take?

    _____

    _____

2. What do I stand to gain by taking this risk?

    _____

    _____

3. What might I lose by taking this risk?

    _____

    _____

4. Why do I want to take this risk? Is it consistent with my goals and ideals?

    _____

    _____

5. What information could I obtain or actions could I take to decrease the amount of risk or uncertainty?

    _____

    _____

6. What kind of schedule should I set for myself?

    There are many types of risks. Some may be worth taking, others definitely not. What risks do you wish to consider taking as you take your train through new territory?

    Risks I am willing to take:

    _____

    _____

    _____

Risks I am not willing to take:

_____

_____

_____

> *I have learned that success is to be measured not so much by the position that one has reached in life as by the obstacles that he has overcome while trying to succeed.*
>
> —Booker T. Washington, *Up From Slavery*

CHAPTER 12

Decision Making

So far in Section Two, you have learned that change is normal throughout life, that you can prepare for change, that you can improve your ability to deal with change by seeking assistance from others, and that you must, at times, be ready to take a risk to accomplish a goal. The next step is making a decision. Life represents a series of decisions—what courses to take, what job to take, what relationships to enter, where to live, what car to buy, and many others. People make these decisions in different ways. It is important for you to understand how you make decisions and how you can take action to improve your decision-making skills.

ELEMENTS OF DECISION MAKING

Think about making decisions in the past. When you were a child, were you encouraged to take risks and make some of your own decisions, or were most decisions made for you? Do you put pressure on yourself to make the *right* decision and therefore feel anxious when you have to decide? Do you enjoy making decisions, or does it make you feel uncomfortable? Do you find yourself using any of the following decision-making strategies?

- **Impulse.** Go with your first reaction. Decide quickly, with little thought given to the process. This technique can actually be effective with some types of decisions, such as what to wear in the morning.

- **Escape.** Avoid a decision or make up an answer to deflect an inquiry. This approach is often used when relatives ask about what you plan to major in or what you plan to do after you graduate. It is also used extensively during the difficult process of job hunting.

- **Procrastination.** Delay until someone else makes the decision for you or until the option before you disappears. In delaying, you actually decide by default to do nothing. An example of this approach would be to cut out job ads from the newspaper and then not follow up on any of them.

- **Compliance.** Let someone else decide for you. When you use this approach, you hand over control of your life to others. An example of this approach is to go along with a plan for an evening with another person or a group without expressing your desires.

- **Agonize.** Consider every detail of every option over and over again. Get wrapped up in the pros and cons until you get stuck and give up. Overthinking a decision can be used as an excuse for not taking action.

- **Play it safe.** Always pick the alternative with the lowest level of risk. This strategy may work well as you drive a car or fill out your annual tax return, but by consistently choosing safety as a primary factor in making decisions, you may close out many options for growth and enrichment of your life.

Consider the approaches you use to make decisions and under what circumstances you tend to use these strategies. Your choice of a decision-making strategy may work very well with certain decisions and not with others. The consequences of using inappropriate decision-making strategies can be very negative, particularly if you consistently use these inappropriate approaches.

Your trust in yourself as a competent decision maker is built slowly over time, and setbacks are an inevitable part of that process. Start with small decisions to build your confidence. One way to become comfortable with making decisions is to choose a decision strategy that fits the circumstances. The decision about which restaurant to go to for dinner, which could be made on impulse, cannot be equated to a career decision, which requires a planning process. Your level of confidence will grow, as will your ability to control your life.

It is possible to become so overly concerned about the outcome of a decision that no action is taken. Stagnation, fear of failure, and even fear of success can be emotional blocks to effective decision making. The elusive goal of seeking perfection in any decision can deter progress. Often it is not possible to predict the outcome of a decision. Base the rightness of your decision on the process you follow and not on the outcome. As you apply effective decision-making techniques, positive outcomes are more likely to follow.

Making a major decision usually causes anxiety, because there is often some risk involved, and there is the potential to lose something in the process. However, as one goes through life, it is often necessary to lose something in order to grow. A lobster must shed its shell to grow a new and larger shell. In the interim, the lobster is at greater risk from predators, but the shell must be replaced with a larger one if the lobster is to grow. As you make career and life decisions, be prepared to lose something in order to grow.

Decisions are:

- Choices made from among alternatives

- Actions taken

- Commitments of resources that cannot be retrieved (for example, something that you buy that is not returnable)

- Controlled by the decision maker (what the choice will be and how it will be made)

- Measured in terms of a good decision or a bad decision by how well the process was used, not by the outcome

THE SIX RULES OF EFFECTIVE DECISION MAKING

1. **Define the decision to be made.** Believe it or not, many of us do not identify precisely what we wish to decide before we start a decision-making process. This can cause frustration and confusion. What is it that you want to decide? If you are unhappy with your career or lifestyle, what do you want to change? Do you want to change careers, change where you work, or change some other part of your life? Don't be impatient to decide how you want to change or what your final decision will be. Rather, spend some time considering just what it is that you want to decide.

   Examples:

   a. Your job has good points and bad points (as most jobs do). You find yourself feeling frustrated and unhappy. You don't quite know why. You know that you need to make a decision about your job. You define your decision as follows: Do I change careers, do I change the place where I work, do I work to improve things where I am, or do I keep feeling frustrated and unhappy?

b. Your commute to work takes you more than an hour each way. You do not like it and find that you are irritable much of the time. You define your decision as follows: Do I look for a better job closer to home, do I move closer to work, do I find a different way to commute, or should I grin and bear it?

You may have several things going on in your life. Try to separate them into specific areas and then define decisions that need to be made in each area. You will probably feel more in control and less confused.

2. **Identify the obstacles you face, and deal with them.** We all have difficulties making important decisions, but it is more difficult to make some decisions than to make others. It may be helpful for you to take stock of what obstacles you face in making a decision. Some typical obstacles to decision making are as follows.

   - The decision you need to make is not defined. You don't know what it is you want to decide.

   - You do not have enough information on which to base a decision.

   - You are impatient and want to make a decision right away, even though you may not be ready to decide.

   - You tend to procrastinate. You may find yourself putting off major decisions.

   - You may be faced with a variety of internal obstacles, such as fear of taking a risk, self-doubt, lack of confidence, fear of failure, and concern over making the wrong decision.

   - You may be faced with external obstacles, such as family responsibilities, time, geographical location, and money.

   - You may be reluctant to take charge of making your own decisions, preferring to let others do it for you or simply by letting things happen. This is decision making by default.

3. **Get adequate information before you make a decision.** Many people try to make a decision without having accurate and complete information. In order to make a decision, you must be able to evaluate several alternatives and then make a choice. You cannot evaluate alternatives unless you have complete information about each. In the case of a career choice, this is particularly important. Before choosing a career, you need to collect information. You need to know many things about a career, a job, a car, a spouse, a house, or a boss before you select one.

4. **Before you make a decision, always compare at least two alternatives.** It is difficult to decide whether or not to do something in the absence of any alternatives. It always helps to have something that you can compare. Think of comparison shopping. It would be pretty dull if you were looking for a new car and had only one choice. It would be downright depressing if you only had one style of house from which to choose. When you make a decision, consider your alternatives. List the advantages and disadvantages of each. Talk with other people. Obtain more information, then decide. Your chances of making a satisfying decision will be much greater than if you considered no alternatives.

5. **Know your most important personal values and rank them in terms of their importance to you.** Major decisions always involve choosing between important personal values. If you want to take a new job that involves moving to a different part of the country and your family doesn't want to move, you are faced with a very difficult conflict between career and family values. Such decisions are never easy, but they can be facilitated by your knowing your most important values *in the order of their importance to you.*

6. **The time comes when you have to make it happen. You should decide. Don't let others, or events, decide for you.** Some people like to delay decisions as long as possible, feeling that things will eventually "work out." Sometimes they do, and sometimes they don't, but it is easy to fall into a habit of making decisions by default. People who do this eventually feel that they have no control over their lives. Events take control over them. This can lead to frustration and a sense of helplessness. This approach does provide an easy out, however, because people who use it can blame what

happens to them on events and on others. You must actively take charge of your decision making by defining the decision, getting information, and choosing among your alternatives. If, after considering all of the alternatives open to you, you decide to do nothing, then it is still a valid decision arrived at after careful consideration. You are much more likely to be satisfied with your situation than if, by default you did nothing .

AVOIDING PITFALLS IN DECISION MAKING

There are several kinds of pitfalls that you may encounter as you make decisions in your life. If you find yourself having problems making a decision, ask yourself the following questions. They may help you to identify the sources of difficulty.

1. **Are you motivated to make the decision?** You have to want to make the decision. It should not be imposed by others. Is this decision something that you really feel is important? If not, perhaps you should reevaluate whether you really should be making this decision.

2. **Are you creating obstacles for yourself?** Are you approaching the decision with a negative attitude? Do you fear making a wrong decision so much that you won't do anything? Are you stereotyping yourself (I'm too old, I'm not smart enough) so that you feel you cannot accomplish something?

3. **If there are external obstacles, how significant are they?** You may have some real obstacles to making a decision, such as family responsibilities, time, and money. However, you may be able to get around these. They may not be as formidable as they seem. Are you using these as an excuse for not taking action?

4. **Do you have the information you need?** You cannot make an adequate decision without knowing about the alternatives you face. What are the merits and problems of each alternative? Don't try to make a decision without first having plenty of information. If you don't have enough information, develop a plan to obtain it.

5. **Have you set a timetable for yourself?** It is easy to put off making a decision. Try to set some realistic goals. Make commitments to yourself and to others. Keep your decision-making process on schedule. Set interim goals for obtaining information and evaluating alternatives.

6. **Are you trying to make several decisions at the same time?** Each change in your life creates stress. Some stress is healthy, because it helps you to grow. Too much stress can be unhealthy and can keep you from making effective decisions. If you are faced with several decisions at once, try to prioritize them and deal with them one at a time.

7. **Do you have your values in perspective?** Every decision involves conflicting values. Do you know what your most important values are in order of priority? If not, take time to analyze your values and rank them. This may help you to make your decision.

8. **Do you have enough alternatives?** Too many alternatives can be confusing, but you should have at least two alternatives for each decision you face. If you do not, this could be the reason you are having problems making a decision. Creatively look at your alternatives and then get the necessary information so that you can choose between them.

9. **Have you allowed yourself incubation time to consider the decision?** Sometimes it helps to think about all aspects of a decision before you take action. It is still important to have a timetable and to avoid procrastination, but give yourself time for careful thought and reflection.

10. **What is your anxiety level?** Some anxiety can be good—it keeps you from being too reckless. However, anxiety can prevent you from taking action. Can you decrease your level of anxiety by controlling those elements of risk that are controllable? Realizing that some risk is involved, ask yourself what the worst thing is that could happen. Realizing that the worst may not be all that bad, you may be able to decrease your anxiety and move ahead.

KNOW YOUR DECISION-MAKING STYLE

Not all people make decisions in the same way. Some people like to analyze their alternatives carefully and then make the decision by themselves, drawing on their own investigative and inner resources. Others like to discuss alternatives with friends. Others prefer to look at the possibilities and then to go with what "feels" right. They like to rely on their intuition as much as an analytical process. Others prefer to get help from a professional such as a career counselor or coach. Some people like to write down alternatives so that they can see them on paper. Others prefer to talk about alternatives rather than to write them down.

There is no single correct way for everyone to make decisions. Information is provided on these pages to help you with the decision-making process, but you must eventually proceed in the way that is best for you. Think about decisions that you have made in the past and answer the following questions.

1. List two or three decisions that you have made in the past about which you have a positive feeling.

    _____

    _____

    _____

2. In the following spaces, write a few comments on why you felt positive about these decisions.

    _____

    _____

    _____

    _____

    _____

3. When you made these decisions, did you:

    (check those that apply)

    _____ consult with others?

    _____ obtain professional help?

    _____ choose from among alternatives?

    _____ accumulate considerable information before deciding?

    _____ make the final decision yourself?

    _____ make the final decision in conjunction with others?

    _____ follow someone else's advice?

    _____ let someone else make the decision?

    _____ write down alternatives and the positives and negatives of each?

    _____ use your intuition in making the decision?

Look back at your responses. What kind of a decision maker are you? Do you like to involve others? Do you like to get as much information as possible? Do you prefer to use your intuition? Do you like to read about your alternatives or talk about them with others? If you prefer a certain approach to decision making, and if it works well for you, then use that approach when the time comes to make a decision. Remember to use the approach that best suits your personal style. As you go about making decisions, remember the following guidelines that apply no matter which approach you use.

1. **Define the decision to be made** and determine what alternatives are open to you.

2. **Obtain sufficient information** about each alternative so that you can make a knowledgeable decision.

3. **Evaluate the alternatives** in terms of the information received, then choose the one that is best for you.

4. **Make a plan** to put your decision into effect and follow through with your plan.

5. **Adjust your plan** along the way.

As you go through this process, be aware of the potential pitfalls described earlier and deal with them as they appear.

One grows or dies. There is no third possibility.

—Oswald Spengler

DECISION-MAKING OUTLINE

The following outline is provided to help you decide between two alternatives. If you have more than two alternatives, make copies of this outline and then compare each alternative with another. Narrow down your alternatives to two, then compare your two final options. If you need to get more information before choosing between two alternatives, go ahead and get the information, but don't procrastinate.

Decision-Making Outline

	Alternative A	Alternative B
Briefly state each alternative		
Advantages of each alternative		
Disadvantages of each alternative		
Unpredictable factors of each alternative		
Risks involved in each alternative		
What is the best thing that could happen?		
What is the worst thing that could happen?		

Now look back at your responses. Based on the relative merits of each, put a check mark after your choice.

Alternative A_____   Alternative B_____

SUMMARY

SECTION *two*

Negotiate Change in Your Life

Change is normal as you go through life. Invite change; manage it based on your needs and values. It is possible to prepare for change by considering your personal characteristics and by having your support systems in place. Risk taking is an important element of change. Be ready to welcome risks while managing the amount of risk involved in any change. By understanding how you prefer to make decisions and by learning about decision-making techniques, you can reduce your anxiety about the unknown and increase your level of confidence in decision-making. Change can make your life exciting and full of opportunities if you are ready for it and are willing to accept the challenges.

ADDITIONAL RESOURCES

Birkel, D. J. & Miller, S. J. (2003). *Career bounce-back! Surfing the emotional wave: The professionals in transition: Guide to recovery and reemployment.* New York; AMACOM.

Bridges, W. (2004). *Transitions: Making sense of life's changes.* 25th Anniversary Edition. Cambridge, MA: Perseus Books.

Bridges, W. (2003). *Managing transitions: Making the most of change.* Cambridge, MA: Perseus Books.

Bridges, W. (2001). *The way of transition: Embracing life's most difficult moments.* Cambridge, MA: Perseus Books.

Coles, R. (1996). *Call of service: Witness to idealism.* NY: Houghton-Mifflin Company.

Deits, R. (2004). *Life after loss: A personal guide dealing with death, divorce, job change and relocation* (4th ed.). Cambridge, MA: Da Capo Press.

Egan, H. & Wagner, B. (2001). *I'm retiring, now what?* NY: Silver Lining Books.

Farley, J. (2004). *Military-to-civilian career transition guide.* Indianapolis: JIST Works, Inc.

Frankl, V. (1946). *Man's search for meaning.* NY: Simon & Schuster.

Gorman, T. (1996). *Multipreneuring: How to prosper in the emerging freelance economy.* NY: Fireside Publishing.

Hammond, J. S., Keeney, R. L. & Raiffa, H. (2002). *Smart choices: A practical guide to making better decisions.* NY: Broadway Books.

Harkness, H. (2005). *Capitalizing on career chaos: Bringing creativity and purpose to your work and life.* CA: Consulting Psychologists Press, Inc.

Hudson, F. M. (2001). *The adult years: Mastering the art of self-renewal.* San Francisco: Jossey-Bass.

Hudson, F. & McLean, P. (2006). *LifeLaunch: A passionate guide to the rest of your life.* Santa Barbara, CA: Hudson Press.

Jacobsen, M. (2000). *Hand me down dreams: How families influence our career paths.* NY: Harmony Books.

Jaffe, D. & Scott, C. (2003). *Managing change at work.* Boston: Course Technology, Inc. (50-Minute Book Series).

Joseph, L. (2003). *Job loss recovery guide.* Oakland, CA: New Harbinger Publications.

Krannich, R. (2002). *Change your job, change your life: Re-careering in the new boom/bust economy.* Manassas, VA: Impact Publications.

Leider, R. J. & Shapiro D. (2002). *Repacking your bags: Lighten your load for the rest of your life.* San Francisco: Berrett-Koehler Publishers, Inc.

Luecke, R. (2002). *Managing change and transition.* Boston: Harvard Business School.

Marston, S. (2002). *If not now, when? Reclaiming ourselves at midlife.* NY: Warner Books.

Menchin, R. S. (2000). *New work opportunities for older Americans.* Lincoln, Nebraska: iUniverse.

Pausch, R. & Zaslow, J. (2008). *The last lecture.* New York: Hyperion Publishing.

Pink, D. (2006). *A whole new mind: Why right-brainers will rule the future.* East Rutherford, NJ: Penguin Group USA.

Pollak, L. (2007). *Getting from college to career: 90 things to do before you join the real world.* NY: HarperCollins Publishers.

Pollan, S. & Levine, M. (2003). *Second acts: Creating the life you really want, building the career you truly desire.* NY: HarperCollins Publishers.

Sanborn, K. & Ricci, W. R. (2003). *Seasons of your career: How to master the cycles of career change.* NY: McGraw-Hill Companies.

Schlossberg, N. K. (2007). *Overwhelmed: Coping with life's ups and downs.* Lanham, MD: Lexington Books.

Schlossberg, N. (2004). *Retire smart, retire happy: Finding your true path in life.* Washington, DC: American Psychological Association.

Scott, C. & Jaffe, D. (2002). *Managing personal change.* Menlo Park, CA: Crisp Publications.

Segalove, I. & Velick, P. B. (2001). *List your life: Listing the risks you can take to enhance your life.* NY: MJF Books.

Syrtash, A. (2006). *How to survive the real world: Life after college graduation.* Atlanta, GA: Hundreds of Heads Books.

Trafford, A. (2004). *My time: Making the most of the rest of your life.* NY: Basic Books.

Vickers-Willis, R. (2002). *Navigating midlife: Women becoming themselves.* Victoria, Australia: Allen & Unwin.

Walker, J. E. (2000). *The age advantage: Making the most of your mid-life career transition.* East Rutherford, NJ: Berkley Trade.

Waxman, B. & Mendelson, B. (2006). *How to love your retirement: Advice from hundreds of retirees.* Atlanta, GA: Hundreds of Heads Survival Guides.

Wendel, R. (2008). *Retire with a mission: Planning and purpose for the second half of life.* Naperville, IL: Sourcebooks, Inc.

Wilson, D. G. (2004). *Back in control: How to stay sane, productive and inspired in your career transition.* Boulder, CO: Sentient Publications.

Online Resources

Empathy Quotient—http://www.glennrowe.net/BaronCohen/EmpathyQuotient/EmpathyQuotient.aspx

The Last Lecture—www.cmu.edu/randyslecture

Resiliency Quiz—http://www.resiliencycenter.com/resiliencyquiz.shtml

Self-esteem Quotient—http://www.performance-unlimited.com/seqeval.htm

Thorson Humor Quotient—www.tinyurl.com/6t7ff/

Time Management Quiz—http://dwp.bigplanet.com/workingresources/timeselfmanagementsurvey/

SECTION *three*

Explore Career Options

Whenever you decide to choose or change a career, it is important to learn as much as possible about the job market. As you learned in Sections 1 and 2, the first step in career planning is to know yourself. The second step is to learn about the world of work. Many people will choose a job on a whim or because a job just happens to be available. Sometimes this approach works, but often it leads to a career blunder. You know that you have made a career blunder when you find yourself on your new job for a day, a week, or a month and you discover that this is not the place for you. When this happens, you are faced with learning a new job and adapting to a new environment while at the same time starting the job search all over again. A career blunder can undermine your self-confidence.

How can you prevent career blunders? There are no guarantees that you can totally avoid career blunders. However, this section will help you to consider the relationships between different kinds of work and the careers that may be most suited to your needs and values. Gathering information can help you avoid a career blunder. This section will help you to learn more about the world of work.

It is essential to investigate your options and to search actively for those organizations that can best use your skills. You will need to continually update your knowledge about your areas of interest and about the constant changes that are taking place. You will need to identify new skills and information that will be required. More than ever before, you will have the responsibility for keeping yourself up to date and positioned to deal with changing career needs. The techniques described in this section will help you to accomplish this goal.

CHAPTER 13

Your Career Options List

What careers have you considered? Have other people recommended possible careers for you? Which of your interests could be turned into careers? In this chapter, you will expand your career options by developing several lists of career alternatives. You will then narrow your alter-natives by looking at each career in terms of your own needs and by using information that you obtain about each career. To begin, try to think of as many careers as possible that interest you. Don't discount creative or unusual career options. Try not to limit your investigation to only those careers that are familiar to you. Be open in considering different career alternatives. The following suggestions may help you to expand your list.

LOOK BACK INTO THE PAST

Start with what you wanted to be when you were a child. What did you see for yourself when you were between 5 and 15 years old? If it's difficult to remember, ask someone who knew you when you were growing up. In the following spaces, list some of the careers you thought about when you were growing up.

_____   _____

_____   _____

_____   _____

_____   _____

_____   _____

CONSIDER CAREER "DREAMS"

In the following spaces list all of the careers that have interested you. Be sure to include those that you have dreamed about but have never considered possible.

_____   _____

_____   _____

_____   _____

_____   _____

GET IDEAS FROM OTHERS

Enlist the assistance of three people who know you well. Ask them to suggest possible careers for you to investigate based on their knowledge of your personality, interests, and skills. You may wish to ask them to think about your request for a couple of days rather than giving you quick answers.

_____   _____

_____   _____

_____   _____

_____   _____

CONSIDER YOUR UNIQUE SELF

Consider your responses in Sections 1 and 2. Based on your analysis of your interests, work values, skills, personal values, and lifestyle considerations, what careers might you want to explore?

_____   _____

_____   _____

_____   _____

_____   _____

CONSIDER YOUR CHOICE OF OCCUPATIONAL ENVIRONMENTS

Consider your choice of occupational environments (realistic, investigative, artistic, social, enterprising, and conventional as described in Chapter 2). Which were your first two choices? Most career resource centers have lists of careers that match each of the six occupational environments. Which careers in the occupational environments of your choice interest you most?

_____   _____

_____   _____

_____   _____

_____   _____

_____   _____

MAKE USE OF INTEREST INVENTORIES

Consider taking an interest inventory that may provide a list of possible career choices based on your interest profile. Some suggestions are:

Strong Interest Inventory

Self-Directed Search

Kuder Career Search with Person Match Inventory

Campbell Interest and Skill Survey

These inventories are normally available at college, community, and private counseling services. In addition, many career resource centers in college, high school, and community libraries have electronic and online systems with which you can identify potential careers based on your interests, values, and other factors. If you are able to take an interest inventory or to use an electronic choice system, write in the following spaces the careers that best matched your interest profile.

_____   _____

_____   _____

_____   _____

_____   _____

Do Some Brainstorming

Another way to expand your career options list is to play the following brainstorming game with a few friends. As you investigate the world of work, consider the following factors.

1. What skill do you wish to use in your career? Do you want to work primarily with:

    data _____

    people _____

    things _____

    ideas _____

    Place a one (1) next to your first choice. Place a two (2) next to your second choice.

2. Do you want to work in a particular field? Examples would be:

agriculture	recreation	arts/humanities
business	construction	transportation
government	communications	marketing
health	manufacturing	military
education	natural resources	product services
personal services	social services	other _____

    List up to three fields that interest you, with (1) being your first choice, (2) your second choice, and (3) your third choice.

    (1) _____

    (2) _____

    (3) _____

3. In which occupational environment would you feel most comfortable? Place a (1) next to your first choice and a (2) next to your second choice.

    realistic _____   artistic_____   enterprising _____

    investigative _____   social _____   conventional _____

4. In what kind of a setting would you like to work? Would it be in a large city, a suburb, or a rural area? Would you like to work inside, outside, or both? Do you want to work in a particular part of the country? In a particular climate? In the following spaces, list up to three of your preferences about the setting in which you would like to work, with (1) being the most important factor.

    (1) _____

    (2) _____

    (3) _____

Now summarize your answers on the following chart.

1. Skill area	First choice _____	Second choice _____
2. Field of interest	First choice _____	Second choice _____
		Third choice _____
3. Occupational environment	First choice _____	Second choice _____
4. Setting	Most important _____	Second most _____ important
		Third most _____ important

You now have choices in each of the four areas that make up the world of work. By yourself or with a few family members or friends, try to brainstorm all of the possible careers that may fulfill each of your first choices in the four areas. Write the suggestions in the following spaces. After you have brainstormed using your first choices, try your second and third choices. Come up with as many possibilities as you can.

_____   _____

_____   _____

_____   _____

_____   _____

YOUR CAREER OPTIONS LIST

By this time, you have several lists of possible careers. Consider your most important interests, work values, skills, personal values, and lifestyle considerations. Now go back over each list in this chapter, sections A through G. Circle those careers that you would like to investigate. After you have circled your choices, write them on your career options list.

My Career Options List

1. _____
2. _____
3. _____
4. _____
5. _____
6. _____
7. _____
8. _____
9. _____
10. _____
11. _____
12. _____
13. _____
14. _____
15. _____

With your career options list, you can now begin to explore the world of work. The information on the following pages will help you to investigate the careers on your list.

If you have run out of space to list your career options, you may wish to use the Continuous Career Options Listing in the Appendix.

CHAPTER 14

How to Investigate Career Information

You now have a list of your career options. You have selected these based on your interests, on the suggestions of others who know you well, and on your evaluation of your unique self. Before you can begin making a career decision, however, you need something that is very important.

INFORMATION!

Too many people try to make a career decision without first having the information they need. Recall the analogy in the introduction of this book that compares your career search to that of buying a car or a house. You may think that your car or your house is the largest monetary investment in your lifetime. However, when you compare your lifetime earnings to the cost of a car or a house, it is apparent that the earnings you accrue throughout your life are your single largest investment. When other possible benefits that you earn—such as health insurance, life insurance, retirement plan, profit sharing, and leave—are added, the amount grows even more. You need to find out as much as possible about a career before you prepare to enter it. There are four basic ways to find out about a career. They are:

- Experience
- Printed material

- The Internet and the World Wide Web
- Talking with people

It is important to get the best, most direct, most up-to-date information available before making a decision. The information that you obtain can prevent career blunders. Here are some guidelines to follow.

EXPERIENCE

The best way to learn what a career is like is to experience it. Working in a field can give you valuable insight into whether or not a particular career is for you. Although it may not always be possible to find a way to get direct experience in a field, there are several actions that you can take to obtain this experience.

1. **Get a part-time job in the field.** You may start at a low level, but you can still get a good deal of exposure to what the career involves. You can find out what the people who work in the field are like

and can learn from talking with them. You can learn about the daily routine and about the advantages and disadvantages of the job.

2. **Do volunteer work.** Many organizations, particularly those in public service and health, have opportunities for volunteers. By volunteering, you can learn the same things that you would learn if you were employed. Volunteer work also gives you the opportunity to ask questions and to get to know as much as possible about the career.

3. **Explore the possibility of cooperative education.** This valuable program, which is offered by most colleges and universities, provides an opportunity to receive on-the-job training, college credit, pay, job experience, and future contacts.

4. **Volunteer to take on an internship.** You do not normally receive pay for an internship, but you do receive valuable on-the-job experience. If you are very interested in a career, explore the possibility of an internship program with those colleges, universities, or other organizations that provide training for that career.

5. **Ask to spend a day or two on the job with someone who does the work in which you are interested.** Even in one or two days, you can find out a great deal about a career. Because people like to talk about their work and like to share their experiences with others, a day or two on the job will be easier to arrange than you might think possible. This technique is often called *job shadowing*.

6. **Take a course.** Check out your interests while you develop expertise and gain knowledge about a field. Adult education programs, community colleges, and continuing education courses offer opportunities to get more information at moderate cost. When you take a course in a field you are investigating, you may be able to meet and discuss related careers with others who work in the field.

Information is your best weapon against career blunders.

WRITTEN MATERIAL

A great deal of written material is available covering career choice, the job market, and information on specific careers. Some general sources of this information are:

- Libraries
- Career resource centers
- Bookstores
- Newspapers and periodicals
- Company reports
- Computerized career information services

- Professional organizations
- Government agencies
- Directories
- Employee handbooks
- In-house newsletters
- The Internet

Written material can be very helpful in obtaining career information, particularly at the beginning of your investigation of the world of work. However, as you read written material on careers, it is important to ask the following questions.

1. **Is the information accurate?** Check more than one source. Keep in mind the relationship between supply and demand. What are the opportunities in the field, and what is the projected growth? How many people are preparing to enter the field?

2. **Is the information up to date?** Career trends often change, sometimes very quickly. What is the date of publication of the material you are reading? If it is several years old, you should check another source. Often, the material in newspapers and periodicals and on Web sites is more up to date. Have there been any recent changes in the economy, in government support, or in society that may affect the outlook for the career? Remember the time lapse between the writing of a book and its publication.

3. **Is the information biased?** Be alert for any age, sex, or minority biases in the material. Many libraries will have screened their materials for apparent sources of bias. In addition, information provided by professional organizations and industries about their own fields may be overly enthusiastic, because these organizations and industries naturally want to present themselves in the most positive way.

4. **Is the information comprehensive?** Use more than one source of information. Learn as much as you can from a variety of resources. Obtain as many specific details as you can. Look up additional sources of information. Many career resource centers have specialists who are familiar with a wide variety of career information. Work with these people.

5. **What other sources of information are available?** As you read written material, be constantly aware of sources of additional information. Write down the names and addresses of professional organizations, companies, and individuals. Check with these sources for additional materials or for personal contacts with whom you can talk about the career.

6. **What conclusions can I make?** If you are very interested in a career, do not make a decision solely on the basis of what you have read. Talk with people and see whether you can do the work as an intern or on a similar basis. Also remember that a poor job outlook does not mean that there will be no jobs available. It simply means that you will have to work much harder at finding a job and will need a backup plan in case you cannot find a job in your field right away.

THE INTERNET

The information networks found on organization Web sites and career-oriented sites provide valuable opportunities for career exploration. You can communicate through email with individuals who may have information that is important to you. You can access any one of over 10,000 newsgroups, many of which have career information that may be relevant to your investigation. You can obtain information and share information through mailing lists, which also help you to learn about the leading people in your field. The Internet provides access to a wide variety of institutions, businesses, and information sites.

Most colleges, universities, and libraries provide free Internet access. The possibilities for doing career research using the Internet are virtually limitless. Many organizations provide a variety of free career planning assistance throughout their Web sites. You can access information on corporations and job trends, and obtain information on training requirements and the availability of internships in some fields. In addition, you can access a multitude of job listings. The Internet has made it much easier to do career research. If you have not had much experience doing career research on the Internet, it is recommended that you take a brief workshop or use a reference book, such as:

Bolles, M E. & Bolles, R. N. (2008). *Job Hunting On-line: A Guide to Using Job Listings, Message Boards, Research Sites, the Underweb, Counseling, Networking, Self Assessment Tools, nichesites.* Berkeley, California: Ten Speed Press.

Dikel, M. R., & Roehm, F. E. (2008). *Guide to Internet Job Searching* 2008–2009 Edition. New York: McGraw Hill.

Schlein, A. M. (2004). *Find It Online: The Complete Guide to Online Research* (4th ed.). Tempe, Arizona: Fact On Demand Press.

For a comprehensive listing of useful Internet sites for career exploration and job hunting, go to Chapter 15, The Internet—Sites for Career Exploration and Job Hunting.

TALKING WITH PEOPLE

One of the best ways to find out about a career is to talk with people who are actually working in that career. This is always preferable to just reading material because of the following:

1. **The information you receive is up to date.** You are talking with someone who is currently doing the work.

2. **The information you receive is more local.** Written material is often addressed to the entire country. When you talk with someone, you get much better information about the career possibilities in your geographic area.

3. **You find out about the job setting.** If you talk with people at their places of work, you can get a sense of what it might be like to work there.

4. **You can get information you wouldn't find in most books.** People are often candid about telling you the advantages and disadvantages of their jobs when you talk with them in person. You have the opportunity to interact, ask questions, and get to know the people.

5. **You develop a network of contacts.** Every person with whom you talk becomes a potential contact when you begin looking for a job.

How do you find people with whom you can talk? Think of all your contacts and then expand your list. Some possible sources of people who can help are:

- Friends and family members
- Contacts made through family or friends
- Officials of unions and professional organizations
- Chambers of commerce
- Community service agencies
- College instructors
- Career counselors
- Resource center directors and librarians
- Company officials
- Personnel directors
- Public relations officials
- Researching the Internet

Once you have identified people with whom you wish to talk, you can plan to interview them. This involves one of the most important components of the career and life planning process: *informational interviewing*.

INFORMATIONAL INTERVIEWING

Each day you have the opportunity to talk with people about their careers. You can do this at work, at social gatherings, with family, with neighbors and friends, and in many other ways. You can formalize this process of finding out about the world of work by selecting people who are in a position to give you firsthand information. The process of talking with people who have careers that interest you is called **informational interviewing.** While you may hesitate to ask people to take the time to talk with you, the results are definitely worth any risk of refusal or discomfort that you may face.

This is your opportunity to ask important questions, the answers to which may be vital to your career search. If you are apprehensive about making that first call for an appointment or visiting a worksite, remember the benefits that you will receive in having the information about the career field. The importance of obtaining the information that you need for your career and life planning outweighs any hesitancy that you may have about contacting people whom you do not know. Remember that people like to talk about their work.

While you may occasionally be turned down for an interview, don't let this discourage you. Move on to the next person whom you would like to interview. Remember, your first priority is to get the information that you need in your career search.

Informational interviewing involves talking with someone who is presently working in a career that interests you. Gathering information that you need in order to make a decision is your goal. The art of informational interviewing is developed with practice. This valuable career and life planning tool can also be incorporated regularly into your work life.

There are four ways to arrange for informational interviews. Choose one or all of the following approaches, depending on your situation:

1. **Walk-in method.** Drop in on a prospective interviewee whom you have identified. Depending on the type of career you are investigating, this may be an effective method of informational interviewing. For example, if you are researching the auto mechanics field, you probably would be welcome on a drop-in basis. On the other hand, most business people prefer appointments, so use your judgment. This method may be less stressful for you initially, but you may not obtain the information during your visit if your interviewee is not available or has very limited time. However, you can use this technique to uncover names and to make future appointments.

2. **Telephone method.** Call an organization and ask for the name of the person who works in an area that interests you. Tell the person that you are doing career research and need additional information in order to make a career decision. Try to make an appointment to see the person at a mutually convenient time: during working hours, at the lunch hour, during a break, or during off-work hours. Informational interviewing is done best *in person* rather than over the telephone. As an alternative to telephoning, you may wish to send an email message and follow up with a telephone call.

3. **Referral method.** Call someone you know or someone who has been referred to you by a friend, and ask the person for an informational interview. This method can be very productive, because you are building on a personal contact. This is a good way to begin informational interviewing, because there is less stress involved in arranging for the interview.

4. **E-mail or letter method.** Obtain the name of the person you wish to interview and write an email message or a letter clearly stating your purpose and desire to speak with the person. The following letter is provided as a guide for requesting an informational interview.

Letter Requesting an Informational Interview

Mr. James Smith
Director of Marketing
ABC Corporation
Anywhere, U.S.A.

Dear Mr. Smith:

In my career exploration research, your name came to my attention as someone who could provide me with valuable advice and information because of your expertise and experience in the field of marketing.

I am currently (employed full-time, attending school full-time, or some other statement about your current status) and I am not at this time looking for employment. I am, however, giving serious consideration to a career in marketing. I would therefore like to talk with you about marketing as a possible career in order to obtain your valuable advice and perspective.

Realizing the demands on your time, I will telephone you on Monday, April 5, to see if we can arrange a brief meeting at your convenience.

Thank you for your interest and help as I explore a variety of career opportunities.

Sincerely,

This letter covers four important points. It:

- Names the person to whom you are writing

- Tells the person why you are writing

- Tells the person you are **not looking for a job**

- Keeps the initiative with **you**

Now it is time to think of people who may be able to help you with your informational interviewing. Use the following diagram to focus on your network of contacts. You are in the center. Work your way around the circle and write on the lines the names of people who might be able to assist you: friends, relatives, friends of friends, spouses of friends, neighbors, acquaintances, classmates, teachers, counselors, professional associates, and any others who can provide contacts or information.

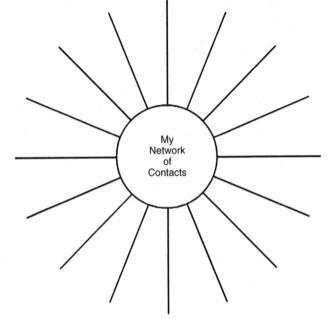

These four methods of arranging for informational interviews: walk-in, telephone or email, referral, and letter can be vital to your career investigation. Use one or more methods to achieve your goal. The advantage of informational interviewing is that it works! Some of the reasons it works are:

- People like to talk about their work.

- People are usually flattered that you are seeking their advice.

- People are empathetic with others who are going through career transitions because most have experienced the indecision and frustration that go with making a career decision.

- People like to help others because it makes them feel good about themselves.

The following are some helpful hints on how to go about informational interviewing. Although interviewing may seem difficult, it is not, and it gets easier with each interview. Follow these simple steps and make informational interviewing work for you.

Know What You Want to Accomplish

The primary objectives of informational interviewing are to:

- Investigate a specific career field

- Uncover areas that may have been unknown to you

- Gain insight into what is happening in a career field and about future trends

- Obtain information that will help you to narrow your options

- Obtain advice on where you might fit in

- Learn the jargon and important issues in the field

- Broaden your own network of contacts for future reference

Identifying People to Interview

Here are some sources to use in developing resources of people you may wish to interview.

- Personal referrals (friends, friends of friends, family, acquaintances)
- Directories
- Company organizational listings and Web sites
- Calling organizations and asking for the name of a person in a specific job or finding the name of that person on an organization's Web site.
- Professional associations
- Yellow Pages
- Newspapers and periodicals
- College departments

Arranging for the Interview

Here are some guidelines for setting up an informational interview.

- Use the method that is most appropriate for the type of career you are investigating: "drop-in," telephone, referral, letter, email.
- Obtain the person's name.
- Explain your purpose.
- State why you are contacting this person.
- Emphasize that you are not looking for a job.
- Consider calling early or late, when you may be able to talk directly with the person.
- Maintain the initiative. Call to follow up after writing a letter or after making an initial inquiry.
- Be prepared for refusals. What is the worst thing that could happen?

Preparing for the Interview

If you do some homework before the interview, you will have a much better chance of conducting a successful interview and acquiring valuable information. You will also make a better impression on the interviewer, which can be helpful when you ask for additional contacts or if, in the future, you ever contact this person about a job.

- Learn as much as you can about the organization. Do your homework through research—look at the organization's literature, annual reports, employee handbooks, and other sources. You absolutely must check out the organization's Web site.
- If possible, learn something about the person you will be interviewing.
- Learn about the career in general—nature of the work, major trends, and current issues.
- If the organization has been in the news, review newspaper and magazine articles about the organization.
- Prepare questions about the **person**, the **field**, and the **organization**.
- Ask questions that are based on the research that you have done. Avoid asking questions that you can answer by reading the organization's Web site.

- Write down the questions that you wish to ask.

- Develop priorities for the interview. Decide ahead of time which information is most important for you to obtain.

- Make sure that you know how to get to the place where you will conduct the interview and leave plenty of time to get there.

Conducting the Interview

- Restate your purpose and why you are talking with this particular person.

- Remember that this is not a job interview, so you don't have to be nervous.

- Develop rapport. Ask open-ended questions. With your questions, show that you have done your homework.

- Try to get the answers to your most important questions. Take notes.

- Ask about alternative ways to prepare for entering the career field.

- Observe the job setting and general atmosphere. How do they match with your expectations?

- Don't ask for a job.

- Obtain the names of other individuals you can contact.

Follow-up

Good follow-up is just as important as good preparation. Here are some suggestions for action after you have conducted an informational interview.

- Send a typed thank-you letter. In many situations, it may be acceptable to send a thank-you note via email. When in doubt, however, send a letter.

- Call later on or send an email message to say how you are progressing.

- Keep the door open to future contacts with the person you interviewed.

- Evaluate your style of interviewing. What could you have done better? Use what you have learned when you conduct your next interview.

- Evaluate the information you received. How does it relate to your plans?

- If appropriate, contact the person you interviewed when you begin looking for a job.

- Keep your notes organized, including dates of contacts, names, addresses, phone numbers, and email addresses.

Informational interviewing is an effective tool and an important resource in your career and life planning. It helps you to discover much of what you need to know in order to make an informed decision.

Informational Interview Guide

This guide provides you with an outline for conducting an informational interview. You can take this two-page guide, along with a notebook, to an informational interview. Questions relate to three important areas: the interviewee, the field, and the organization. Of course, not all questions listed here can be used because of time limitations. Go through the list before the interview and choose the most important questions to ask. Ask other questions as time permits.

The Interviewee

You can find out about the person you are interviewing, the **interviewee**, by asking some of the following questions.

1. How long have you worked in this field?
2. How did you decide to enter this field?
3. How has your career progressed?
4. How would you describe a typical day on your job?
5. What skills do you use in your job?
6. What kinds of experiences prepared you for this job?
7. What challenges do you face? daily? long term?
8. What are the rewards that you get from your job? What gives you the most satisfaction?
9. What are the frustrations that you experience?
10. What does it take to be successful in your job?
11. How does this job fit into your career plan?
12. What is your major contribution to your profession?
13. Are there opportunities to continue to learn on your job?
14. What expertise have you developed?
15. Looking back, would you have done anything differently in your career?
16. What effect does your career have on your lifestyle and your family?
17. Would you enter this field again if you could start over?

The Field

You can research the **field** you are investigating by asking some of the following questions.

1. What type of preparation, credentialing, and training must one have to enter this field?
2. Is there growth in the field? What is the job potential?
3. What are the current needs in the field?
4. What can I do, if I enter the field, to make myself marketable and competitive?
5. What are the future directions in the field? What changes are expected?
6. Will there be new opportunities for employment as a result of future changes?
7. What kinds of skills and what type of commitments are necessary to be successful in this field?
8. What are the advantages and disadvantages of working in this field?
9. What are the characteristics of people who become successful in this field?
10. What experiences would be helpful for someone entering this field?

(Continued)

(Continued)

11. What are the typical entry-level salary and benefits?
12. What are the opportunities for professional growth?
13. How mobile are people in this career? Are there opportunities in a variety of geographic locations?
14. What technologies are important in this career?
15. What recommendations would you have for an entry-level person considering this field?

The Organization

You should try to do some research on the **organization** that you will be visiting. Never ask the interviewee something that you could easily have learned through reading or the Internet. Do your homework and ask questions that build on your knowledge about the organization. Here are questions that you may wish to ask your interviewee and others whom you may meet. Keep in mind that some interviewees may be reluctant to give candid answers to some of these questions. If you sense reluctance to answer a question, move on to another question. Don't push.

1. How does your position fit into the organization's structure?
2. Who are the organization's leaders? How long have they been with the organization? How are the leaders perceived?
3. Where does the organization's funding come from? Is there stability in this funding?
4. What is the management philosophy of the organization? Do decisions come from the top down or are decisions made by work groups?
5. Are there frequent staff meetings? How do people feel about attending?
6. What are the opportunities for growth? Is there a professional development program? Are people encouraged and promoted from within?
7. What is the style of supervision in the organization?
8. What kind of hours do people work? Are the hours standard for everyone or flexible? Is overtime encouraged? Are vacations encouraged?

You can learn more about the organization by making some of the following observations. Remember that some of these questions can be thoroughly answered only through extended observations. However, even if you can only make a brief visit, your initial impressions are very important.

1. What is the atmosphere of the organization? Do people seem happy to be there?
2. Do people seem willing to communicate and to share ideas and work with their colleagues?
3. Do people enjoy going to meetings?
4. Do the supervisors spend time with the people that they supervise?
5. Is there a group approach to decision making? Do people feel that they are included in the process?
6. Is there a cooperative or a competitive atmosphere in this workplace?
7. What is the physical environment? Is there good lighting, ventilation, workspace allocation, equipment, privacy, and security?
8. Do employees have access to health and fitness services as a part of the job?
9. Does the organization support professional development in terms of providing tuition assistance, encouraging people to develop new skills, and providing time for professional development activities?
10. What is the dress code for the organization? Are employees dressing informally? Notice the details of dress for future employment interviewing.

CHAPTER 15

The Internet—Sites for Career Exploration and Job Hunting

The Internet has already changed the way we communicate, shop, and plan for travel, and will continue to change how we conduct our businesses and our lives. The possibilities seem to be limitless. The Internet has certainly made it easier to do career research and to identify possible employment opportunities. This chapter provides a listing of useful Web sites that relate to career planning and job hunting. While all of these sites have been checked for accuracy as of this writing, be aware of the rapid changes that continually occur.

CAREEER WEB SITES

General Career and Educational Planning

America's Career InfoNet (www.acinet.org/acinet)
This site is part of the America's Career Kit from the U.S. Department of Labor. It provides excellent general information on the U.S. job market and valuable resources for career planning.

Black Collegian Online (www.black-collegian.com)
The online version of this comprehensive magazine provides very good career planning, job search, and career resource information.

Career Key (www.careerkey.org/)
Gives you expert help with your career search and career choices—career change, career planning, job skills, and choosing a college major.

Career Kiosk (www.careerkiosk.org)
This is a comprehensive, well-maintained site which provides up to date links to sites in the following areas: self-assessment, career planning, networking and interviews, resumés and letters, and job listings. It also provides information on how to use career Web sites.

CareerOneStop (www.careeronestop.org)
A U.S. Department of Labor-sponsored Web site that offers career resources and workforce information to job seekers, students, businesses, and workforce professionals to foster talent development in a global economy.

Career Magazine (www.careermag.com)

Good search paths, career resource, job bank information, and industry specific career channels.

Career Resource Center (www.careers.org)

This site provides job information resources including government, nonprofit, freelance, seasonal employment, and more. Also provides extensive educational exploration resources.

Career Wizard (www.career-wizard.com)

Presents information, resources, tools, and educational programs to build a better career.

College Grad.Com (www.collegegrad.com/careers/all.shtml)

Targets college students and recent grads providing job views which include Nature of the Work, Working Conditions, Training, Other Qualifications, Advancement, Employment/Job Outlook, Earnings, Related Occupations and Sources of Additional Information.

Consulting Psychologists Press, Inc. (www.cpp-db.com)

This is the publisher of the Strong Interest Inventory, Skills Confidence Inventory, the Myers-Briggs Type Indicator, the Career Beliefs Inventory, the Adult Career Concerns Inventory, and many related books and materials.

Internet Career Connection (www.iccweb.com)

This site provides: career advice, information on job hunting techniques, career testing, help with resumé writing, searchable databases, reference information, and more. Career counseling via email is offered for a fee.

Occupational Information Network (www.doleta.gov/)

This is a list of products provided by the U.S. Department of Labor with information about occupations, skills, and training.

Occupational Outlook Handbook: (www.bls.gov/oco/)

This is the online version, recently updated, of the book published every two years by the U.S. Department of Labor. It provides succinct information on a variety of careers.

O*Net Online (http://online.onetcenter.org/)

Developed for the Department of Labor, this site provides information about an occupation (work performed, skills, education, training, and credentials) and also provides a crosswalk of Military Occupational Classifications (MOC) to Standard Occupational Classifications (SOC).

Online Sports Career Center (www.onlinesports.com/pages/careercenter.html)

This site provides job information for careers in sports other than being a professional athlete. There are also shopping links.

Quintessential Career and Job-Hunting Resources Guide: (www.quintcareers.com)

This is a very extensive and well-organized site for many aspects of a job search.

Psychological Assessment Resources, Inc. (www.parinc.com)

This is the publisher of the Self Directed Search, the Occupations Finder, and all related Holland materials. They also publish My Vocational Situation, a brief checklist, useful for beginning job searchers.

The Riley Guide: Employment Opportunities and Job Resources on the Internet (www.rileyguide.com)

This is a comprehensive, detailed guide to using the Internet for job search and other services.

Twolingos (www.twolingos.com)

Includes resources related to language education, studying and working abroad, making new friends, and more!

Vocational Information Center (www.khake.com)

Provides comprehensive information on career choice and academic support in various fields.

Job Search/Listings

America's Job Bank and America's Talent Bank (www.ajb.org)
This Department of Labor site links 1800 state employment service offices, providing over 1000 new listings daily. The applicant must register, but there is no charge.

Best Jobs in the *USA Today* (www.bestjobsusa.com)
This site includes all national regional and local ads from *Employment Review* magazine with emphasis on recruiting and help with job searching.

CareerBuilder.com (www.careerbuilder.com)
This interesting site gives help in the search process covering over 40 career sites. This is one of the largest job listing sites. The listings come from two sources: the help wanted ads of the nation's leading newspapers and the Web sites of leading employers. User must register.

Careerbuzz.com (www.careerbuzz.com)
This is a good, lively place to access the job bank and also get advice on dress, current business news, and links to other information.

Career Journal (http://online.wsj.com/careers)
This site provides interesting, interactive, up to date information on a variety of current career issues and advice on job hunting, resumés, networking, and salaries.

College Grad Job Hunter (www.collegegrad.com)
This is a detailed site including a job bank for entry level positions, resumé posting, internships, employer search, and Internet job search strategies.

Cool Works (www.coolworks.com)
This is a very interesting site for up to date information on seasonal jobs in unusual places.

Dice.com (www.dice.com)
Specific information is provided for high tech jobs in this lively site, with listings by metropolitan areas, and help with job search.

Diversity Link (www.diversitylink.com)
The mission of Diversity Link is "to bring outstanding female, minority, and other diversity professionals together with equally outstanding employers who have career opportunities."

Employment Guide (www.EmploymentGuide.com)
The Employment Guide offers many resources to search by geographical area and apply online. There are many industries and levels of jobs posted.

Five O'clock Club (www.fiveoclockclub.com)
This site is maintained by a national career counseling network, which provides career coaching, an outplacement network for professionals, managers, and executives, a newsletter, access to local seminars, and help with resumé development, interviewing, and salary negotiation. There is an access charge of $49.00 per year.

Fortune 500 (http://money.cnn.com/magazines/fortune)
This is a good source of information on companies.

Hire Diversity (www.hirediversity.com)
This site provides career resource services for African Americans, Asian-Americans, the disabled, gays and lesbians, Hispanics, mature workers, Native Americans, veterans, and women.

Hoover's On-line (www.hoovers.com)
This is a research site for obtaining information about public and private companies.

HotJobs.com (www.hotjobs.yahoo.com)

This up-to-date, accessible site, sponsored by Yahoo!, offers a job bank, notifies the applicant of openings that meet stated criteria, and provides various career tools.

Idealist/Action Without Borders (www.idealist.org)

An interactive site where people and organizations can exchange resources and ideas, locate job, internship, and volunteer opportunities, and take steps toward building a world where all people can lead free and dignified lives.

Indeed.Com (www.indeed.com)

A search engine for jobs with a different approach to job search. In one simple search job seekers get free access to millions of employment opportunities from thousands of Web sites.

Job Bank USA (www.jobbankusa.com)

This site offers job listings by field, company, and location, employment resource sites, and links to other career related sites.

Job Hunt (www.job-hunt.org)

This is a complete, comprehensive listing of online job search resources.

Job Hunters Bible (www.jobhuntersbible.com)

This companion Web site to Richard Bolles, *What Color Is Your Parachute* is an extensive selection of well organized links.

Job Profiles (www.jobprofiles.org)

This interesting, somewhat "folksy" site provides first-hand accounts of what it is like to work in different careers. Information on academic programs is also included.

Job Source Network (www.jobsourcenetwork.com)

This is a comprehensive source of links to many job sites.

Job Web (www.jobweb.com)

This is a well-done job and employer database sponsored by the National Association of Colleges and Employers.

Jobs.Com (www.jobs.com)

This is a comprehensive site with state-by-state job listings.

Monster Board (www.monster.com)

This excellent site, one of the most comprehensive, enables the job seeker to register and then set up a personalized job search center.

Monstertrak (www.monstertrak.com)

This very good job and resumé bank requires registration because access is limited to students and alumni of over 900 colleges and universities that participate in the service.

Nation Job Network (www.nationjob.com)

There are very general categories and the seeker must sign up for job search.

Net Temps (www.net-temps.com)

The leading job board for temporary, temp-to-perm, and full time employment through the staffing industry.

NowHiring (www.NowHiring.com)

Formerly CareerSite, this service is free, but the applicant must register to obtain anonymous profiling. Provides good career information, personalized search agents, job matching, and advice.

Overseas Jobs (www.overseasjobs.com)

There are over 50 categories of international jobs here and interesting sidetracks and ads. Free registration is required for full use of resources.

Recruiters Online Network (www.recruitersonline.com)
    A network for recruiters, job-seekers, and employers.

Saludos Hispanos (www.saludos.com)
    This is an employment service for bilingual Hispanic college graduates including job listings, links to other sites, and resumé posting.

Spherion (www.spherion.com)
    This is the Web site of a comprehensive recruiting, staffing, and workforce solutions company.

SpotLight247 (http://www.spotlight247.com/index.asp)
    Founded in 2007, this is a free interactive job portal that connects job seekers to employers all across the world. Video resumés can be used to effectively market applicants to employers.

TopJobs (www.topjobs.net)
    TopJobs provides access to job listings in the UK. It specializes in management, professional, technical, and graduate positions.

True Careers (www.TrueCareers.com)
    This site is associated with Sallie Mae. Most users have a college degree. Various job search tools are provided, in addition to an employer database.

VaultReports.com (www.vault.com/index.jsp)
    This interesting, detailed site requires a no fee membership, and provides industry articles, career advice, and company snapshots.

Wetfeet.com (www.wetfeet.com)
    This is a comprehensive career site that provides a variety of career services as well as a job listing service.

Salary

Abbott-Langer Association Surveys (www.abbott-langer.com).
    This site contains salary ranges for jobs as well as averages for each geographic area.

JobStar Central (www.jobstar.org)
    This site provides links to salary surveys, career guides, resumé helps, and a personal electronic library.

Relocation Salary Calculator (www.homefair.com)
    This site provides cost of living comparisons in the 50 top U.S. employment markets.

Salary.com (www.salary.com)
    This site provides salary information that is specific to geographic areas throughout the U.S. Information on benefits is also provided, along with other useful information.

Salaryexpert.com (http://.salaryexpert.com)
    This site provides a free salary calculator along with a variety of salary information.

Wage Web (www.wageweb.com)
    This site provides information, including specific salaries, on 150 benchmark positions. National data is free, but there is a fee for local data.

Federal Employment/Service

AmeriCorps (www.americorps.gov)
    AmeriCorps is a national network of programs that engages more than 70,000 Americans each year in intensive service to meet critical needs in communities throughout the nation.

Federal Jobs Digest (www.jobsfed.com)

This is a private company site where the user must subscribe, free, to get job specifics. The information is up to date, and wide ranging.

Fedworld.gov (www.fedworld.gov)

This Web site is a gateway to government information. It is managed by the National Technical Information Service, an agency of the U.S. Department of Commerce. It has a search program for federal jobs.

Firstgov.gov (www.firstgov.gov)

This is the official U.S. gateway to all government information. It provides extensive online information from the United States Government, with search capabilities for more than 50 million web pages from federal and state governments. This is the most comprehensive site for government information on the Internet.

Peace Corps (www.peacecorps.gov/index.cfm)

This site provides all the necessary information and application details for volunteer services in the Peace Corp.

U.S. Agency for International Development (www.usaid.gov/careers/)

This is very specific for Foreign Service jobs, but also includes work opportunities in humanitarian efforts worldwide.

U.S. Department of State (http://careers.state.gov/officer/selection.html)

Information on and application materials for jobs in the Foreign Service, embassies, Iraq, and civil service.

USAJobs (www.usajobs.opm.gov)

This is the official site for Federal jobs and employment information provided by the United States Government Office of Personnel Management.

CHAPTER *16*

What to Look for When You Investigate a Career

You now have your list of career options that you plan to investigate. You also know how to go about obtaining information through experience, printed material, the World Wide Web, and talking with people. As you seek information from these resources, what is it that you want to find out? What are some of the things that you should look for when you are investigating a career?

GENERAL QUESTIONS

Consider the **who**, **what**, **where**, and **when** of career investigation:

Who

- Who are your coworkers likely to be? Are you likely to share their interests, values, and personal characteristics?
- Who is likely to be your supervisor?
- If you will be dealing with the public, who will you be serving, and in what capacity?

What

- What will your duties be?
- What will a typical workday be like?
- What skills will you use?
- What are the education and training requirements?
- What are the salary and benefits?
- What are the current job possibilities in this field?
- What important interests, work values, life values, and lifestyle needs are you likely to fulfill in this career?

Where

- Where are you likely to be working? by yourself? in a large office with many others? inside? outside?

- Where, geographically, are you likely to work? Will your career allow you to work in various parts of the country or will you be limited to certain locations?

- Where, in terms of the type of organization, are you likely to be working?

- Where will your skills take you? Can you work with a variety of organizations? Will you be restricted to one type of organization?

When

- When can you expect promotions to occur? What lateral and developmental opportunities are available?

- When can you expect to increase your earning power and your benefits?

- When you want to do something different, can you move within the organization?

- When you want to change jobs, how easily will you be able to find another job in a different organization?

- When a few years pass, what is the job outlook likely to be?

EMPLOYMENT PROJECTIONS

Evaluate how many jobs will be available in the career you are investigating and where these jobs will be. Ask yourself the following questions.

Exactly how many jobs will be available?

If information you read indicates a 30 percent growth rate in an occupation over the next five years, what is the starting point? If there are 20,000 total jobs in the field, a 30 percent growth rate would mean that 6,000 jobs would be created. If there are 100,000 jobs in a field, the same 30 percent growth rate would create 30,000 jobs. All other things being equal, the second would be a better choice, because five times as many jobs would be available.

Will the career be affected by fluctuations in the economy?

Some occupations, such as construction and travel, may be much more dependent on a good economy than others, such as information systems, health, and accounting.

How many people are preparing for the occupation at the present time?

If a certain occupation is growing modestly but is also seen as highly desirable, with many people entering the field, the number of job seekers may soon outstrip the demand.

Do you wish to work in a specific geographic area?

If your choice is limited by the area in which you plan to live, good employment projections in your field of interest may be of no value to you if they do not include your locality.

TRAINING REQUIREMENTS

Consider the amount and type of training required for entry into a career. Ask yourself the following questions:

Is a college degree required for entry, even at a basic level?

In some fields, there are so many people who want jobs that the entry-level requirements are driven up to a high level. For example, someone who wishes to become a social worker may need a master's degree simply to compete for jobs with others who have master's degrees.

Is certification required?

People who wish to enter many of the health professions must meet state certification requirements and may have to take qualifying exams. Some software and hardware providers have developed their own certification requirements for specialty areas.

How important is experience in finding a job in a given field?

The job market for some careers dictates the need for hands-on experience as well as education. Part-time work, cooperative education, or volunteer work can be useful in such situations.

Are there alternative ways to get training for an occupation?

If so, is one better than the others? For certain occupations, you may have a choice between a public college, a private college, or a proprietary specialty school. It is important to evaluate the costs, the type of training provided, and the merits of each as preparation for the job market.

How long will the training take?

Some careers require a long-term commitment for entry. Others can be entered in a relatively short time with minimal training. What commitment can you realistically make to training for a particular career?

Can a career be entered with the skills you already have?

Is additional training really necessary? If you have worked before, you have transferable skills. Does the new career you are considering really require new skills, or can you transfer the same skills you used in your past work, with simply a different focus?

Are there union or on-the-job training programs?

Some unions run apprenticeship programs and some companies have extensive training programs for their employees.

If a college degree is required, must it be in a specific field?

Some potential employers may require a degree with specific training as a part of the academic program. Other employers may want a more general degree that stresses overall thinking and problem-solving skills.

SALARY AND BENEFITS

Your informational interviewing, reading, networking, and Internet search should provide you with some information on the general salary range you can expect in a given career. Consider the following questions.

1. **How important are salary and benefits to you?** If high salary and good benefits are primary values for you, they should be significant factors in choosing a career.

2. **What is the salary range?** Some careers offer a low starting salary but have good potential for raises and bonuses. Other careers have relatively fixed maximum salaries and limited chances for advancement.

3. **What is the method of payment?** Some of the alternatives include:

- annual salary
- commission
- wages plus tips
- payment of a fee for services rendered

- hourly wage
- wages plus commission
- payment by the piece
- payment of a retainer for services to be rendered

4. **What benefits are provided?** Some jobs provide numerous benefits, others very few. Some of these benefits include:

- health insurance
- retirement program
- paid vacation and holidays
- profit sharing
- tax sheltered compensation plans
- credit union
- free parking
- tuition assistance
- medical facilities
- telecommuting

- life insurance
- sick leave
- expense account
- bonuses
- disability insurance
- company car
- clothing and equipment
- discount privileges
- recreational facilities
- technological devices

NONMONETARY REWARDS AND OTHER FACTORS

In addition to salary and benefits, there are other, less tangible, rewards that may be important to you. You should consider the following questions.

1. **What is the work environment?** Do people seem to get along well together? What style of supervision is provided? Is it appropriate for you?

2. **Do you want to work with other people around or by yourself?** Do you need an environment free from distractions, or do you like it rather hectic?

3. **Are there opportunities for positive reinforcement?** Do people compliment one another, or is the atmosphere highly competitive?

4. **Can you be independent, or must you do someone else's bidding most of the time?** To what extent is the work you do dependent on someone else's work?

5. **What kind of hours are required?** Do people work long hours with no overtime pay? What kind of *flexibility of time* would you have? Are you locked into a fixed schedule or do you have some control over the hours you work?

6. **How will the job affect your family responsibilities?** Will it take a considerable amount of time away from your family? Is this acceptable to you?

7. **Is there variety?** Will you be doing the same thing every day? What opportunity is there for personal and professional growth?

8. **Are you philosophically in agreement with the job and with the organization?** Do you believe in what you would be doing? Is the job consistent with your values?

9. **Can you transfer your work from one geographic location to another?** Once you have settled in a job, are you tied to that area or are you mobile?

10. **Are there visible end products so that you can see what you have accomplished, or are the results of the work more vague?** What kind of payoffs do you need?

11. **Does the job allow you to make use of your most important skills and abilities?**

12. **Some other factors you may want to consider include:**

   - travel requirements
   - challenge
   - risk
   - opportunities to learn

   - prestige
   - physical setting
   - work culture
   - upward mobility

WORKSHEET FOR INVESTIGATING A CAREER

Make several copies of the worksheet on the following page. Use it as a guide for summarizing information about each career you investigate.

Career Option _____

1. What would I do? How would I spend a typical day at work?

2. Training requirements—how long will it take to get ready to enter the field?

3. Projections—what is the future job market?

4. Salary and benefits—what can be expected?

5. What are the nonmonetary rewards?

6. What are the opportunities for career mobility?

7. With what type of people would I be working?

8. What are the liabilities and limitations of this career?

9. What learning opportunities will I have?

10. What will I be able to contribute?

CHAPTER *17*

Evaluation of Career Options

After completing the previous chapters, you have now identified at least two or three potential career options that intrigue you. How do you evaluate the information that you have uncovered about yourself and your career options? How do your career options reflect your skills, values, interests, and lifestyle requirements? Compare your unique mixture of needs with the information that you have gathered through research and informational interviewing. Perhaps one or more of these options will fulfill most of your requirements for a satisfying career. This evaluation will assist you in merging the work you have done so far in self-assessment and collection of career information. The evaluation may point to areas that you need to investigate more thoroughly.

PRESENT OPTIONS

The career options I am considering now are:

1. _____

2. _____

3. _____

EVALUATION OF CAREER OPTIONS

It is now time to evaluate your career options in terms of your preferences and priorities. On the following three pages are checklists you can use to assess whether the career options you have identified represent a good match with your assessment of your values, interests, skills, and other requirements. Make a check mark (✓) in the appropriate column to indicate whether the match is good, okay, not a match, or if more information is needed. Use this evaluation to assess your alternatives and to identify what additional information is needed. Try to complete one checklist for each of your three career options.

This is the moment of truth when your hard work pays dividends!

Career Option One _____

How closely does this option match my preferences in the following categories? Make a check mark (✓) in the appropriate column for each factor.

	Good Match	Okay Match	Not a Match	More Info Needed
My work values				
My interests				
The skills and abilities I want to use				
My personal values				
My lifestyle preferences				
The working conditions I prefer				
Number of job opportunities				
Potential for career growth				
Financial rewards				
Nonmonetary rewards				
The type of people I work with				
My ideal workday				
Professional development opportunities				
The geographic location I prefer				
Education or training requirements				
Daily job responsibilities				
Making a valued contribution				
Opportunities to learn				
Others:				
Totals				

Total your check marks in each column for your evaluation of career option one. What additional information do you need? How can you obtain this information?

Career Option Two _____

How closely does this option match my preferences in the following categories? Make a check mark (✓) in the appropriate column for each factor.

	Good Match	Okay Match	Not a Match	More Info Needed
My work values				
My interests				
The skills and abilities I want to use				
My personal values				
My lifestyle preferences				
The working conditions I prefer				
Number of job opportunities				
Potential for career growth				
Financial rewards				
Nonmonetary rewards				
The type of people I work with				
My ideal workday				
Professional development opportunities				
The geographic location I prefer				
Education or training requirements				
Daily job responsibilities				
Making a valued contribution				
Opportunities to learn				
Others:				
Totals				

Total your check marks in each column for your evaluation of career option one. What additional information do you need? How can you obtain this information?

Career Option Three _____

How closely does this option match my preferences in the following categories? Make a check mark (✓) in the appropriate column for each factor.

	Good Match	Okay Match	Not a Match	More Info Needed
My work values				
My interests				
The skills and abilities I want to use				
My personal values				
My lifestyle preferences				
The working conditions I prefer				
Number of job opportunities				
Potential for career growth				
Financial rewards				
Nonmonetary rewards				
The type of people I work with				
My ideal workday				
Professional development opportunities				
The geographic location I prefer				
Education or training requirements				
Daily job responsibilities				
Making a valued contribution				
Opportunities to learn				
Others:				
Totals				

Total your check marks in each column for your evaluation of career option one. What additional information do you need? How can you obtain this information?

Compare the results from your career options evaluation by recording the following summary of totals.

	Matches	More Information	No Match
Career Option 1			
Career Option 2			
Career Option 3			
Totals			

Based on your assessment of your career options and on the assessments that you completed in Sections 1 and 2, consider completing the following tentative career outline. If you do not feel ready to complete this outline, do not be concerned. Perhaps you need to do more research and to talk with more people. A conference with a career counselor may help. In any case, when you are ready, complete your tentative career outline.

TENTATIVE CAREER OUTLINE

1. What are your life and career goals, now that you have summarized your results and weighed your list of career options? Be as specific as you can.

2. What conflicts, if any, exist between your lifestyle needs and your career options? For example, if a top need is money, will your career options provide this for you? What compromises are acceptable to you? What compromises are unacceptable?

3. What interests would you like to use in your career and what interests would you like to reserve for your leisure and noncareer activities?

4. What skills and abilities would you enjoy using in your career? Do you need to build on these skills through continuing education? How do you plan to increase your skills and abilities?

5. How will your self-esteem be enriched by your career options? How will you continue to be challenged in your career?

6. What would you like the *purpose* of your work to be? What accomplishments would you like to look back on ten years from now?

7. Where would you like to live and work? In what setting and geographic area would you be happiest?

8. For whom would you like to work? In what kind of organization—size, purpose, type of work—would you feel most comfortable?

9. What additional information do you need to narrow your options and to make decisions about your career options?

10. Is anything holding you back from accomplishing what you want to accomplish? What barriers and fears do you need to confront?

TIMETABLE OF EVENTS

Example: John

John's career goal is to become a professional accountant. His timetable shows one route to achieve this goal.

Timetable of Events

Career Goal: Professional Accountant—as an entrepreneur or employed by an organization.

Step	Goals (Education and/or Experience)	Time Required
1.	A.S. degree, Business Administration Part-time work as teller in a local bank	2 years
2.	B.S. degree, Accounting Part time work, with some accounting functions	2 years
3.	Full-time work, with primarily accounting functions Miscellaneous courses toward M.B.A.	3 years
4.	Finish M.B.A. degree Prepare for and successfully complete C.P.A. exam	about 4 years

---

Now put your tentative career outline to work by assigning a specific timetable to it. Remember that this is a tentative timetable. You control this plan and you are free to change and review it at any time. Estimate your timetable on the following form, using John's sample as a guide. Think in terms of how long it will take to reach your desired goals. Then consider the steps needed to move toward these goals and plot a timetable for the events.

In the following space, write your tentative career timetable.

Career Goal _____

Step	Goals (Education and/or Experience)	Time Required
1.		
2.		
3.		
4.		
5.		
6.		
7.		
8.		

CAREER SURPRISES

You are satisfied with your job and have not been actively involved in career planning for some time. Suddenly, your boss, a friend, or a colleague lets you know about an opportunity to make a change. The new job is yours if you want it. But do you want it? Often, career opportunities arise at unexpected times. How do you decide if the time is right for you to seize the opportunity? Common approaches are to make lists of positives and negatives and to talk with friends and family members. While these approaches can be helpful, they may not be sufficient. The following checklist will help you deal with an unexpected career opportunity—a career surprise!

1. **Personal values.** What are your top five to ten personal values in order of importance? If necessary, go to Chapter 4, Personal Values. Examine your top personal values in light of your career surprise. Does the job support your values or do value conflicts exist? For example, if your family values are most important, will the job require you to spend more time away from home or will it require you to move? In the space below, write your most important values and how they relate to your new job opportunity.

_____

_____

_____

_____

2. **Work values.** What are your most important work values? Again, you may wish to review Chapter 1, Work Values. Is your new job opportunity in harmony with your work values or are there potential conflicts? For example, some people accept promotions and then find that most of their workday consists of unfulfilling activities. In the space below, write your work values and how they relate to your prospective new job.

_____

_____

_____

_____

3. **Growth, learning, and challenge.** Consider the learning opportunities that your career surprise will provide. Will you be able to expand your repertoire of skills and knowledge by accepting the job? Will this opportunity challenge you to grow personally and professionally? How will this experience position you in relation to achieving your long-range goals? In the space below, write some of the learning and growth opportunities provided by your career surprise.

_____

_____

4. **Lifestyle.** How would your career surprise affect your lifestyle? Would you have to relocate, alter your commute, travel out of town, or change your working hours? Think about your most important lifestyle considerations and how these relate to your new job opportunity.

_____

_____

_____

_____

5. **People.** What people would you be working with in your new job? Who will serve as your supervisor? Satisfaction in many jobs is closely linked to the people with whom you work and especially to your supervisor. In the space provided, jot down your impressions of your prospective new boss and colleagues. Do you need to find out more about them before you make a decision?

_____

_____

_____

_____

6. **Benefits.** Does your career surprise mean a higher salary range? Are the benefits superior to those of your present job? Are there more intrinsic rewards, such as the personal satisfaction of contributing to your community? Do these potential benefits outweigh any potential disadvantages of making the change?

_____

_____

_____

_____

7. **Risks.** What are the risks involved in accepting the new job? Is the organization stable? Do the funds that will cover your salary come from the organization, or are they dependent on grants or other less predictable sources? Is the job environment preferable to your present job? Does the job reflect your interests and skills, thereby enhancing your chances for success? In the space below, write the risks involved if you take this job. What are the risks of refusing this job?

Risks in taking the job	Risks in refusing the job

8. **Future growth.** Does your new job opportunity have as much potential for growth as your present job? more? less? Some jobs seem attractive at first but may lead to a dead end. In the space below, write the potential for growth in both your present job and in your career surprise.

_____

_____

_____

_____

9. **Pros and cons of your career surprise.** Now you can list the positives and negatives of your new job opportunity in relation to your values and preferences. One or two factors may be much more important than all the others combined, so be sure to rank your priorities. This is a good time to ask your mentors and your board of directors for their input on your decision. It may be helpful to talk with a professional career counselor to objectively evaluate your options. In the spaces below, summarize the pros and cons of accepting your career surprise.

Pros	Cons

_____ _____

_____ _____

_____ _____

_____ _____

10. **Intuitive reaction.** This section has addressed a logical and sequential process for dealing with your unexpected career opportunity. Now consider your "gut" reaction to your career surprise. What are you saying to yourself? If you are feeling scared or nervous, this is a natural response to change. In the space below, write about what your intuitive sense is telling you about your career surprise.

_____

_____

_____

_____

_____

The checklist for dealing with a career surprise is designed to assist you in making a thoughtful, but rather quick, decision, since these opportunities usually require a quick response. Every career decision requires some risk of the unknown. Make your decision, maintain your confidence, and go with it. Even if you decide not to accept the career surprise, you may feel better about your present job since you will have made a conscious decision to stay.

> **By learning to trust your intuition, "miracles" seem to happen.**
> —Susan Jeffers, *Feel the Fear and Do It Anyway*

CHAPTER 18

Resources for Career Investigation

There are many sources of information about careers. The following is an annotated bibliography of some of the major career resources. They are separated into four categories:

1. Occupational handbooks, job facts, and trends

2. Employer handbooks and directories

3. Educational resources

4. Online directories

They are included in this chapter to provide a handy reference for a variety of career and job market information.

SELECTED RESOURCES

There are many sources of information about careers. The following is an annotated bibliography of some of the major career reference books. They are included in this chapter to provide a handy reference for a variety of career and job market information. Many handbooks and directories are available electronically.

Occupational/Educational Handbooks, Job Facts, and Trends

The Big Book of Jobs 2007–2008, **The United States Department of Labor, New York: McGraw-Hill, 2007.**
Helps explore various career options; write cover letters and resumés; build job-hunting networks; and master the interview. Describes more than 250 career possibilities, providing such data as: working conditions, employment, job outlook, earnings, related occupations, training, other qualifications, and advancement.

The Big Guide to Living and Working Overseas: 3,045 Career Building Resources, Fourth Edition Revised, **Jean-Marc Hachey, Toronto, Canada: Intercultural Systems, 2007.**
Provides insights into international employment trends and offers inspirational advice to short and long-term job seekers.

Brickers International Directory, Peterson's, **Therese DeAngelis (Editor), Lawrenceville, NJ: Peterson's 2008.**

A valuable resource for individuals looking to advance their careers through education. Myriad worldwide opportunities abound in this guide, from programs in e-commerce and general management to seminars on technology, human resources, and more. Detailed analysis of trends in executive education. Essential program details, from cost and location to faculty. Demographic information on past participants.

Career Opportunities Series, **New York: Facts on File, 2003–2008.**

Each volume contains in-depth profiles of approximately 60 to 100 jobs, providing thorough information on salary ranges, advancement prospects, employment trends, necessary experience, and helpful unions and associations. Each profile presents an overview of the main duties and features of the job, a Career Ladder that illustrates frequent routes to and from the position, and comprehensive descriptions of certification, education, special skills, and training required.

Career Guide to Industries, 2008–2009, **Department of Labor, Washington, DC: United States Printing Office, 2008.**

Provides information on available careers by industry, including the nature of the industry, working conditions, employment, occupations in the industry, training and advancement, earnings and benefits, employment outlook, and lists of organizations that can provide additional information.

Chronicle Occupational Briefs, **Moravia, NY: Chronicle Guidance.**

Updated on a four-year cycle. 650 four-page comprehensive descriptions of professional, technical, blue-collar, and white-collar jobs with information on more than 2,100 careers. They also write and publish up to eight new and original Occupational Briefs each year. Chronicle Occupational Briefs are available in print, on CD-ROM, and as an Internet application.

Cities Ranked and Rated: More than 400 Metropolitan Areas Evaluated in the U.S. and Canada, 2nd Edition, **Bert Sperling, Peter Sander. Hoboken, NJ: Wiley Publishing, Inc., 2007.**

Provides timely facts and unbiased information on over 400 U.S. and 30 Canadian cities in an easy-to-access format. Categories include: economy and jobs, cost of living, climate, education, health and health care, crime, transportation, leisure, and arts and culture

College Majors and Careers, **Paul Phifer. Garrett Park, MD: Garrett Park Press, 2003.**

Describes 60 of the most popular college majors and cites occupations closely related to them.

College Majors Handbook with Real Career Paths and Payoffs, **Neeta P. Fogg, Thomas F. Harrington, Paul E. Harrington. Indianapolis, IN: JIST Works, 2004.**

Actual jobs, earnings, and trends for those considering a college major and for graduates of 60 college majors.

Encyclopedia of Associations, Vol. 3, **Detroit, MI: Gale Research Company, 2008.**

A guide to national and international organizations that includes addresses, membership tallies, publications, and conference schedules.

Encyclopedia of Careers and Vocational Guidance, **Chicago, IL: J.G. Ferguson Publishing, 2007.**

This set covers more than 900 careers, giving a general description of the job or career field, the personal and professional requirements, salary statistics, work environment, future outlook for the field, and sources for more information.

International Jobs: Where They Are, How to Get Them, **6th ed. Eric Kocher. Boston, MA: Addison-Wesley, 2003.**

Provides all the tools necessary for understanding the complex international job market and finding the right employment options. A valuable resource for those interested in working abroad.

National Trade and Professional Associations of the U.S., **Washington, DC: Columbia Books, 2008.**

A great directory for finding the association that has information related to a variety of career areas. More than 7,500 national organizations are listed.

Occupational Outlook Handbook. Washington D.C.: U.S. Government Printing Office, Updated every two years.

> This book, published by the Department of Labor, sketches thousands of different occupations, including nature of the work, places of employment, qualifications needed, earnings, and working conditions, and even future employment outlook. (http://www.bls.gov/oco/home.htm).

Occupational Projections and Training Data 2008–2009, Washington, D.C.: U.S. Government Printing Office, 2008.

> An indispensable aid for those interested in job trends and job outlooks. A statistical supplement to the Occupational Outlook Handbook. (http://www.bls.gov/emp/optd/optd.pdf).

O*Net Dictionary of Occupational Titles, Michael Farr, J. Michael Farr. Indianapolis, IN: JIST Works, Inc, 2007.

> The Occupational Information Network—O*NET™ database replaces the Dictionary of Occupational Titles (DOT) as the nation's primary source of occupational information. (http://online.onetcenter.org/).

Places Rated Almanac, David Savageau. Foster City, CA: IDG Books Worldwide, Inc., 2007.

> Rates and ranks 379 metropolitan areas on factors including climate, cost of living, jobs, arts, recreation, health care and environment, education, transportation, and crime.

Salary Survey Reports, National Association of Colleges and Employers, Bethlehem, PA. Updated four times annually.

> Gives the monthly beginning salary offers to college graduates organized by curriculum and type of employer (http://www.naceweb.org/).

Vault Career Guides, New York: Vault, Inc. 1997–2008.

> These guides are available in print or PDF format and cover a variety of career fields. Often referred to as "Cliffs Notes for Careers" by *Forbes* magazine, Vault guides have been published since 1997 and are the premier source of insider information on careers. Vault surveys and interviews thousands of employees each year to give readers the inside scoop on industries and specific employers to help them get the jobs they want. (http://www.vault.com).

WetFeet Insider Guides. San Francisco, CA: WetFeet Inc., 2007–2008.

> These guides offer an in-depth look at what it's really like to work in various careers, from Accounting to Consulting to Investment Banking to Real Estate. (http://www.wetfeet.com/asp/careerlist.asp).

Employer Handbooks and Directories

Adams Job Bank Series, Robert L. Adams, Holbrook, MA: Bob Adams, Inc.

> Potential employers, locations, contact persons, phone numbers, and descriptive information are supplied for the following major United States job markets: Atlanta, Boston, Chicago, Dallas, Denver, Detroit, Florida, Houston, Los Angeles, Minneapolis, New York, Ohio, Philadelphia, San Francisco, Seattle, St. Louis, and the Washington, D.C. metropolitan area.

Adams Internet Job Search Almanac, Robert Kehn, Holbrook, MA: Adams Media Corp., 2002.

> Comprehensive and authoritative career directory with 16,000 entries including 2,000 new listings.

Adams Jobs Almanac, 9th ed. Carter Smith, Holbrook, MA: Adams Media Corp, 2006

> Over 10,000 employers are profiled in this guide plus industry forecasts of the hottest industries and companies in each region of the country.

Almanac of American Employers, 2009, Jack W. Plunkett, Houston, TX: Plunkett Research Ltd., 2008.

> A guide to America's 500 most successful large corporations profiled and ranked by salaries, benefits, financial stability, and advancement opportunities.

Book of U.S. Government Jobs: Where They Are, What's Available and How to Get One, (10th ed.)
Dennis Damp, Moon Township, PA: Brook Haven Press, 2008.
> Provides up to date information on all of the changes in the federal hiring process and what federal job seekers must know to take advantage of these changes.

Business Organizations, Agencies, and Publications Directory, **Detroit, MI: Gale Research Company, Updated annually.**
> A listing of trade, business, and commercial organizations, government agencies, labor unions, stock exchanges, chambers of commerce, trade and convention centers, trade fairs, publishers, data banks and computerized services, educational institutions, business libraries, information centers, and research centers.

Career Guide: Dun's Employment Opportunities Directory, **Parsippany, NJ: Dun and Bradstreet Information Services, Updated annually.**
> This reference offers comprehensive, accurate coverage of the more than 5,000 major U.S. companies that have indicated that they plan to recruit during the year. Information is easy to access and is cross referenced by company, geography, industry classification, and educational discipline sought.

Career Opportunities for Bilinguals and Multilinguals: A Directory of Resources in Education, Employment, and Business, **Vladimir F. Wertsman, Lanham, MD: Rowman & Littlefield Publishers, Inc. 2002.**
> Lists resources in the U.S. and Canada for learning languages other than English and for identifying American and foreign employers interested in hiring bilingual or multilingual American professionals and paraprofessionals. Included are some 3,800 annotated items (national and international institutions, firms, organizations, etc.), and coverage of over 300 languages

Directory of American Firms Operating in Foreign Countries, **20th Ed., 3 Vols. Millis, Massachusetts: Uniworld Business Publications, Inc., 2009.**
> Authoritative source of information on American firms which have branches, subsidiaries, or affiliates outside the United States. Designed to aid anyone interested in American business activities abroad.

The Directory of Public School Systems in the United States 2004–05, **Columbus, Ohio: America Association for Employment in Education, Inc., 2004.**
> This directory lists over 15,000 public school systems in the United States. Each entry contains the school system name, address, hiring official's name and title, phone number, Web site and two codes indicating approximate student population as well as which grades are taught within that district. School systems are listed alphabetically by state, then by city.

Directory of Websites for International Jobs: The Click and Easy Guide, **Ronald and Caryl Krannich, Manassas, VA: Impact Publications, 2002.**
> This unique book reveals over 1,000 Web sites of special interest to anyone seeking an international job. Includes practical information on key steps in conducting an effective job search.

The Encyclopedia of Global Industries, **4th Ed. Millerton, NY: Grey House Publishing, 2007.**
> This guide includes detailed articles which discuss the origins, development, trends, key statistics, and current international character of the world's most lucrative, dynamic industries, including a revised and expanded look at more than 125 business sectors of global significance.

The Encyclopedia of Emerging Industries, **5th Ed. NY: Grey House Publishing, 2007.**
> Details the inception, emergence, and status of nearly 120 U.S. emerging industries in a broad-based, readable fashion.

Federal Yellow Book, **New York: Leadership Directories, Inc., Updated quarterly.**
> Gives the telephone numbers of top people in government. Includes departments, independent agencies, and regional offices.

Government Job Finder: Where the Jobs are in Local, State, and Federal Government, **Daniel Lauber & Jennifer Atkin, River Forest, IL: Planning Communication, 2009.**

> Details some 1,400 sources of vacancies for professionals, labor trade, technical, and office support positions in local, state, and federal government in the United States and overseas. Also includes federal agency personnel office phone numbers, and salary surveys.

Hoover's Handbook of American Business, **Austin, TX: Hoover's Books, 2008.**

Hoover's Handbook of Emerging Companies, **Austin, TX: Hoover's Books, 2008.**

Hoovers Handbook of Private Companies, **Austin, TX: Hoover's Books, 2008.**

Hoover's Handbook of World Business, **Austin, TX: Hoover's Books, 2008.**

Hoover's Master List of U.S. Companies, **Austin, TX: Hoover's Books, 2008.**

> In-depth information on 2,550 of the world's largest, fastest-growing and most influential public and private companies. Handbooks are updated annually.

National Directory of Internships. **Sally Migliore, (Ed.). Springfield, VA: The National Society for Experiential Education, 1998.**

> A complete description of more than 26,000 internship opportunities across the country from high school through graduate school and beyond. Contains indexes by field of interest, location, and name of organization.

National Directory of Nonprofit Organizations, Vol. 1, **Thomson Gale, Farmington, MI: The TAFT Group, an imprint of Thomson Gale. 2006.**

> A rich database of hard-to-find information on individual, corporate, and foundation philanthropy.

Nonprofits Job Finder: Where the Jobs Are in Charities & Nonprofits, **Daniel Lauber & Deborah Verlench, River Forest, IL: Planning Communications. 2009.**

> This book reports the details on over 2,000 online and print sources of positions at all levels with charities and nonprofits: online and print job listings, online job and resume databases, email job notifications, online and print directories, salary surveys, and much more. Job sources are organized by profession and by state.

Weddle's Directory of Employment-Related Internet Sites, **Peter Weddle, Stanford, CT: Weddle's, 2007–2008.**

> Directory provides the Internet address or URL for over 9,000 Web sites that specialize in employment. It lists sites that post a wide range of jobs, and those that specialize in openings for a specific career field, industry, geographic location, or affinity group; sites in every state of the USA, plus those in over 25 countries; sites that post full time positions, and those that post part time, contract and consulting opportunities; sites that serve corporate recruiters, staffing firm recruiters, and executive search consultants.
>
> Additionally, updates to the guides are provided at the Weddle's Web site. FREE email newsletter for job seekers also available at: http://www.weddles.com/register.htm.

Weddle's Guide to Association Web Sites, **Peter Weddle, Stanford, CT: Weddle's, 2007–2008.**

> Extensive directory of Web-based professional associations and societies. This comprehensive list of more than 2,500 such associations from around the world ensures that readers can find them. Each listing indicates whether the association offers a job board, a resume database, and a discussion forum, and the sites are organized by career field, industry, and geographic location to ensure that searches remain focused.

Weddle's Guide to Employment Web Sites, **Peter Weddle, Stanford, CT: Weddle's, 2007–2008.**

> This guide helps make smart choices among some of the best of 40,000 job boards and career portals on the Internet.

Educational Resources

Bear's Guide to Earning Degrees By Distance Learning, John Bear, Tom Head, Mariah Bear, Thomas Nixon. Berkeley, CA: Ten Speed Press, 2006.

> Describes over 100 programs that offer fully accredited education degrees and teaching certificates that can be earned online.

Graduate Schools in the U.S. 2009, Peterson's. Lawrenceville, NJ: Peterson's, 2008.

> Compact, annually updated guide to graduate and professional schools in the United States. Readers can compare hundreds of institutions offering regionally accredited masters and doctoral programs in a wide variety of academic disciplines.

Guide to Career Colleges 2009, Peterson's. Lawrenceville,, NJ: Peterson's, 2008.

> Annually updated and comprehensive guide to more than nearly 1,000 Career College Association (CCA) member institutions in the United States that offer career-specific degree and certificate programs. Additionally, more than 400 schools offering the Imagine America scholarship program, sponsored by the Career College Foundation (CCF), are profiled.

Guide to Distance Learning Programs, Peterson's. Lawrenceville,, NJ: Peterson's, 2008.

> Peterson's *Guide to Distance Learning* comprises more than 4,600 annually updated profiles of more than 1,100 accredited degree-granting institutions offering distance learning programs in the United States and Canada. It also includes detailed two-page descriptions written by admissions personnel for more than 160 distance learning programs.

Guide to Online Learning, 1st Ed., Peterson's. Lawrenceville,, NJ: Peterson's, 2006.

> A guide to help you understand if online learning is right for you and how to make the most of your experience.

2006–2007 National Directory of Scholarships, Internships, and Fellowships for Latino Youth.

> A valuable resource compiled by the Congressional Hispanic Caucus Institute (CHCI).

Scholarships, Grants and Prizes 2008, Princeton, NJ: Peterson's, 2007.

> Compact, how-to-pay-for-college reference book provides updated listings of the 500 most lucrative financial awards available from private organizations—foundations, clubs, corporations, religious groups, unions, veterans groups, and more—giving students the means to continue their education.

Undergraduate Guide: Four-Year Colleges 2008, Princeton, NJ: Peterson's, 2007.

> A valuable resource including information on every accredited four year undergraduate institution in the United States and Canada—more than 2,100 institutions all together! It also includes detailed two-page descriptions written by admissions personnel for nearly 1,000 colleges.

Online Directories

Career Info-Net Employer Locator http://www.acinet.org/acinet/employerlocator/employerlocator.asp

> Searchable database of over 12 million employers by industry, state, occupation, and name.

EDGAR (Security and Exchange Commission Reports) http://www.sec.gov/edgar/searchedgar/webusers.htm

> Detailed financial information on US companies. After searching for a company, select the 10-K report which is similar to an annual report.

Education Resource Organizations Directory http://wdcrobcolp01.ed.gov/Programs/EROD/

> Helps job hunters, students, and educators locate organizations that provide information and assistance on many education-related topics, such as multicultural education, at risk persons, standards, teaching methods, and much more.

Federal Job Titles-Handbook of Occupational Groups and Families http://www.opm.gov/fedclass/text/HdBktoc.htm

Lists the "series" or occupational group for professional positions. Use the outline (p. 13) or the alphabetical index (p. 97).

Federal Agencies Directory http://www.lib.lsu.edu/gov/fedgov.html

Identify possible agencies and find the employment, job, or career section on their Web sites.

Headhunters Directory.Com http://www.headhuntersdirectory.com/

A free directory of professionals that help real people find real jobs including headhunters, executive recruiters, employment agencies, executive search firms, staffing and personnel agencies.

Hoover's Online http://www.hoovers.com

10,000+ companies with direct links to their corporate Web sites, SEC filings, and other company information. Also includes job listings and points to the best business directories on the web.

IRIN http://www.irin.com/

The Investor Relations Information Network (IRIN) provides a single point of reference for accessing electronic annual reports—considered by many investors to be the most valuable means of communication between a company and its shareholders. More than 10,400 current and historical annual reports are available for viewing and printing. And if you want to request a hard copy of an annual report, IRIN will forward your request to the appropriate company. In addition to providing free access to more electronic annual reports than any other site, IRIN offers other useful information, including company statistics.

Military Connection http://www.militaryconnection.com/

Government jobs, up to date information on military schools, federal jobs, as well as military loans and detailed information on military pay charts. Online directories of resources and information feature vital information on military education and benefits including the GI Bill, employment opportunities, the latest military job postings, pay charts, and salary calculators.

Salary Surveys http://jobstar.org/tools/salary/index.cfm

Search by job title, level (entry, mid-career, etc.) and city for many different professions. Includes data from over 70 surveys plus help with salary negotiation.

Thomas Register of American Manufacturers http://www.thomasregister.com

More than 165,000 companies with indexing for more than 57,000 product and service headings. Free registration required.

Top Company Listings

Fortune Magazine http://money.cnn.com/magazines/fortune/fortune500/2008/

Inc. Magazine http://www.inc.com/inc500

Forbes Magazine http://www.forbes.com/lists/

Wetfeet http://www.wetfeet.com

Information on employers and industries.

Work At Home Directory http://www.work-at-home-directory.com/index.html

A directory of legitimate opportunities for working at home or starting an online home based business.

YAHOO's Listing of Companies by Industry http://dir.yahoo.com/business_and_economy/directories/companies/

Connections with employer Web pages in highly specialized areas.

SECTION four

Conduct an Effective Job Campaign

You have evaluated your unique self, considered how to deal with changes and life transitions, and have investigated the job market. In this section you will learn some traditional and nontraditional ways of looking for a job. You will consider methods that can give you more control over a job search than you might think possible. The section includes an outline on conducting a job campaign, making the best use of your time, and protecting your ego. It continues with a chapter on resumé writing, including samples of different kinds of resumés. It will show how you can use some of the same principles for resumé writing when you fill out employment application forms. It will provide information about using the Internet and the World Wide Web in conducting a job campaign. Finally, it will provide advice and information on how to prepare for and conduct an employment interview.

CHAPTER 19

The Job Campaign

The process of looking for a job can be a difficult experience. It is stressful and it is easy to feel that you do not have much control over what is happening. You may even find yourself procrastinating or denying that you need to start the process of job hunting. It is natural to avoid something that you think is going to be painful. This is particularly true if you are unemployed. It is important to remember, however, that you *do* have more control than you might think. You have specific actions that you can take and there is specific information that you need to uncover. By developing a goal and a plan to reach that goal, you can assume more power over the job-finding process. You can develop a strategy in which you act on events and opportunities rather than react to the wishes of others. To begin, however, you should be aware of some of the cold, hard facts of job hunting. You can then develop a positive job campaign and reduce the negative aspects of the job-hunting process.

JOB HUNTING—THE COLD, HARD FACTS

1. **Job hunting can be very stressful.** The process creates fear and anxiety for most people and can damage a person's ego.

2. **People who are job hunting often feel that they have little control** over the process and outcome. This feeling of powerlessness can undermine a person's self-confidence.

3. **People often take the path of least resistance** by approaching the job hunt in a very passive way. For example, staying home, searching for jobs advertised on the Internet, and sending out letters and resumés is not very stressful in the short term, but can lead to a great deal of stress in the long run when rejections come rolling in. This is passive job hunting.

4. **People sometimes put more energy into buying a car than into choosing a job.** Some will take almost any job, just to get the process over with. The uncertainty in job hunting can be painful.

5. **Even very secure people have trouble taking action** when it comes to job hunting. Every job interview becomes a potential rejection. Every telephone call holds the possibility of a turn-down.

6. **Active job hunting requires a significant investment of time, money, energy, and ego.** Job hunting demands hard work.

7. **Rejection is an unavoidable part of the job-seeking process.** The following can be expected to be part of any job campaign.

   - obstacles
   - barriers
   - turn-downs
   - rejections
   - disappointments
   - fear
   - missed opportunities
   - self-doubt
   - unfulfilled expectations
   - unresponsiveness
   - disinterest
   - ambiguity

   All of these can be damaging to the ego if they are not balanced with positive approaches and activities.

8. **Looking for a job without defined career goals can lead to uncertainty and discouragement.** It is important to make self-assessment the first part of the job-hunting process.

9. **It is important to use time effectively** by investing the most time in the job-hunting methods that will produce results and by having a clear idea of what types of jobs to pursue.

10. **The job-hunting process involves positioning one's self to be in the right place at the right time.** Planning, assessment, and actively pursuing goals can help you do exactly that.

Take care of yourself during your job hunt. Your ego is your most precious resource.

Rejection Shock

Before considering how to deal with the realities of a job campaign, there is a significant problem to be aware of. This problem is *rejection shock*. This is a term used to describe a withdrawal from the job hunting process after someone receives one or more rejections. Rejection shock can become severe if you allow it to hurt your ego. People protect themselves from further rejection by simply not initiating any new contacts. They develop elaborate rationalizations for not making contacts and for not continuing to actively look for a job. They wait for something to happen. They are afraid to continue their job search for fear that they may again be rejected. Some people can even remain unemployed for years as a result of rejection shock. The longer they go without taking action, the more difficult it becomes for them to overcome rejection shock. Your primary responsibility as a job hunter is to protect your ego and avoid rejection shock.

How can you guard against rejection shock? Here are some suggestions.

The Ten-Point Rejection Shock Avoidance System

Point One	After you have been rejected for a job, **immediately** begin initiating other contacts.
Point Two	Try not to take a rejection personally. Many other factors over which you have no control, such as quotas and preselection, may influence hiring decisions.
Point Three	Use your support system of family and friends to serve as a buffer and to lighten your spirit.
Point Four	Join or form a job club with one or more job hunters. Get together at least once a week to share your feelings, exchange ideas, and swap job leads.
Point Five	Develop a plan for your job campaign. Expect rejections as a normal part of the campaign.
Point Six	Beware of investing too much time in activities that may bring a large number of rejections, such as blanket mailings of resumés, applying for jobs for which you are minimally qualified, or using the Internet exclusively.
Point Seven	Make use of community support services, such as courses, groups, and mental health centers. Find a career counselor who can help you to clarify goals and to develop your job-hunting strategies.
Point Eight	Avoid the temptation to engage in long-term career planning instead of looking for a job. If you are not working, invest your energy in finding a job.
Point Nine	Instead of looking for your ideal job, be willing to compromise. This is especially true if you are not working. Use state employment agencies and other services that can be of help in your job search.
Point Ten	Set goals for yourself each day. Most jobs are found through personal contacts. Make a special attempt to arrange contacts with others, including those in your personal network and those in professional organizations.

WHAT IS AN EFFECTIVE JOB CAMPAIGN?

An effective job campaign involves the following:

1. Have a specific plan of action and a career goal that you want to attain.

2. Use your time effectively. Plan to spend a great deal of time on your job campaign and schedule daily activities. Balance difficult and rewarding tasks.

3. Develop a system to protect your ego and to avoid procrastination and rejection shock.

4. Do job market research using:

   - Experience
   - Printed material
   - The Internet
   - Talking with people

5. Expand your network of personal contacts by using informational interviewing.

6. Spend the most time on the methods that hold the most promise for finding a job.

7. Write a good resumé, and know how to accurately complete employment applications.

8. Rehearse your interviewing techniques and be prepared for job interviews.

9. Follow up on contacts, interviews, and referrals, including timely thank-you letters, phone calls, and email messages.

10. Reward yourself periodically for sticking to your job campaign.

Remember that the person who finally is hired for a given job may not be the most qualified for the job. It's the person who knows how to get hired that most often gets hired.

ORGANIZING YOUR JOB CAMPAIGN

Planning, preparation, and follow-through are essential in the job-hunting process. The following information will help you to organize your job campaign.

1. Have a specific plan of action and a goal that you want to attain.

   - Analyze your unique self and determine what jobs will best fulfill your needs. You can probably find *a* job, but you want a job that is more than just *a* job.

   - Concentrate your search in areas that hold potential for future growth and expanded opportunities.

   - Define the specific type of job that you want. Target your efforts to the type of job that is on your career path. Expand the places where you might find this type of job.

   - Develop a plan that incorporates several short-term goals to help you reach your major goal. Set a time schedule for the achievement of these short-term goals.

2. Use your time effectively.

   - A job campaign is demanding. Expect to spend many hours thinking, planning, and assessing your alternatives.

   - Plan to call prospective employers and write follow-up letters every day. Job hunting may require a full-time commitment if you are unemployed.

   - Plan a variety of activities each week, including:

     - Planning
     - Self-research
     - Job market research
     - Telephone calls
     - Nonjob trips (to library, to meet friends)
     - Writing letters and email messages
     - Letters
     - Informational interviews
     - Job interviews
     - Third-party meetings
     - Thinking and processing

   - Plan some rewards for yourself for using your time effectively.

   - Remember how much time you spend at work every day. Keep in mind that it's worth it to spend a great deal of time finding a job that you will enjoy.

   - Distribute your time among different job-hunting activities.

3. Develop a system to protect your ego and avoid rejection shock.

   - Make regular commitments to yourself and to others and keep them.

   - Maintain your support systems with family and friends.

   - Keep active. Stay with your plans.

   - Become familiar with time management techniques.

   - Regularly get together with other job hunters or career changers to share feelings and information.

   - Seek out institutional support: community colleges, churches, local clubs, and professional organizations.

   - Acknowledge your needs and seek out support. Affirm your skills and abilities, use self-esteem-building exercises, and develop positive approaches to your everyday activities.

   - Take care of yourself every day.

4. Do job market research, using experience, written material, the Internet, and talking with people.

Experience

- Consider cooperative education programs and internships as a means of obtaining a job, experience, and contacts.

- Do temporary work in order to make money, to get experience, and to make contacts for a full-time job.

- In your spare time, do volunteer work to obtain experience and be well situated when a job opening occurs.

- Write a proposal or develop an idea that solves a problem for a company or organization.

Written Material

- Newspapers and want ads are usually good sources of specific job openings, but remember that many job vacancies are not listed in newspapers. You also need to be aware of ads that are come-ons. These ads may feature positions that sound much better than the jobs that are actually available. Newspapers can also be a good source of general information. Pay particular attention to:

  - Articles on future trends
  - Grand openings
  - Contracts awarded
  - Promotions

  - New businesses
  - Companies that are hiring
  - Articles on careers
  - Potential informational interviewees

- The Yellow Pages can provide useful information. You can identify companies and organizations where you can inquire about available positions or about future job openings. This is particularly useful if you are looking in a new geographic area.

- Professional journals, newsletters, and trade magazines often have listings of available jobs, but are also useful in other ways. You can identify key people to contact; you can find out what is going on in the field; you can obtain information on new jobs that are likely to appear; and you can learn the jargon of the profession. All of this can be particularly helpful when you go for an interview.

- Company websites, literature, employer handouts, and in-house newsletters can provide useful information on the organization and often have sections on available positions. These may give you a chance to learn about openings before they are advertised on the outside. Check the website and call the specific organization for these materials.

- Directories of organizations, associations, and businesses can be used as sources of names and addresses of individuals who can give you information. These individuals may also be prospective employers. Check at your local library or career resource center for directories, journals, and other print material that might be helpful in your job search. Ask the reference librarians for assistance and to verify that you have not overlooked an important source of information.

- The Internet should be used as a primary source of information on organizations, job listings, and general career planning assistance. This information is usually more up to date than print material and is much easier to access. For a comprehensive listing of career-related websites, see Chapter 15.

Remember that the person who gets hired may not be the most qualified. It is the person who knows how to get hired that gets the job.

Talking with People

- Friends, family members, and contacts made through friends and family can be good sources of information. Don't be reluctant to let others know that you are looking for a job. Most people want to help.

- Through newspapers, journals, contacts, and other sources, identify the names of individuals who might have jobs available or know where or when jobs might become available. Contact these individuals and ask for informational interviews.

- State employment agencies provide some assistance in finding jobs and often have a data bank of available jobs. Most colleges and high schools also have job search information and job listings available for students.

- Human resource offices in private and public organizations can be sources of job information. It is important to remember, however, that these offices primarily screen candidates. They do not usually hire. If you are interested in an organization, it is important that you meet people who are in a position to hire you.

- Private employment agencies can help you to find a job, usually for a fee paid by the employer. Some companies prefer that agencies do their recruiting for them, and thus the primary loyalty of many agencies is to the employer. They will attempt to match you to whatever jobs they have available at the time, which may not be in line with your career goals. **The best person to help you find you a job is you!** However, these agencies can be a useful resource in your job search.

5. Expand your network of personal contacts and use informational interviewing.

   - Almost 80 percent of all jobs are obtained through personal contacts of one kind or another. Therefore, it is essential that you expand your personal contacts.

   - Use friends, family, associates, and all of the resources described previously. Expand your contacts and identify people who may be in a position to hire you or to know where jobs are available.

   - Make your skills and abilities known to as many people as possible. Ask for referrals. Form a job-finding group. Encourage suggestions. Use the telephone and the Internet to make contacts. Arrange face-to-face meetings with as many people as possible.

   - Make use of **informational interviewing**. The basic techniques are the same as those described in Section 3. However, you will now use informational interviewing as a means of meeting people who may have a job available or who may know of a job that would interest you. Recall the job hunter's number one responsibility, which is to protect the ego and avoid rejection shock. If this is number one, then the process of informational interviewing becomes an invaluable, nontraditional technique in job hunting. Informational interviewing can help you to:

     - Decide on the job

     - Decide whom to interview

     - Decide what organizations to explore

     - Decide whether you are interested

     - Decide whether the combination of job, people, and organization matches with your goals, skills, interests, values, lifestyle, and self-esteem

   What other method offers so much valuable information that can help you make decisions about jobs? The procedures for informational interviewing remain the same, so check back in Section 3. However, make the following changes in the informational interviewing techniques, since you are now actively looking for a job.

- Use the process of informational interviewing wisely and honestly. How do you really know that you want to work for an organization if you do not know the details that would help you make a quality decision about a job?

- Interview for the information that will help you to make an employment decision that blends with your goals, skills, values, and lifestyle preferences.

- Keep the information part of the informational interview flowing with questions about available positions, required qualifications, and potential contacts.

- Do not ask for a job either on the telephone or during the interview. You will probably be referred to human resources. Your goal is to obtain information; then you will make a decision about the organization.

- Do not produce a resumé or a completed application form. The focus of the interview shifts from the interviewee, who offers the information to you, the interviewer. This "bait and switch" approach weakens the potential benefits derived from informational interviewing.

- Ask the person you are interviewing for other sources of information or about jobs that may soon be available.

- Arrange informational interviews with people who might be in a position to hire you.

- Remember that potential employers may like to have the opportunity for a preliminary interview with you before an actual job interview is arranged.

- Write a letter requesting an informational interview that clearly states your purpose. This can be somewhat different from the letter you would write if you were not looking for a job. While a letter is preferable, it may be okay to use email in this situation. After the interview, if you are interested in an organization, send a follow-up letter and a copy of your resumé. Be sure that:

  - It is addressed to a specific person.
  - It tells the person why you are writing.
  - It tells the person your situation.
  - It keeps the initiative with you.

  Samples of both types of letters are on the following pages.

- If appropriate, send your resumé or completed application form with your letter of appreciation for the informational interview.

6. Spend the most time on the methods that hold the most promise for finding a job.

- Since most jobs are obtained through personal contacts, spend the most time pursuing and increasing these contacts.

- Be aware of new developments that may create jobs, such as emerging problems, unreleased plans, impending retirements, expansions, reorganizations, and jobs that will be advertised in a few weeks.

- Organize and maintain a diversified, active job campaign.

- Less effective methods include:

  - Shotgun letters and resumés
  - Relying heavily on newspaper want ads
  - Relying heavily on employment agencies
  - Relying solely on human resource offices
  - Relying solely on Internet sites

You may wish to use these methods, but don't depend solely on them. Your job campaign strategy can be summarized by looking at the following diagram. You can then move to the next important steps in an effective job campaign.

- Resumé writing
- Completing applications
- Employment interviewing

Letter for requesting an informational interview— written by someone who is looking for a job

Jane Doe
5000 Ivory Lane
Wichita, Kansas 45678
406-555-5555
jdoe@hotmail.com

March 23, 2009

Mr. James Smith
Director of Institutional Research
XYZ Corporation
Anywhere, U.S.A.

Dear Mr. Smith:

In my personal career exploration research, your name came to my attention as someone who could provide me with some valuable advice and information because of your experience in the field of institutional research.

I am currently considering a career transition. I have experience in managing research projects on a small scale and I have found it stimulating to gain expertise in the technological advancements in the area of institutional research. I have investigated the field and have some specific questions related to current trends, technical developments, and skills that may be needed in the future. I would like to talk with you to learn more about these and other issues from your very valuable perspective.

Realizing the demands on your time, I will telephone you during the week of April 6 to see whether we can arrange a brief meeting at your convenience.

Thank you for your interest and help as I explore a variety of career opportunities.

Sincerely,

Jane Doe

Follow-up letter from someone who is looking for a job, has conducted an informational interview, and is interested in a job with the organization

Jane Doe
5000 Ivory Lane
Wichita, Kansas 45678
406-555-5555
jdoe@hotmail.com

April 20, 2009

Mr. James Smith
Director of Institutional Research
XYZ Corporation
Anywhere, U.S.A.

Dear Mr. Smith:

I would like to thank you for meeting with me yesterday to discuss career possibilities in the field of institutional research. The information and insight you provided were most helpful. I appreciated your sharing your expertise and time with me. I especially enjoyed hearing about the recent advances in technological applications in institutional research.

I was pleased to learn from our discussion that you feel I have the skills and qualifications necessary to enter the field of institutional research. I would appreciate your considering me for a position when a vacancy does occur. Your organization and your personal approach are very appealing to me, and I feel that I could make some significant contributions to your program.

I am enclosing a copy of my resumé for your reference. I will be contacting you in the near future to discuss future employment possibilities with you. Thank you very much for your consideration and for the information and assistance you have given me.

Sincerely,

Jane Doe

JOB CAMPAIGN ANALYSIS

If you are presently in the process of looking for a job or you can recall the last time you engaged in a job campaign, this section will be helpful. You will have the opportunity to

- Consider the four stages of job hunting

- Review the expenditure of your most valuable personal resources

- Analyze the results of your job campaign

This chapter has presented the hard, cold facts of job hunting and the organization of an effective job campaign. The challenge now is for you to evaluate the specific components of your job campaign. The process of job hunting may make you feel out of control and powerless. This analysis will help you to regain some control. Remember that looking for a job produces stress. Use this stress to your advantage by turning it into energy and action.

Evaluate the Job-Hunting Stages

Job Hunting Stages

1. Flip-flop

2. Fledgling

3. Focused

4. Flight

These are the four stages of job hunting. Identify the stage that you are presently going through and consider how you can move to a new stage by upgrading the techniques in your job hunt.

Four Stages of Job Hunting				
	Stage 1 Flip-flop (Trying-on)	**Stage 2 Fledgling (Testing)**	**Stage 3 Focused (Committed)**	**Stage 4 Flight (Action)**
Risk	None–Low	Minimal	Significant	High
Personal Visibility	None	Minimal	Significant	High
Confidence Level	Tentative	Testing	Less ambivalent and clearer	Purposeful Determined
Decison Making	Unsure	Clarifying	Commitment	Commitment to action
Action Taken	Reading want ads Preliminary investigation	Resumé ready Initial contacts Talk with counselor Convenient discussions	Writing letters Sending resumés Informational interviewing Articulating decision	Active job hunting Letting go of old job Interviews Poised for movement
Internal Talk	I could do this.	I think I can do this.	I am going for it.	I am going to make it happen.

Description of the Job-Hunting Stages

Stage 1. Flip-flop

Stage 1 is named "flip-flop" because you are trying to figure out where you fit into the world of work. Reading the want ads is a low-stress, low-risk job-hunting method. It is also not very effective. It is one task to define your career and quite another to locate a job that supports your goals. The answers to your questions in this stage are critical to your moving to the next stage. If you have a "can do" attitude, movement to the next stage will be assured.

Evaluating the appropriateness of jobs based solely on the information found in a want ad or in a listing on a Web site limits your possibilities. Want ads and job descriptions often present jobs in jargon and technical terms. Each person molds a job description to fit individual skills, personality, goals, expertise, and style. Don't be daunted by words that describe a job.

The trying-on of different jobs is characterized by your internal talk of, "I could do this job or I could do that job." Indecision, frustration, and a feeling of uncertainty about fitting into a job may cloud your thoughts. This internal debate is a natural part of the process. This stage may take a long time. The low risk and low commitment may be attractive, but it is important to set a deadline for moving into the next stage. Calculate the risks of going forward to the next stage of job hunting versus the price of not moving forward. The risks of movement to the next stage may be worth taking when compared with doing nothing, especially when you consider your career goals, self-esteem, and professional growth.

Stage 2. Fledgling

Stage 2 is named "fledgling" because you begin to take small, comfortable risks related to your job hunt. You start to branch out by engaging in convenient conversations about your objectives, digging out your resumé, and consulting with those closest to you or with a counselor. This period of testing is also critical to your movement to the next stage. The information you uncover in this stage may propel you into a job commitment, or you could remain in this stage in order to avoid a job commitment. Only you can judge. As in stage 1, there is minimal risk. The leap to the next stage requires courage and trust in your decision-making abilities. To help make this leap, ask yourself the following questions.

- Will this job provide me with learning opportunities?
- Will the learning opportunities provide me with necessary skills?
- Does the job fit into my career and life plan?
- Am I excited about what I would learn?

If you have answered "yes" to most of the questions, you are ready to move to stage 3. Remember, you do not have to possess all the expertise **before** you apply for a job. It is quite acceptable to be in process, that is, to be gaining the expertise through course work, apprenticeship, or self-directed learning. Your in-process status demonstrates commitment to potential employers, builds self-confidence, and serves to verify that this is the job area for you. Remember, the commitment that you make in moving to stage 3 is not permanent. It means that right now in your career and life plan, this is the way you choose to direct your job-hunting energies. By making a decision, you save a valuable human resource—you.

Stage 3. Focused

The leap to stage 3 is no small task. This stage is named "focused" because you have made a decision, you are ready to risk more of your personal resources, and you are occupied with the tasks ahead. The resumé or sample application has been revised and cover letters written. You are sending your package (resumé or application plus letter) to selected employers. You are actively involved in informational interviewing with peers in other organizations or in your organization. As your visibility increases, the knowledge about your interest in other areas is spreading. As you articulate your career and life goals, you are clarifying them for yourself and for others.

The decision is in clearer focus and there is relief in knowing that you are moving toward a goal. The exact picture may not yet be in full view, but the movement is a goal in itself. The variables of job market, geographic area, economy, and personal limitations you have placed on your job hunt may encourage or thwart the process at this stage. The only variable that you have control over is the personal limitations that you have placed on your job hunt. If you are in this stage for a long time—and only you can be the judge of time—then reexamine the lifestyle considerations and work values in Section 1. You may have placed too many restrictions on your job hunt. Examples of some restrictions include the person who restricts the job hunt to a 5-mile radius from home or one who will only apply for a job that is part-time. Negotiation is a part of the process. Consider breaking your own barriers to employment.

Stage 4. Flight

Stage 4 is named "flight" because you are ready to take off into another job. You have listened to your inner voice that said it was time to leave your present job and are in the process of letting go on an emotional level. The risk is high because your visibility is high. Active job hunting requires confidence and direction. In this stage you feel purposeful and clear about your direction. You do not second-guess yourself. You are poised for employment interviews or are already engaged in employment interviews with several organizations. Flight to the next job is just a matter of time. The goal in this stage is to work toward a job offer.

Many variables must come together before you are offered a job. Some of these variables involve matches between:

- Job requirements and your skills and abilities
- Salary and benefits package and your financial needs
- Demands of the job and your lifestyle considerations
- Culture of the organization and your personality
- Supervision style and your work values
- Potential for learning and your career and life plan

In stage 4, you may have one foot in and one foot out of your present job. Before you leap into another job, consider these variables and return to Section 1 if you need further clarification of your personal goals.

Review the Expenditure of Your Personal Resources

Recognize that job hunting is one of life's most stressful challenges. Since you may feel somewhat out of control during your job hunt, it will be helpful for you to regain some of your control by quantifying those factors over which you do have control—your valuable personal resources. Guard them vigilantly and spend them wisely. Your personal resources can be divided into five categories.

1. **Energy.** Do you seem to spend a great deal of time lost in thought and strategizing the "what ifs" in your job hunt? Visualizing and daydreaming use up emotional energy during the job hunt. How much energy do you spend on thinking, processing, and planning in each job-hunting method?

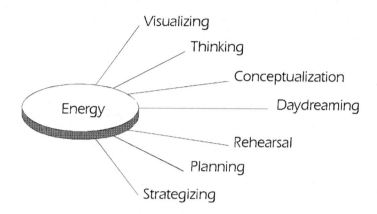

2. **Action.** Do you seem to be overwhelmed with all the details involved in job hunting? Follow-up calls, thank-you letters, informational interview letters, and organizational research require action on your part. Action in your job hunt requires effort. Approximately how much action are you devoting to writing, calling, traveling, researching, and reading in your job hunt?

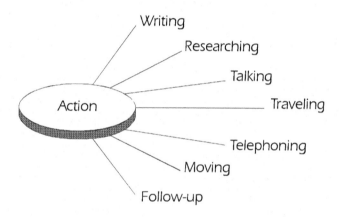

3. **Money.** What financial resources are you expending on your job hunt? Have you invested in additional training, newspaper subscriptions, interview clothing, and professional development to market yourself effectively? These expenses are a part of the overall cost of job hunting. How much money have you spent on your job hunt?

4. **Ego.** How are you feeling about yourself during your job hunt? Your self-esteem is your most precious resource during these times of uncertainty. In every interview, phone call, and contact you initiate, your ego is on the line. Your motivation, your creativity, and your enthusiasm are interwoven with your ego. In the job hunt all of these resources are needed to make an impact and get the job. How much ego do you risk on each job-hunting method?

5. **Time.** Do you question the time you spend on your job hunt and feel guilty if you do not spend every waking moment on an activity related to finding a job? Rather than feeling guilty, analyze and decide how much time you are willing to allocate to each job-hunting method. Your time is the sum total of your expenditures of all the other personal resources. In the list below, consider the approximate amount of time you spend on each method of job hunting.

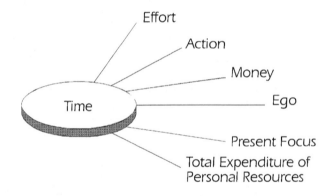

Analyze the Expenditure of Your Personal Resources

Several job-hunting methods are listed in the left column of the following chart. Fill in any additional methods that you are currently using in the space marked "other." Mark something in each box. Identify the amount of energy, action, money, ego, and time that you expend on each of the job-hunting methods listed. Your personal investment in job hunting is significant, and these five personal resources are critical to your success. Since you possess a finite amount of each resource, you need to use them wisely. Assign the following values to each of the job-hunting methods listed.

0 = No expenditure of resources in the method

1 = Low expenditure of resources in this method

2 = Medium expenditure of resources in this method

3 = High expenditure of resources in this method

Expenditure of Your Personal Resources					
Job-Hunting Methods	**Energy**	**Action**	**Money**	**Ego**	**Time**
1. Internet job sites, newspaper ads, other want ads, research					
2. Contacts with personnel or human resources offices					
3. Contacts with employment agencies					
4. Sending resumés, letters, applications					
5. Using federal, state, or local employment commissions					
6. Utilizing college career centers or local agency assistance					
7. Networking in professional organizations					
8. Informational interviewing in person					
9. Telephoning for appointments and follow-up					
10. Researching the job market and general company investigation					
11. Internet networks					
12. Other methods:					

Analyze the Results of Your Job Campaign

If you have only so much effort, action, ego, money, and time to spend on your job hunt, it makes sense to allocate these resources carefully and weigh them in terms of present and probable results. By evaluating your job-hunting efforts you can save valuable personal resources. What job-hunting methods are working for you, and what job-hunting methods are draining your valuable resources? The same listing of job-hunting methods is provided for you to evaluate the results of your labor.

With some approximation, analyze the results of your job hunt thus far by counting how many

- contacts made in each method
- responses you have received by telephone, letter, or fax
- employment interviews you have gotten through each method
- job offers or negotiating sessions you have experienced using the methods listed

Analysis of Your Job Campaign				
Job-Hunting Methods	Number of Contacts Made	Responses Letter/Phone	Employment Interviews	Job Offers
1. Internet job sites, newspaper ads, other want ads, research				
2. Contacts with personnel or human resources offices				
3. Contacts with employment agencies				
4. Sending resumés, letters, applications				
5. Using federal, state, or local employment commissions				
6. Utilizing college career centers or local agency assistance				
7. Networking in professional organizations				
8. Informational interviewing in person				
9. Telephoning for appointments and follow-up				
10. Researching the job market and general company investigation				
11. Other method:				
12. Other method:				

Your present job campaign may be ineffective. Continue to evaluate your job campaign by answering the following questions.

1. Does your job campaign have balance? Does it allow you the time and energy to process information and consider alternatives, or are you always running from place to place?

2. Are your present job-hunting methods getting results?

3. Are there some methods that are not worth the investment of your energy, action, time, money, and ego? Should you continue to use them?

4. If the expenditures of your resources are not yielding the results that you desire, then how can you strive to improve the efficiency of your job campaign?

When your cart reaches the foot of the mountain, a path will appear.

—Chinese Proverb

Job Hunting in Cyberspace

The Internet provides the most rapidly growing resources for job hunters. There is an explosion of information available to anyone who takes the time to access these networks. Much of this information is updated constantly and therefore represents a source of career information and work opportunities that should be used by anyone who is conducting a job campaign.

In addition to information on jobs, it is possible to gain access to a wealth of information on organizations, to communicate with other people, and to send resumés and applications electronically. The potential of the Internet for job hunting and career exploration is unlimited and there will continue to be constant enhancements in the information and opportunities that are available. This chapter will outline the uses of the Internet and provide resources for further investigation.

JOB HUNTING USING THE INTERNET

1. **Research specific careers.** You can use Web browser and other sites to find information about the career in which you are interested. You can learn about the latest developments in the field and where jobs might be found. You can become familiar with the jargon of the field.

2. **Research information about specific organizations.** If you are conducting an informational interview, or if you have a job interview with a company or organization, it is essential that you visit the company or organization's Web site. You will be better informed about the organization and will be better prepared for an informational interview. In an interview, you can demonstrate your interest by referring to information you obtained from the Web site.

3. **Research job leads.** You can learn about available jobs by going to online job banks (see Chapter 15) and through newspaper listings, journals, association newsletters, and organization Web sites.

4. **Networking.** You can use mailing lists and newsgroups to correspond with others who work in areas that interest you. Through these you can make contacts for possible informational interviews.

5. **Resumé posting.** You can post your resumé online for possible review by potential employers.

6. **Expanding your job search.** You can find out about jobs that are available in different geographical areas.

7. **Applying for jobs.** You can respond to specific job announcements by sending an online cover letter and resumé.

8. **Obtain essential job information.** You can research salary and benefits information so that you can be better prepared for negotiations after you have received a job offer.

Getting Started with Online Research

1. You need to have access to the Internet. If you do not have access at home, most libraries provide access. In addition, most schools, colleges, and universities provide access for students. Also, cyber-cafés and some copy centers may provide access.

2. Use virtual libraries, Internet directories, and search engines to obtain information. There are many sources that you can use to browse and search the Web.

3. The following three-stage procedure for researching a specific employer is recommended by Dikel and Roehm (2008) in the *Guide to Internet Job Searching*. 2008–2009 ed., pp. 10–22.

   a. Begin employer research at the employer's Web site. Be sure to print out pages of special interest. Pay special attention to any section that says "news" or "what's new." Find out how the organization describes itself. Check out the human resources area for job openings. Get an idea of the organization's mission.

   b. Check business directories and other employer information sources. Recommended sites for this purpose are:

      hoovers.com   sec.gov/edgar.shtml

      vault.com   wetfeet.com

   c. Use search engines to find additional information. Conduct a search using the employer's name, products, or names of people in the organization.

NETWORKING THROUGH THE INTERNET

The importance of networking in the job search process is emphasized in Section 3 of *Training for Life*. The Internet provides many opportunities for networking. You can use the Internet to make initial contacts and to participate in dialogues with people who may be sources of job contacts.

There are thousands of online discussion forums in which you can participate and learn about current trends and issues in your field, as well as possible employment opportunities. For example, many professional associations provide opportunities for online interaction with members of the association.

Online communities, message boards, Web forums, and chat rooms provide opportunities for communication with people of like interests. Examples of these sites are vault.com and peopleconnection.aol.com. Many people use social networking sites such as linkedin.com and networkingforprofessionals.com to make contacts and communicate with people who share their interests. Be sure to review carefully each site's privacy policy before participating. You can also subscribe to a mailing list from which you will automatically receive messages. Two useful directories of mailing lists are www.lsoft.com/lists/listref.html and groups.yahoo.com.

Alison Doyle, in *Internet Your Way to a New Job* (2008), recommends using the following sites to create a professional profile on the Web: http://linkedin.com, http://facebook.com, and http://jobfox.com. She provides practical advice for online career networking and makes a powerful case for using this tool in your job search.

While online networking is strongly recommended by most job search consultants and writers, they do offer some cautions. It is important to remember that employers often "Google" job applicants to see what they can find on the Internet about the applicant. Be careful about what you post regarding yourself on various sites. In addition, it is important to follow the simple rules of "Netiquette." Margaret Dickel and Frances Roehm, in *Guide to Internet Job Searching* (2008), provide a useful description of "Netiquette," which includes learning the site's rules of conduct and accepted discussion topics, looking for a list of frequently asked questions, learning the tone, language, and culture of a group, and never posting your resumé or asking someone for help to land a job unless the forum is dedicated to job searching.

If you do not have your own personal email address, two of the most popular free email services are gmail.google.com and mail.yahoo.com. You may want to establish a separate email address just for career networking.

USING JOB LISTING WEB SITES

1. There are many job listing Web sites that are worthwhile to explore as part of your job search.

2. Try several of the Web sites listed in Chapter 15. When you are reviewing them, check how recent the listings are and the availability of other useful information. Consider who runs the service and ask others for their opinions about Web sites they have found useful. Check on whether the site provides additional information and help, such as with writing resumés and cover letters.

3. You may wish to consider posting your resumé online. While this may be useful in some fields, such as information technology, it is not generally recommended by most experts in job searching. They place emphasis on networking first and then sending a resumé after you have found someone who is interested in you. Simply posting your resumé on one or more sites is not a very effective way to go about job hunting. In their book, *Job-Hunting on the Internet,* Bolles & Bolles (2008) assess the effectiveness of posting a resumé online at less than one half of 1 percent, unless you are seeking a job in a computer field, where the effectiveness rises to 20 percent.

SENDING YOUR RESUMÉ ELECTRONICALLY

The next chapter will provide information on how to create a good resumé. After you have developed a resumé that you feel represents you effectively, you then need to make some adjustments in the resumé in order to email it to potential employers.

1. Follow all of the directions for developing a good resumé. You must begin with a good product.

2. Determine whether you can send your resumé as an attachment, in the body of an email message, or whether it must be copied and pasted into an online application program. If you can send it as an attachment, you can keep bullets, boldface print, and other features that make your resumé look good. Make sure that you send your resumé as an attachment to yourself and to a friend ahead of time to see of there are any problems in its transmission that must be resolved.

3. If you must include your resumé in the body of an email message or if you are required to copy and paste it into an online application program, reformat your resumé as follows:

    a. Do not use any boldface, underlined, or italicized words. Do not use any special symbols, such as bullets.

    b. To draw special attention to certain words, use all capital letters.

    c. Left justify all text. Do not use the tab key for spacing.

d. In a paragraph or sentence, keep typing to make your text continue on the next line. Do not use the return button or enter key to go on to the next line. Do not use the tab key or space bar to indent the second line.

e. Set the left margin of your text at 1 and the right margin at 1.75. Your text should not have more than 65 characters and spaces per line.

f. Select a simple font with 12-point type.

g. Use all caps for your name and major headings. Use parentheses around your phone number area code.

h. Save your resumé as a text only file, making sure that you double-check all information and run a spell check. Close the file, reopen it, and fix any spacing problems with your space bar.

i. E-mail your resumé to a friend so that you can see how it transmits.

j. Follow up with a printed resumé and a cover letter, if possible.

SENDING A COVER LETTER VIA E-MAIL

The importance of cover letters will be discussed in the next chapter, along with guidelines for writing a good cover letter. When sending your resumé electronically, do not neglect to send a cover letter if possible. A cover letter allows you to relate your skills and experience to a specific job and to address your application to a specific person or organization. A good cover letter may help your application to receive special consideration, since it demonstrates your interest in the specific job that the organization has available. Take time to craft a cover letter using the guidelines in the next chapter and include it as the first section of your email message when you send your resumé to a prospective employer.

BE CAREFUL!

The explosion of information available through the Internet can be an extremely useful resource in career planning and job hunting. But it can be captivating and can easily distract you from the important work-finding activities that have been described in this chapter. You can access the information using your (or someone else's) computer. You can interact with others online and send your resumé online. There is even a possibility that you may be able to find a job online.

However, there is no substitute for the face-to-face meetings, the interpersonal contacts that are essential to the job campaign. You can easily allow yourself to spend hours in front of the computer accessing all of this wonderful information. Remember that you must get out and around and talk with people in order to conduct an effective job campaign. The computer can be an extremely useful tool in the career exploration and job-hunting process. Use it as a tool, but don't let it overwhelm you by taking your energy and time away from the other techniques that will help you to find the work of your choice.

THE MOST IMPORTANT CYBERSPACE APPLICATION TO CAREER PLANNING AND JOB HUNTING

While the use of the Internet can be helpful in the job search, as described in this chapter, there is a more important application of the new technology to your career planning. The developments in technology are becoming pervasive throughout the workforce in the 21st century. Most planners maintain that we have just begun to see the effects of the technological and information revolution. No matter what career field you enter, you will gain an advantage by taking every opportunity to learn how to use new technologies. Learn about new developments. Try out new software applications at your work. Volunteer to be a part of work groups exploring new technological applications. Take courses and workshops whenever they are given. Be open to change and to the new technologies that will come with change. By welcoming new technologies and learning how to use them, you will open yourself to new career opportunities.

ADDITIONAL RESOURCES FOR JOB HUNTING IN CYPERSPACE

Bolles, M. E. & Bolles, R.N. (2008). *Job hunting online: A guide to using job listings, message boards, research sites, the underweb, counseling, networking, self assessment tools, nichesites.* Berkeley, CA: Ten Speed Press.

Dickel, M. R. & Roehm, F. E. (2008). *Guide to internet job searching: 2008–2009 edition.* New York: McGraw-Hill.

Doyle, A. (2008). *Internet your way to a new job: How to really find a job online.* Cupertino, CA: HappyAbout.info.

Kallos, J. (2004). *Because netiquette matters: Your comprehensive reference guide to email etiquette and proper technology use.* Philadelphia, PA: Xlibris Corporation.

Strawbridge, M. (2006). *Netiquette: Internet etiquette in the age of the blog.* Ely, Cambridgeshire, UK: Software Reference Ltd.

Weddle, P. D. (2007). *2007/2008 guide to employment sites on the internet: For corporate and third party recruiters, job seekers, and career activists.* Stamford, CT: Weddle's.

CHAPTER 21

Resumé Writing

Your resumé is an important part of your job campaign. It presents in writing the skills, accomplishments, and qualifications that you bring to a potential employer. The process of writing your resumé is an efficient way of organizing your qualifications so that **you** know what you have to offer an employer. For this reason, it is very important that you spend a good deal of time writing and rewriting your resumé. It is not a good idea to have someone else write your resumé for you.

Think of the skills and abilities that you have developed that would contribute to your career goals. No one can write these attributes better than you because no one knows you better than you do. Your resumé should be neat, clearly written, and positive. The process of writing your own resumé will help you to focus on your skills and abilities, communicate your strengths, and interview effectively.

CHARACTERISTICS OF A GOOD RESUMÉ

What do you want your resumé to do for you? Here are some characteristics of a good resumé.

1. A resumé presents your **accomplishments.** It should show how **well** you perform, rather than just presenting descriptions of previous jobs that you have held.

2. A resumé demonstrates how your qualifications will **meet the needs of employers.** It should focus not on what you want but on what you have to **offer** the employer.

3. A resumé describes **your major strengths and potential** without being too long.

4. A resumé shows **your own unique personality** and experiences and should make an employer want to talk with you.

5. A resumé **is interesting to read** rather than challenging to read.

Questions to Ask Before You Write Your Resumé

1. What is your purpose in writing a resumé? Are you changing jobs in the same career area or are you changing careers? It will make a difference in how you organize your resumé.

2. What type of job are you seeking? It helps to have a specific objective.

3. What type of person and experience are required for the job? You can find this information through research, informational interviewing, and networking.

4. What skills and abilities do you have to offer an employer?

5. Which skills, abilities, and accomplishments do you want to stress? Focus on those that support your career objective.

Organization of Your Resumé

There is no specific resumé format that is best for everyone. Choose the style that is best for you. Although there are many variations in format, most resumés can be categorized in two types.

1. **Chronological resumé.** The chronological resumé, by far the most common, is the format employers normally expect, and is appropriate when your most recent experience is your most qualifying experience. If you are looking for a position that is a logical next step in your career, this is the format that may best fit your needs. Your work history is presented in chronological order, with your most recent experience first. The usual order of basic information for each position is position title, name of employer, city, state, and years. There is no need to right-justify dates or to include months or days.

2. **Combination chronological and functional resumé.** This format may be helpful if you want to place up front a summary of your skills and accomplishments that are especially relevant to your goal. It is particularly useful when the skills that you have used in your most recent position are not as relevant to your goal as the skills that you used in previous positions. This format is good for people who are changing careers and want to show how their transferable skills and accomplishments relate to the position for which they are applying.

    While your most relevant accomplishments will be featured on the first page of a combination resumé, it is still important to list your experience in reverse chronological order. You should describe the positions that you have held and provide examples of your accomplishments, just as you would do with a chronological resumé.

Contents of Chronological and Combination Resumés

Heading

Include your name, address, telephone number, and email address. You may want to include additional information, such as cellular telephone number or fax number. Consider making your name at least one font size larger than the other information and use boldface type. If you include an academic degree or professional certificate, place it after your name. Try centering your heading in the middle of the page.

Profile or Qualifications Summary

After your heading, it is important to include a statement that summarizes your experience and qualifications that are most relevant to the type of work that you want to do. This is a statement of what you have to offer an employer **now**. This brief section, usually three to five sentences in length, gives you the opportunity to place up front in your resume the information about you that you want a prospective employer to see first.

A general guideline is to include the name of the career field, your level of experience, the number of years of relevant experience, where the experience has been applied, specialized skills and experience, and your knowledge, training, and/or education relating to the position. You may also wish to include special certifications, clearances, language skills, and other specialized skills if they are relevant to your goal.

There are other titles that you could give this section of your resume. In addition to qualifications summary or profile, other titles are career profile, executive summary, professional summary, and skills summary. You can also use a specific job title, such as accountant, human resource professional, or teacher.

The most important function of a profile or qualifications summary is to feature in your resume a brief summary of your qualifications that are most relevant to your goal. While it is most common to write your profile as a paragraph, you can also choose a different format, such as an introductory sentence followed by bullets.

Experience and Accomplishments

This is the most important part of your resumé. Remember that it is **not** a series of job descriptions. Show what you have achieved, the special contributions you have made, the responsibilities you have assumed, and the recognition you have received. If you can quantify what you did, by all means do so.

Example: Developed a new inventory system that resulted in annual savings of $25,000.

Include any awards and indicate how proficient you are in specific terms. Avoid general grandiose statements that are self-serving. In describing your experience and accomplishments, use action verbs such as:

• Sold	• Designed	• Developed	• Managed
• Planned	• Initiated	• Promoted	• Performed
• Trained	• Implemented	• Established	• Created
• Supervised	• Coordinated	• Negotiated	• Researched

Remember to demonstrate what you have done and what you are capable of doing in the future. Show results of your work whenever possible. Possible titles for this section of your resumé include experience, professional experience, professional experience and accomplishments, work experience, work history, career history, employment history, and professional highlights. The usual order of basic information for each position is position title, name of employer, city, state, and years. There is no need to right justify dates or to include months or days.

For Chronological Resumés

Show your best experience first. Generally start with your most recent experience (unless it does not support your objective) and work backward. List your experience in reverse chronological order. Include titles, employers, and dates. You do not have to include all of your experience. Go back at least ten years, but you may want to go back further if that experience is relevant to your goal. When describing your experience, emphasize your accomplishments.

Quantify and give results if possible. Avoid extensive use of job description language that would apply to anyone holding the position. Emphasize the special contributions that you have made in your career. Include part-time and summer work if it was moderately recent and is relevant to the type position for which you will be applying. Show the sequence of your career and present your career as a series of progressive accomplishments.

For Combination Chronological and Functional Resumés

After your qualifications summary, use the heading of "Professional Accomplishments" or something similar for this section of your resumé. You may wish to use two to four subheadings to describe your accomplishments that are most relevant to your goal. For example, if you are applying for a position that involves both supervision and project management, you can create subheadings for both areas and list accomplishments under each. Examples of these areas of expertise are:

- Organization
- Budgeting
- Purchasing
- Supervision
- Communication
- Programming
- Teaching
- Coordination
- Repairing
- Writing
- Marketing
- Installing

Give two or three specific examples of your expertise for each area. Write in a manner that illustrates your results and accomplishments. Use a variety of strong action verbs. Draw on every aspect of your life, including any volunteer work, in addition to paid employment. After your listing of functional expertise, provide a chronological listing of your experience and accomplishments, just as you would for a chronological resumé.

Special instructions for this section
- Define abilities rather than duties.
- Stress your accomplishments.
- Use correct dates.
- Use concise descriptions that focus on how you have performed.
- Write clearly and simply. Do not use long paragraphs.
- Use strong action verbs.

Education and Training

After describing your experience, list your education in reverse chronological order. While education is usually listed after experience, put education before the section on experience if it is your most qualifying experience. For example, someone who has just completed a degree in nursing and has passed the National League of Nursing examination may want to place this information on the first page of the resumé, right after the qualifications summary and before the section on experience.

The usual order for listing basic educational information is degree, major, school, city, state, and year of graduation. When describing your education, list your highest degree first and then work backward. If high school or vocational school is your highest level, include it. Otherwise, high school education is usually not included. Provide names of schools and colleges attended, degree(s) received, academic honors, grade point average (if it is outstanding and recent), and major subject areas. If you have a substantial number of credits but no degree, you can list the number of credits (or the name of the program), major, school, city, state, and years. You may prefer not to include the years of your education. This is perfectly acceptable unless the employer has asked for dates of your education.

You may want to include training or have a separate category for training. List the relevant training that you have completed in reverse chronological order. If you have completed many training courses during your work experience, consider including your most recent training and the training courses and programs that are most relevant to your goal.

Special Skills, Memberships, Military Service, and Awards

If you have special skills, clearances, and certifications that are relevant to your goal, you can create a special category. If you have military experience, be sure to include it in this section, unless you have already included it in the description of your experience and accomplishments. You may wish to include information on publications, licenses, computer skills, professional affiliations, community service, presentations, and awards, if this information is relevant to your goal. If you have received awards, you can describe them in this category, although it is usually preferable to use the earning of an award as an example of results that you have accomplished in the experience and accomplishments section of your resumé.

Interests and Community Contributions

Include special interests, travel, skills, licenses, certifications, community activities, or any other information that:

- Relates to your objective
- Puts you in a positive position so that a potential employer may want to meet you

References

Never list your references on your resumé. You do not need to indicate that they will be furnished on request. Although this was common in the past, it is assumed that you will have references. You will want to select particular references depending on the position you are considering. Choose people who can attest to your work-related skills and work habits.

GENERAL TIPS ON WRITING YOUR RESUMÉ

- Use your own language. You are the best person to write your resumé.
- Emphasize your accomplishments. Show the amount and quality of your experience. Whenever possible, use numbers to quantify your experience.
- Avoid long paragraphs. Use bullets and boldface type to draw attention to your accomplishments. Be consistent in your use of indentations, bullets, boldface, italics, and capitalization. Try to keep margins at approximately 1" on all four sides.
- Place the most significant and powerful information in the beginning of your resumé and in the beginning of each heading. Don't hide information that packs a punch.
- Generally limit your resumé to 2–3 pages unless longer resumes are expected in your area of interest, such as in academic work.
- Use the "I, understood" format. Begin your sentences with action verbs such as managed, supervised, coordinated, created, etc. Avoid using "I."
- Check for grammar, syntax, and spelling. Use spell check, but don't depend on it. Proof your resumé and have two other people proof it. Never have a misspelled word.
- Avoid extensive use of abbreviations and acronyms unless they are very relevant to your goal. Use simple terms rather than complex ones.
- Use 8½" × 11" quality bond paper (24 pound cotton fiber) in a light neutral color, or good quality printer paper. Use the best printer available. If your printer at home doesn't provide crisp, clear print, use a friend's printer or a printer at an office supply store.
- Use a clear font, such as Arial, Antiqua, Bookman Old Style, or Times New Roman, in a readable size (11 or larger for text, 12 or larger for headings). Leave plenty of white space to make reading and scanning easy.

- As a general guideline, single space between lines and double space between sections.

- Pay careful attention to tense. Use present tense for your current job and past tense for previous jobs. Use correct dates throughout your resumé.

- If you are mailing your resumé, do not fold it. Mail it flat in a 9" × 12" envelope.

- Do not include your salary history, unless you are writing a federal resumé.

- Avoid self-congratulatory language, such as "Wrote an excellent report." Instead, indicate if you received a commendation on what you wrote or if your report was accepted and influenced policy.

- Number each page after the first page and put your name on each page, either on the same line as or near the page number.

MAKE TWO VERSIONS OF YOUR RESUMÉ

It is recommended that you prepare at least two versions of your resumé:

1. Your primary resumé should look attractive, with appropriate use of boldface and capitals, different size fonts, and bullets. It is important that you be consistent throughout in the use of these features. Your resumé should look professional and be easy to read. Have several people look at your resumé and get their feedback.

2. Once you have completed your primary resumé, save it and then make a copy so that you can use it to create an electronic version of your resumé. See Chapter 20, Job Hunting in Cyberspace, for specific instructions on how to create an electronic version of your resumé.

Use your primary resumé whenever possible, since it will be visually more appealing and easier to read than the electronic version. If you are asked to mail or fax your resumé, use your primary one. If you go for an interview and take copies of your resumé with you, the copies should be of your primary resumé. If you send a copy of your resumé to someone who requests it after an informational interview, again, use your primary resumé. Use the electronic version of your resumé only when instructed to do so by an employer or if you are required to copy and paste your resumé into an online application system.

ELECTRONIC SCANNING OF RESUMÉS

With increasing capabilities to scan materials and put them in an organization's database, more and more resumés are being scanned electronically. Many companies in the United States sell resumé scanning software and automated applicant tracking systems. People in organizations can review resumés and applications on their computer screens, making this process much more efficient.

In addition to scanning resumés so that they can be entered in a database, the software allows an organization to search resumés for certain experiences, skills, or training that are deemed important for a particular position. Resumés can also be scanned for certain factors and routed to appropriate offices within an organization. The applicant tracking software can also generate letters of rejection or letters offering interviews and can also store resumés or selected applicant information for potential future openings.

What does this approach to the review of resumés and applications mean to the job hunter? It is more important than ever to construct a good, well-organized resumé. However, since scanning programs will be used much more frequently in the future, here are some factors to consider.

1. Since scanning programs search out key words, use more nouns in your resumé in addition to action verbs. Specific experience, training, and skills should be described using accepted names and the jargon appropriate to the field. Here are some examples:

   - Certified Public Accountant
   - Microsoft Office 2000 Suite Trainer

- Certified Novell Engineer (CNE)
- Training in A.D.A. compliance
- Experienced in conflict resolution techniques
- Certified A.S.E. mechanic
- Experience in contract management and acquisitions

Check position descriptions on the Web sites, classified ads, and organizational newsletters as a source of these words. Include them in your objective, which can also incorporate a summary of your skills, experience, and education.

2. Use common fonts no smaller than a 10 and no larger than a 14. Scanners can more easily deal with your resume if your document is not too fancy.

3. Use boldface only for section headers, not for your name and address. Do not use underlining or italics. If you want to draw attention to a section, you can use caps.

4. Print your resume on good quality paper with a good printer. Do not send a photocopy.

5. Use plain white or ivory paper and don't use borders. When mailing your resume, use a large enough envelope so that you do not have to fold your resume. All of these make scanning your resume easier. When attaching your cover letter, use a paper clip. Stapling or folding your resume may result in it being misread by a scanner.

Make sure to continue to send a cover letter with each resume and keep up to date with the latest technology.

SAMPLE RESUMÉS

On the following pages, sample resumés are provided in two different formats. In most cases, these sample resumés are presented on one page since they are designed to illustrate different approaches. For an actual job application, the resumés could easily be expanded to two pages.

- Chronological
- Combination chronological and functional

There is no one right way to write a resume. Use the format that most favorably presents your experience, your background, and your career goal. Once you have written a resume, you will need to update it frequently. The best time to revise your resume is when you do not feel pressured to do so. Try to keep an accurate resume on file at all times. You never know when opportunity will knock. Resumé writing is usually considered a difficult task because it is hard to write about yourself. However, writing a comprehensive, positive resume is a worthwhile process, because it can reinforce your self-worth and can increase your self-confidence.

A note of caution: Relying too heavily on your resume in the job-seeking process can be discouraging as well as counterproductive. How you use your resume in your job search is as important as developing your resume. A survey of human resource executives reported that they spent less than one minute scanning the average resumé they received and that only 5 percent of all resumés sent resulted in an interview. The resume is merely a tool. It will never replace the value of networking and other job search techniques. You may wish to review the job-seeking techniques described earlier in this chapter to enhance your job campaign.

Remember, the best person to compose your resumé is YOU!

Antoine Jackson
1000 Main Street
Chicago, IL 60673
Home: 312-555-5555
Cell: 312-555-9000
e-mail: ajackson@msn.com

Qualifications Summary

Over 14 years experience in retail sales. Significant experience in direct marketing to customers, supervision of staff, and managing a sales program. Proven record of productivity and ability to meet and exceed sales targets.

Experience

Manager, Assistant Manager, XYZ Department Store, Chicago. IL, 1998–present

- Manage all operations of the men's department, with annual sales in excess of $15 million. Supervise a sales staff ranging in size from 15 to 30. Work closely with buyers in planning sales campaigns. Assist in the selection of men's merchandise.

- Train new sales personnel; designed and implemented a training program that has served over 100 new employees.

- Coordinated and completed comprehensive modernization plans for the men's department.

Assistant Manager, J.C. Company, Peoria, IL, 1994–1998

- Started as a clerk in retail shoe sales. After six months was promoted and transferred to a new outlet as assistant manager. Coordinated all display work, newspaper advertising, and sales promotion.

- In four years, helped to build the store's sales volume to third highest of a 12 store chain.

Communications Specialist, United States Army, 1991–1994

- Supervised a communications group of twelve enlisted personnel who dealt with top secret information on a daily basis.

- Served in Germany and at the Pentagon.

Education and Training

B.S. in marketing, University of Illinois, 1991

Completed extensive training in customer service, human resources, supervision, and quality assurance. Earned certificate in project management, 2007.

Sarah Kozlowski

100 Main Street
Minneapolis, Minnesota 67854
Telephone: Home (612) 555-0032
Cell (612) 555-1111
E-mail: sarahk@gmail.com

Profile

Database manager with extensive problem-solving skills and experience, knowledge of six programming languages, and ability to adapt to organizational needs and challenges.

Education

A.A.S. 2006, Minneapolis Community College. Majored in computer information systems. Completed cooperative education in computer information systems and took additional course work in accounting and business management. Elected to Phi Theta Kappa academic honor society. Graduated magna cum laude.

Experience and Accomplishments

Information Systems Technologist, ABC Corporation, St. Paul, Minnesota, 2006–present. Began as a trainee and was moved into a programmer position within six months. Write programs and assist in coordinating all aspects of the information systems of the company. Use JAVA and C++ extensively. Promoted to assistant manager of the data system.

Secretary to the human resources director, BCD Corporation, Minneapolis, Minnesota, 1998–2004. Supervised two full-time employees. Developed and administered a new records system. Wrote letters and reports for the director. Monitored the office budget and initiated all work orders and purchase requisitions.

Bank teller, Second National Bank, Minneapolis, Minnesota, 1996–1998. Assisted customers and monitored money flow. After one year, promoted to supervisor of the evening shift.

Special Skills

Have a working knowledge of three computer languages including JAVA, C++, and EVENT-DRIVEN BASIC. Took extra courses in mathematics to develop good analytical skills. Have worked with ORACLE and ACCESS database programs.

Chronological Resumé

RICHARD E. MOSSER
123 South Taylor Street
Lima, Virginia 22204
E-mail: RMosser@earthlink.net

Home: (804) 111-1111   Cell: (804) 555-5555

ELECTRICIAN

More than 12 years experience in all phases of the electrical field. Expertise in troubleshooting electrical circuits and providing necessary maintenance. Effective supervisor of tradespeople.

EXPERIENCE

Lima City Government, Lima, Virginia, 2003–present
ELECTRICIAN

- Repair, install, and test electrical systems and devices for 300,000 square feet of office space, including:

  —Electrical panels   —Fluorescent   —Magnetic starters
  —Conduit   —Computer   —Switches, receptacles
  —Motors   —Breakers   —Incandescent lights
  —Ballasts   —Wire   —Data lines

- Evaluate and prepare purchase orders for more than 1,000 electrical items
- Trained two apprentices on electrical maintenance procedures
- Supervised as many as four tradespeople
- Read blueprints and schematics for wiring of new equipment, new additions, and new buildings
- Work with voltages up to 480-volt 3-phase systems

XYZ Management Company, Lima, Virginia, 1996–2003
ELECTRICIAN
Coordinated the total electrical renovation of more than 500 apartments. Replaced fixtures, switches, receptacles, and wiring

ABC Electric Company, Lima, Virginia, 1995–1996
ELECTRICIAN HELPER
Installed new wiring in single-family homes and townhouses. Completed commercial electrical work on mid-rise office buildings in the Central Virginia area

EDUCATION

Best Community College, Lima, Virginia, 2004–2007
A.A.S. Degree in electronic technology
Dean's List with G.P.A. of 3.68

Training Community College, Highland, New York, 1992–1995
Electrical Construction, 1,920 hours of study, certificate awarded 1995.

SPECIAL LICENSE

Virginia Journeyman's License # 5678-JK, April 6, 1996

THOMAS DiVINCENZO

100 Exeter Street
Springfield, CA 90111
916-555-0321
tdivincenzo@earthlink.net

QUALIFICATIONS SUMMARY

Extensive experience in administering and delivering social services, including supervising professional staff, managing caseloads, and training professional, paraprofessional, and support staff. Skilled in preparing and administering budgets and dealing with budget reductions due to changing state and municipal funding levels. Experienced in developing and assessing the effectiveness of programs. Skilled in developing cooperative relationships with other non-profit agencies and community groups.

PROFESSIONAL EXPERIENCE

Director of Social Services, Springfield, CA, 2002–present

Administer a comprehensive program of social services for a city of approximately 100,000 residents, 4,000 of whom are currently receiving some form of social service assistance. Supervise a staff of approximately 50 professional, paraprofessional, and support personnel. Analyze community needs and develop programs designed to meet these needs. Administer an annual budget in excess of $11 million.

- Created and administer a program designed to enhance job skills to make aid recipients self-sufficient. The number of people requesting and receiving aid has decreased by 18% since the program was started.

- Developed and administer a comprehensive training program for all levels of social service staff which involves staff in identifying training needs and how they can improve services. In the past four years since this program has been in effect, turnover of staff has decreased by 40%. This program has been used as a model by four other agencies.

- Supervised the creation of an electronic record keeping system that has decreased administrative costs by 50%, resulting in the retraining of five administrative staff members to provide direct paraprofessional service to clients.

- Worked with other government and non-profit agencies to develop and maintain a system to cooperate in providing a variety of services to city residents. These services derive their support from both public and private funding sources.

Associate Director of Social Services, Mountain View, OR, 1999–2002

Assisted in the management of social services for a city of approximately 75,000 residents with a population of approximately 3,000 who were receiving services. Provided support to the director and served as acting director in her absence, as well as providing direct services to clients.

- At the request of the director, developed and ran a comprehensive training program for approximately 40 professional, paraprofessional, and administrative staff members. Provided direct training and arranged for other professional training support when needed. Involved staff in planning the program and developed a system for assessing the value of the training. After the program had been in effect for a year, staff turnover decreased by 30%.

- Created a workforce transition program. Worked with colleagues and provided direct services to clients. Conducted individual counseling appointments and led groups that were primarily focused on helping clients to enter the workforce.
- Managed the creation of a new system of providing health support services for eligible clients. Identified providers and established systems for referrals, payment for services, and follow up. This resulted in more than 500 clients receiving regular health care who had been without organized health service in the past.

Social Worker, Valley View, OR, 1995–1999

Provided individual counseling, group assistance, and training to clients who were receiving social services. Managed a caseload of 200 clients. Provided follow up and arranged for support to meet clients' needs.

- Created back-to-work support groups that were designed to assist clients make a transition to gainful employment. After two years of follow-up, participants in these groups had a 50% higher success rate of staying in their jobs for at least one year.
- Led a committee of staff members tasked with identifying training opportunities that could be pursued both at and outside their work setting. This resulted in a significant increase in the number of staff members who participated in some form of training.

Social Service Intern, Eugene Public Schools, Eugene, OR, 1993–1995

While enrolled as a graduate student, provided direct services to high school students and co-led groups of students as an intern with the Eugene, OR school system.

EDUCATION

Master's Degree in Social Work, University of Oregon, Eugene, OR, 1995.

Bachelor of Arts Degree with a major in psychology, St. Lawrence University, Canton, NY, 1993

TRAINING AND CERTIFICATIONS

Licensed, Certified Social Worker in California and Oregon

Certified Professional in Learning and Performance, American Society of Training and Development

Fellowship for study of the developmental needs of adults at the University of California, Los Angeles

Completed training in project management and human resources management. Have completed numerous courses and workshops on providing effective training and workforce development programs.

Combination Resumé

This resumé has substantially the same text as the preceding resumé, but is presented in the combination format to emphasize the person's training experience for a potential position as training coordinator.

THOMAS DIVINCENZO

100 Exeter Street
Springfield, CA 90111
916-555-0321
tdivincenzo@earthlink.net

QUALIFICATIONS SUMMARY

Accomplished trainer with broad experience in developing training programs and providing direct training for professional, paraprofessional, and administrative staff. Extensive experience in administering and delivering social services, including supervising professional staff and managing caseloads. Skilled in preparing and administering budgets and dealing with budget reductions due to changing state and municipal funding levels. Experienced in developing and assessing the effectiveness of programs. Skilled in developing cooperative relationships with other non-profit agencies and community groups.

PROFESSIONAL ACCOMPLISHMENTS

Training

- Developed and administer a comprehensive training program for all levels of social service staff which involves staff in identifying training needs and how they can improve services. In the past four years since this program has been in effect, turnover of staff has decreased by 40%. This program has been used as a model by four other agencies.

- As Associate Director of Social Services, developed and ran a comprehensive training program for approximately 40 professional, paraprofessional, and administrative staff members. Provided direct training and arranged for other professional training support when needed. Involved staff in planning the program and developed a system for assessing the value of the training. After the program had been in effect for a year, staff turnover decreased by 30%.

- Led a committee of staff members tasked with identifying training opportunities that could be pursued both at and outside their work setting. This resulted in a significant increase in the number of staff members who participated in some form of training.

Management

- Created and administer a program designed to enhance job skills to make aid recipients self-sufficient. The number of people requesting and receiving aid has decreased by 18% since the program was started.

- Supervised the creation of an electronic record keeping system that has decreased administrative costs by 50%, resulting in the retraining of five administrative staff members to provide direct paraprofessional service to clients.

- Managed the creation of a new system of providing health support services for eligible clients. Identified providers and established systems for referrals, payment for services, and follow up. This resulted in more than 500 clients receiving regular health care who had been without organized health service in the past.

Workforce Development and Community Service

- Worked with other government and non-profit agencies to develop and maintain a system to cooperate in providing a variety of services to city residents. These services derive their support from both public and private funding sources.

- Created a workforce transition program. Worked with colleagues and provided direct services to clients. Conducted individual counseling appointments and led groups that were primarily focused on helping clients to enter the workforce.

- Created back-to-work support groups that were designed to assist clients make a transition to gainful employment. After two years of follow-up, participants in these groups had a 50% higher success rate of staying in their jobs for at least one year.

PROFESSIONAL EXPERIENCE

Director of Social Services, Springfield, CA, 2002–present

Administer a comprehensive program of social services for a city of approximately 100,000 residents, 4,000 of whom are currently receiving some form of social service assistance. Supervise a staff of approximately 50 professional, paraprofessional, and support personnel. Analyze community needs and develop programs designed to meet these needs. Administer an annual budget in excess of $11 million.

Associate Director of Social Services, Mountain View, OR, 1999–2002

Assisted in the management of social services for a city of approximately 75,000 residents with a population of approximately 3,000 who were receiving services. Provided support to the director and served as acting director in her absence, as well as providing direct services to clients.

Social Worker, Valley View, OR, 1995–1999

Provided individual counseling, group assistance, and training to clients who were receiving social services. Managed a caseload of 200 clients. Provided follow up and arranged for support to meet clients' needs.

Social Service Intern, Eugene Public Schools, Eugene, OR, 1993–1995

While enrolled as a graduate student, provided direct services to high school students and co-led groups of students as an intern with the Eugene, OR school system.

EDUCATION

Master's Degree in Social Work, University of Oregon, Eugene, OR, 1995

Bachelor of Arts Degree with a major in psychology, St. Lawrence University, Canton, NY, 1993

TRAINING AND CERTIFICATIONS

Licensed, Certified Social Worker in California and Oregon

Certified Professional in Learning and Performance, American Society of Training and Development

Fellowship for study of the developmental needs of adults at the University of California, Los Angeles

Completed training in project management and human resources management. Have completed numerous courses and workshops on providing effective training and workforce development programs.

Functional Resumé

For Someone Who Is Moving from a Clerical Position to a Different Career Objective

Theresa Munoz
100 South Main Street
St. Petersburg, FL 34567
Home: 555-413-3000 Cellular: 555-111-1111
e-mail: theresamunoz@hotmail.com

PROFILE

Over ten years' experience in design, management, analysis, writing, and customer service. Skilled in supervision of staff and organizing the preparation of high-quality publications. Extensive experience in working with members of the public.

SELECTED ACCOMPLISHMENTS

Public Relations and Management

Manage the career information resources for the career service of a major university. Serve as the primary contact with employers and schedule more than 500 employer visits to the campus each year. Organize several job fairs each year with as many as 100 employers at each event. Supervise an office staff of five. Coordinate work schedules, organize work flow, train new personnel, and serve as the office manager. Assist students in the use of career information.

Document Preparation

Respond to student and employer requests for information about the service. Publish a monthly newsletter for the career service and write more than half of the articles. Compose justifications for new equipment and tuition assistance requests. Create guidelines for students to use in researching career information. Experienced in the use of Microsoft Office Suite, McIntosh Operating System, QuarkXPress, Adobe Photoshop, and Adobe Illustrator.

Art/Design/Production

Coordinate the preparation of all publications for the office. Edit, organize, and design layout and artwork for brochures, fliers, and booklets for career services. Serve as the contact person for contracted printers. As a self-employed freelance artist, prepared brochures, with appropriate design and artwork, for businesses and government agencies.

EMPLOYMENT HISTORY

Career Information Specialist, Administrative Assistant, Career Services, Florida University, St. Petersburg, FL, 2002–present

Administrative Assistant and Bookkeeper, First National Bank, St. Petersburg, FL, 2000–2002

Freelance design assignments, 1993–2000

EDUCATION

Completed 24 semester hours toward M.B.A. degree, Florida University, 2007–present.

B.A. degree, Florida University, 1997. Majored in public relations and communications.

A.A.S. degree, St. Petersburg Community College, 1995. Majored in commercial art.

Combination Chronological-Functional Resumé

For Someone Who Is Changing Careers

ZAIDAN SYED

1000 Main Street
Washington, D.C.
Telephone: Home (202) 555-0032
Cell (202) 555-1111
E-mail: Zaidansyed@yahoo.com

Qualifications Summary

Accomplished convention and classroom manager. Skilled in coordinating the work of employees and students. Able to deal with multiple responsibilities while establishing clear priorities. Excellent organizational and leadership skills.

Professional Accomplishments

Organization
- Developed a comprehensive program for teaching college-level English to high school seniors
- Supervised up to ten workers at various convention assignments
- Organized and led overseas educational trips for high school students
- Initiated and followed through on more than twenty educational trips for high school seniors to various cities and theater programs
- Assisted the director of the New Orleans Convention and Visitors Bureau in the staffing of convention sites throughout the city
- Coordinated the work of a team of English teachers
- Developed skills in use of Microsoft Office, PowerPoint and other presentation software, web page design

Teaching
- Developed instructional programs for students at all grade levels (9–12) in high school English
- Completed 20 years of successful teaching at the high school level
- Supervised various student organizations, directed plays, served as advisor for a variety of activities
- Elected as faculty representative to local educational association

Professional Experience

Convention Work
Assistant administrator, program coordinator, New Orleans Convention and Visitors Bureau, 1993–1997. Organized the staffing of conventions, worked with various associations in the planning of conventions, provided direct assistance at convention sites

Teaching
High school English teacher, Alpha High School, Washington, D.C. 1997–present. Developed advanced placement programs. High School English Teacher, Beta High School, New York, New York, 1985–1993

Education

M.S., Counseling and Development, George Washington University, Washington, D.C., 2000
B.A., English, New York University, 1985

Memberships

National Council of Teachers of English, 1985–present
American Association of Convention Planners, 2006–present

Resumé Worksheet

Use this worksheet to record as much information as you can think of that you might want to include in a resumé. Then take the information and organize it according to the format that you prefer.

Qualifcations Summary

Education

Experience

Special Skills

Awards, Honors

Professional Memberships and Community Activities

COVER LETTERS

When you apply for a position, you should send a cover letter along with your resumé. Your cover letter gives you the opportunity to focus your qualifications on the specific position for which you are applying. As a general principle, draw attention to **what you can do for the organization, not what you expect to get** from the organization. Here are some guidelines for writing cover letters.

Guidelines for Writing a Good Cover Letter

1. Indicate the position for which you are applying.

2. Address your letter to the appropriate person. Do some research to find the person's name. Avoid the use of: Dear Sir or Madam, Gentlemen, or To Whom It May Concern.

3. State why you are interested in the position.

4. Demonstrate how your skills and experience would be appropriate for the position.

5. Select one or two specific accomplishments in your experience that are particularly relevant to the position, and draw attention to them in your letter.

6. Maintain the initiative by stating that you will call to see whether an interview can be arranged.

7. Try to keep the length of the letter to one page.

8. Use good quality stationery and, by all means, do not handwrite the letter. The following is a sample cover letter. It is very brief in order to give a concise example of a format. Yours could be longer to allow you to focus more on appropriate accomplishments.

Your Heading Here
name, address, telephone
numbers(s), email address

Date

Mr. James Smith
Director of Marketing
ABC Corporation
Anywhere, U.S.A. 50000

Dear Mr. Smith:

It has come to my attention that you have a position available in your office as Assistant Director of Marketing. I am very much interested in being considered for this position.

I have several years of appropriate experience in marketing as described in my resumé, a copy of which is enclosed. I would especially like to draw your attention to my work in marketing with XYC Corporation, in which I created and implemented a new marketing program for the company which resulted in a 25 percent increase in sales. I feel that I can offer you and your organization my experience and skills in program development and my administrative skills, which I have used in marketing for more than five years.

I would appreciate your consideration of my application for this position. Realizing the demands on your time, I will call you next week to see whether we can arrange for an interview. I look forward to meeting with you in the near future.

Sincerely yours,

APPLICATIONS

Applications are generally disliked by employers and applicants alike, but knowing how to complete application forms or online applications is a necessary part of your job campaign. Your application should reflect your best skills, abilities, and accomplishments. An application is different from a resumé. Where resumés can be tailored to disguise unemployment, job hopping, or underemployment, an application usually tells all in chronological sequence. Some general application hints will be offered in this section.

Employment interviewing is difficult enough without having to complete a long application form while you wait. Request that the employment application be sent to you ahead of time so you can complete it at your own pace. Many organizations will ask you to enter application data into the organization's information network or may provide access to their applications through their web sites. In other cases, you will have to enter information at the work site.

Some General Application Do's

- Communicate your background clearly with action verbs.

- Type your application or use a word processing program, if possible, and proofread it twice.

- Include all dates of employment and verify those dates.

- Complete all blocks on the form. If an item is not applicable, write N/A.

- Always attach a well-written resumé.

- Include a cover letter if you are mailing your application.

- If possible, customize your application by cutting and pasting additional lines in the "Description of Work" area to accommodate your experience. The use of a word processing program makes this much easier. Unlike a resumé, in which you narrow your employment description to a few lines, on an application you may be called on to explain and list your duties, responsibilities, and, especially, your accomplishments. You might list them as follows, expanding each as fully as possible

    - My responsibilities were . . .

    - The skills used were . . .

    - My accomplishments were . . .

- Include all relevant experience—paid and volunteer.

- Make your application interesting—use action verbs.

- Use references who can attest to your work ability and can remember you. Ask for their permission ahead of time so that you will be ready to write their names on an application.

Some General Application Don'ts

- Don't misspell words.

- Don't omit your signature and the date that you completed the application.

- Don't attach former job descriptions, transcripts, or letters of recommendation unless specifically requested.

- Don't omit relevant volunteer work.

- Don't overlook special sections such as honors and awards, if they are relevant to the job for which you are applying.

- Don't include anything negative about previous positions, or about anything else.

- Don't make your application a challenge to read. If it is hard to read, people will ignore it.

How You Can Compensate for Gaps, Job Hopping, and Underemployment

a. **Unemployment gaps.** If your employment gap is more than one year, you should normally account for this time. Rather than putting "unemployed" on the form, which is negative, state what you were doing—traveling, enhancing your education, consultant, home improvements, self-employed. It is not necessary to list your experience in months and years. Just giving years of employment is sufficient. This may help if you have an employment gap of less than one year.

b. **Job hopping.** Lump a few jobs in the same space, especially if they were for three months or less, and give a general description of what you accomplished during that period. You may decide not to list some jobs that lasted less than a few months.

c. **Underemployment.** Underemployment is a term used to describe an employee whose skills and abilities are not being fully used in a job. If this is your situation, you may wish to change or upgrade your job title and description to better reflect what you are doing in your job. You can always list your accomplishments and the skills you used in the experience section of the application, thus helping to clarify the expertise you use on the job. If you have few accomplishments thus far, then get going and start thinking of some creative projects you could initiate, design, and implement in your job.

Knowledge, Skills, and Abilities Statements (KSAs)

Some organizations, such as the United States government, encourage or require the inclusion of KSAs in job announcements and require all applicants to address the KSAs. Typically, the position announcement will list three or more KSAs, which the applicant is required to address. A KSA is a statement of required knowledge, skills, and abilities that are either essential or very important to the performance of the advertised position. Here are two examples of KSAs:

- Ability to effectively communicate orally with people at all levels within an   organization, including executives, managers, and staff, and to articulate concepts verbally.

- Ability to collect and analyze information, prepare reports, and present studies, recommending courses of action as appropriate.

Rather than approaching KSAs as another chore to be endured in the job-hunting process, it is important to look at KSAs as opportunities to show how your knowledge, skills, and abilities relate to the needs of the employer. Use KSAs to give examples of how you have demonstrated the skills that are listed in the KSAs. For example, if a KSA statement includes supervision, your introductory response might be:

> For XYZ Corporation, I supervised seven administrative staff members. I organized a weekly work plan and distributed work assignments. I conducted regular meetings and encouraged my staff to suggest improvements and changes in how we could better accomplish our unit's goals.

You would then go on to give specific examples of supervisory experience.

It is perfectly all right to use "I" in a KSA response. In fact, it is preferable, as it emphasizes what you have accomplished and how you have performed. When applying for most positions, you may only have your resumé and cover letter to relate your skills and experience to a position. KSAs give you the opportunity to take skills and accomplishments from any part of your experience and put them together to relate to the needs of a potential employer. Be sure to take advantage of any opportunity that you have to relate your experience to an employer's needs. If a job announcement requires KSAs, you can welcome the opportunity to prepare your responses.

Some employers are beginning to use online application programs that require you to answer a series of questions and to give narrative explanations of some of your answers. Use the same approach in writing these responses as you would in writing KSAs.

Online Application Programs

Increasingly, large businesses and government agencies are using specialized online application programs that are specifically directed to meet the requirements of an organization. They require the applicant to complete an extensive online application.

One program used by all United States Department of Defense agencies, and also by the Disney Corporation, is *Resumix*, which requires the applicant to build a resumé within the system. This is a "keyword/skill" system, which can be programmed to scan for keywords and skills that are identified by managers. In addition to the resumé, there are up to 20 supplemental questions that the applicant must answer. If you are applying for a position that uses *Resumix* or another keyword system, you should adjust your resumé and carefully complete the online application. A useful reference for preparing an application for a keyword selection system is:

Peterson's (1996) *The job hunter's word finder*, Munising, MI: Peterson's Publishing Co.

QuickHire is a different type of online application system that is used by many federal agencies and other organizations. Applicants can copy and paste their resumés into the system and there is a limit to the size of the resumé. Applicants must then answer a series of questions, many of which are multiple choice. Some questions may require an essay to support a response. Some organizations that use *QuickHire* and other similar systems may initially screen applicants on the basis of their responses to the multiple choice questions or by using responses to a combination of short answer, multiple choice, and essay questions.

When applying for a position that uses an online application system, it is very important to find out what system is being used and on what basis the screening of applicants will take place. If you are uncertain about how your application will be screened, check with the hiring official who is usually listed on a vacancy announcement or with the organization's human resources office. Because the Federal Government uses many of these systems in its hiring, a worthwhile resource in preparing online applications is

Troutman, K. K. (2007) *Federal resume guidebook* (4th ed.). Indianapolis, IN: JIST Works.

CHAPTER 22

Employment Interviewing

It is rare that someone is hired for a job without an employment interview. Interviews are a necessary and critical component of your job campaign strategy because:

- An interview gives the employer the opportunity to meet you in person and to evaluate your attitude, appearance, personality, confidence, and knowledge about yourself.

- An interview gives you the opportunity to meet the employer, to look over the organization in person, and to evaluate the specific job for which you are applying.

This two-way appraisal includes the employer asking, "Will this applicant fit into our organization?" and you asking, "Will this position fit in with my career goals?" Both are equally important. Employment interviewing can be stressful if you give all the decision power to the employer. However, with proper preparation, conducting an employment interview can be a very positive and valuable part of your job campaign. How can you maintain as much control as possible over employment interviewing? Here are some strategies that you can use to develop effective job interviewing techniques.

KNOW WHAT YOU WANT TO ACCOMPLISH

Keep your purpose in mind. Why are you at this interview? According to Richard Lathrop (1989, p. 194), there are three primary objectives of a job interview.

1. To convince the employer to hire you because you have the appropriate skills, abilities, personality, and interests for that job.

2. To evaluate the job, setting, employer, coworkers, and company. Do you want to work here?

3. To demonstrate how the employer would benefit if you were hired. Discuss the employer's needs—not yours.

BE PREPARED—USE THE 4 R'S

Preparation is vital. Planning improves your performance, especially in employment interviewing. You can reduce the discomfort that usually accompanies employment interviewing by investing time and energy in preparation. This is the one aspect of the job-hunting process where you have complete control. Candidates who are uncomfortable with employment interviewing often report feelings of powerlessness and fear of the unknown. Preparation is one action that you can take to allay the negative feelings that can interfere with your ability to conduct a good interview. The 4 R's present ways that you can maintain control and feel positive about the process of employment interviewing.

Reflect

- Reaffirm your skills and abilities.

- Review your self-assessment in Section 1.

- Determine what aspects of your experience relate to the job and the employer's needs.

- Make a list of your accomplishments that relate to the position for which you are applying. Write them down. This will help you to remember them during an interview.

- Consider what you can contribute to the organization and be prepared to talk about this.

- Compare your values to the organization's philosophy.

- Know what aspects of your experience and skills you want to share in the interview.

- Think through your career goals in relationship to this job.

Research

- Obtain information about the organization through human resources, the public relations office, and the Internet. Some examples are:

  - annual reports
  - policy statements
  - employee handbooks
  - employee newsletters

- Use the Internet and libraries to access literature, including any recent newspaper articles, about the organization.

- Develop appropriate questions that reflect your research. Be prepared to ask questions that relate to the needs of the employer.

- Obtain a copy of the job description.

- Visit before interview day so that you are sure of the location and to get a feel for the atmosphere.

- If possible talk with employees about the organization.

- Try to learn something about the individuals who will be interviewing you.

- Use the technique of informational interviewing, if appropriate.

Rehearse

- Practice your interviewing technique in front of a mirror, with an audio or videotape recorder, and do a mock interview with a friend.

- Review your body language.

- Use gestures that emphasize your points rather than detract from your interview.

- Be yourself—allow your uniqueness to show through.

- Remember to smile in practice sessions and during the interview. It relaxes the facial muscles and communicates positive feelings to the employer.

- Have in mind those accomplishments that you really want to talk about in the interview and plan how you can bring them up.

Remember

- Pack your resumé, a blank pad of paper, a good pen, questions that you have developed, references' names and addresses, and data on the organization.

- Select work samples, portfolios, brochures, letters, and reports that display your skills.

- Choose clothing that corresponds with the work environment and the position that you are seeking. When in doubt, overdress.

- Reduce all unnecessary stress on the actual day of your interview.

- Allow extra time to arrive early. Be sure to get the interviewer's name and phone number. Get good directions to the interview site.

- Never go to an interview without first checking the organization's Web site.

- Before the interview, turn off your cell phone.

USE NONTRADITIONAL METHODS OF GETTING INTERVIEWS

Be creative in arranging for interviews. This can be particularly important if you are changing careers. Some possible approaches include:

1. **Uncover the informal hiring system** by talking with employees. The formal hiring system usually involves the human resources office, and you want to have other options available to you.

2. **Be referred by an employee.** By developing a comfortable relationship through informational interviewing, you could be recommended for a particular job. Most people get their jobs through people they know. Employers usually prefer to hire people who are known quantities.

3. **Develop your referral network.** Talk with people who do what you would like to do. Some clever ways of meeting contacts are in elevators, the company cafeteria, a local restaurant, the ladies' or men's rooms, or local night spots where employees gather. You may choose their offices also, but sometimes the clever ways pay off.

4. **Informational interviewing is the most effective way of uncovering unadvertised job openings.** Calling a potential employer for information is less threatening than asking for a job interview. Informational interviewing is one of the best ways of finding out about possible job openings and how your qualifications may relate to those openings.

CONDUCT YOUR EMPLOYMENT INTERVIEW WITH STYLE

There is no one right way to interview. Relax and be yourself. Remember that this process is a two-way appraisal that requires active listening and active participation. Passivity is not an effective strategy in employment interviewing or in job hunting. Remember the following guidelines for job interviewing.

1. Use the 8 E's of interviewing.

   Enthusiasm for the position and the organization shows you at your best.

   Energy is demonstrated through your attitude and in your resume. Show that you can take action.

   Eye contact between you and the interviewer is essential.

   Elaborate on the questions but be succinct. Don't use one-sentence answers.

   Exchange ideas because the interview is a two-way appraisal. Don't forget to do your evaluation of the organization.

   Equality exists in the interviewing relationship. Retain your personal power.

   Ease in interviewing comes from practice. Breathe deeply and smile to aid relaxation.

   Etiquette is also important in interviewing. Shake hands, thank your interviewer, and immediately write a follow-up letter, thanking the interviewer for the opportunity to interview.

2. The person interviewing you may not be a good interviewer because he or she may not know how to guide the interview to bring out your skills. If the interview gets sidetracked, take the initiative in getting back on track.

3. Explain how you could meet the needs of the organization by contributing your expertise.

4. Demonstrate your experience. Offer suggestions or ideas that may help the organization.

5. Do not bring up questions regarding pay, vacations, and benefits. Wait until the employer mentions them.

6. Don't volunteer negative information about yourself and don't criticize former employers or coworkers. Show pride in your past performance.

7. Don't accept or reject a job offer on the spot. Allow yourself some time to discuss it with others and think about it yourself.

8. Do not misrepresent yourself. Falsifying skills or experience can backfire.

9. Have some solid questions about the organization and the position for which you are applying. Research your questions through the use of company information.

10. If the employer indicates that you will not be selected, ask for other referrals or advice.

11. The interview practices of organizations vary. Attempt to clarify the type of interview that will be used so that you can prepare effectively for the event.

SAMPLE INTERVIEW QUESTIONS

The following questions are representative of those that you might be asked during an interview. Think of how you would answer them. It will help you to be better prepared. Avoid memorized or "canned" answers because they may show through in your interview. Be honest, be yourself, be natural, and be responsive. Listen carefully to each question asked.

- What has brought you to this point in your career?
- What did you like and dislike about your previous jobs?
- Why do you want this job?
- How does this position fit into your future plans?
- What do you want to be doing five years from now? ten years?
- What are your strengths? What are your weaknesses?

- What could you have done better on your last job?

- What can you do for this company?

- What interests you about our service or product?

- What are your salary requirements?

- What do you like to do with your leisure time?

- How do you respond to pressure?

- What would you like to accomplish during your lifetime?

- How do you plan to achieve your goals?

- How important is job satisfaction in your life?

- What kind of people do you enjoy working with? dislike working with?

- What have you done recently that shows your initiative and willingness to work?

- How would you describe yourself to others?

- How do you feel about overtime?

- What was the last book you read?

- What type of supervision do you prefer?

- Are you able to list some character and employer references?

- How do you feel about our organization so far?

- What is your ideal job?

- Describe your concept of success.

STRUCTURED INTERVIEWS

Many organizations use "behavior-based" questions in employment interviews. These are questions that require you to explain how you dealt with a specific problem, how you made a decision, how you resolved an issue, or how you achieved a goal. Typically, these interviews are conducted by a panel of interviewers who ask the same questions of all the candidates. This approach helps to provide a consistent, thoughtful way of conducting interviews in which all candidates are treated equally. However, it requires more preparation on the part of candidates. Here are some examples of interview questions that might be asked:

- Describe a situation in which you were able to use persuasion to convince someone to see things your way.

- Describe a time when you were faced with a stressful situation that challenged your coping skills.

- Describe a specific example of a time when you used good judgment and logic in solving a problem.

- Tell me about a time when you had to go above and beyond the call of duty in order to get a job done.

- Tell me about a time when you had too many things to do and you were required to prioritize your tasks.

- What is your typical way of dealing with conflict? Give me an example of a situation in which you resolved a conflict.

- Describe two examples of specific situations in which you showed initiative and took the lead.

- Tell me how you go about motivating others and then give a specific example of a situation in which you motivated others.

- Tell me about a time when you delegated a project effectively.

- Describe a time when you anticipated potential problems and developed preventive measures.

- Tell me about a time when you were forced to make an unpopular decision.

- Describe a situation in which you had to deal with people who were upset about a problem.

These questions require specific responses. Unless you have done a considerable amount of preparation, you may forget actions or accomplishments in your past that you could use in answering these questions. Therefore, plan to do the following well ahead of your interview:

1. Carefully reread the vacancy announcement and the job description.

2. Think about all of your past experience, not just your current position. Write down as many accomplishments and actions that you have taken that you might be able to use in answering interview questions. Organize these in categories, based on how you might use them to address different types of questions.

3. In reviewing your accomplishments, there will probably be several that are very relevant to the position for which you are applying. You want to be sure to talk about these in the interview, so plan to use them when you craft your responses. Write down these special accomplishments. Make them part of your list.

4. Before the interview, review your list several times. You will probably not remember all of the accomplishments and actions that you have written down, but you will remember and use many more of them than if you had not prepared for the interview.

5. Identify your strengths and your weaknesses and be prepared to respond to a question about them. Have a specific example in mind to give for each strength. In sharing a weakness, consider discussing something that was not a strength but that you have worked on to improve your skills.

6. It is very possible that you will be asked to say something about yourself. You want to give a thoughtful response that is not too long. Here is a suggested approach to responding to this request.

Tell Me About Yourself: Constructing the Two Minute Drill*

Start with the present. Briefly describe your current role in plain English.
I'm an accountant with the Government Accountability Office here in Washington. I work with a team of six accountants in the agency's Financial Investigation section. Right now, I am working on the audit of an agency that has an annual budget of more than $10 billion.

Then summarize your past experience.
Before coming to the GAO, I worked at the General Services Administration for five years and with Price-Waterhouse for three years. I spent much of my time helping both organizations to automate their accounting systems. I also trained staff teams to use customized accounting software. I got my CPA in '96 and am looking at area MBA programs.

Share some future possibilities. Mention your plans for the future and consider including what you hope to gain from this particular conversation.
Because of my experience in both the private and federal sectors, I have gained a broad exposure to large accounting operations. I'd like an opportunity to integrate what I've learned from both environments and advise organizations on new technologies and best practices. That is why I am very interested in this position.

*Used with permission from materials adapted by Dr. Barbara Suddarth, Career Development Alliance

7. In responding to structured interview questions using specific examples that demonstrate your qualifications, consider the following three part approach:

Situation, problem or task.
Describe the situation or problem that you confronted or the task that you needed to accomplish. You must describe a specific event or situation, not a generalized description of what you have done in the past. Be sure to give enough detail for the interviewer(s) to understand. This situation can be from a previous job, from a volunteer experience, or any relevant event.

Your action.
Describe the action you took and be sure to keep the focus on you. Even if you are discussing a group project or effort, describe what you did, not the efforts of the team. Don't tell what you **might** do. Tell what you **did**.

Results you achieved.
What happened? How did the event end? What did you accomplish? What did you learn?

8. After you have answered, you may wish to verify with the interviewers that you have answered the question, especially if the question has several parts. Don't be disturbed if the interviewers take notes.

9. If you have the opportunity to ask questions, demonstrate your interest in meeting the needs of the employer by asking questions about the employer's needs, challenges, and goals. With your questions, show your interest in the organization.

TEN KEY CONSIDERATIONS FOR EFFECTIVE INTERVIEWING

According to Richard Lathrop (1989, p. 197), the following are the ten most important factors that employers consider when evaluating an interviewee.

1. Appropriate clothing

2. Good grooming

3. A firm handshake

4. The appearance of controlled energy

5. Pertinent humor and a readiness to smile

6. A genuine interest in the employer's operations and alert attention when the interviewer speaks

7. Pride in past performance

8. An understanding of the employer's needs and a desire to serve them

9. The display of sound ideas

10. Ability to take control when employers fall down on the interviewing job

FOLLOW-UP

After the interview, it is important for you to follow up with your contacts. Perseverance pays off.

- Review what happened in your interview. What could you have done to make it better? What else could you have emphasized?

- Send a typed thank-you letter to the employer, preferably within 24 hours of the interview. If you know that regular mail will take more than a few days to arrive, consider sending your thank-you letter via email.

- Call the following week to express your continuing interest in the position.

- If you are not offered the job, leave the door open for future contact. Another job may open up. Ask for other suggestions and alternatives. It is generally not a good idea to ask why you were not selected, as this may put the employer in an awkward situation and may foreclose your opportunity for future contacts with the employer.

- Keep in contact with the employer.

INTERVIEW CHECKLIST

Preparation

_____ Know your skills and abilities—what you have to offer.

_____ Know your career goal(s).

_____ Research the company or organization through print and electronic resources.

_____ Have a resumé with which you feel satisfied.

_____ Know about your field of interest—openings, salary ranges, possible jobs.

Filling Out the Application

_____ Always try to fill out the application before you arrive for the interview.

_____ Read the instructions carefully.

_____ Use your correct name, not a nickname.

_____ Answer every question that applies to you, or use N/A if not applicable.

_____ Have available the correct names and addresses of people that you can use as professional and personal references.

_____ Employers expect you to state the kind of work in which you are interested. Therefore, state clearly your particular interest. Do not write the word "anything" in answer to this question.

_____ If there is a blank for "Salary Desired" only give a salary range if you have an accurate idea of what can be expected of this position.

_____ Check the application fully upon completion for possible errors.

_____ When describing your past work, be sure to emphasize your accomplishments.

For the Big Day

_____ Dress appropriately.

_____ Make arrangements for transportation necessary to get you to the interview on time.

_____ Arrive ten minutes early for the interview.

_____ Know the interviewer's name.

_____ Do not take friends, parents, or children with you to the interview.

_____ Be prepared to state your qualifications briefly and intelligently.

_____ Bring your resumé.

_____ Bring pen and paper with you.

The Interview Itself

_____ Introduce yourself, shake hands, and state the purpose of your visit.

_____ Smile and look directly at your interviewer(s).

_____ Be a good listener; make sure you listen carefully to the interviewer(s) questions.

_____ Answer all questions briefly and intelligently.

_____ Ask questions that show your interest in the organization and your willingness to contribute.

_____ Make sure that you present your skills and accomplishments that relate to the position for which you are applying.

_____ Be sincere, honest, and enthusiastic.

_____ Do not bring up salary questions, but be prepared to respond if asked. (See Negotiating a Salary.)

_____ Leave family or personal problems at home.

_____ Show pride in your past performance.

_____ Do not be critical of former employers or coworkers.

_____ Once the interview is over thank the person for her time and consideration.

Afterwards (Phew!)

_____ Make each interview a learning experience.

_____ How could you improve your next interview?

_____ What points could you stress more strongly?

_____ Practice will help you with your next interview.

_____ Send a thank-you letter.

Frame your previous experiences positively!

TYPES OF INTERVIEWS

Panel Interviews

In these type of interviews, a panel of people will interview you. Members of the panel typically will take turns asking questions. In your responses, try to make eye-contact with all of the panel members but pay special attention to the person who asks you the question. Try not to get upset if panel members are making notes while you are responding.

Behavioral Interviews

A behavioral interview, which is often called a structured interview, can be conducted by an individual or a panel, but the primary feature of this type of interview is its emphasis on specific actions that you have taken. You will be asked to give examples of what you have done and may be asked to describe how you would handle hypothetical situations. In responding to behavioral questions, be as specific as possible. State the problem or situation that you confronted and what your role was at the time. Then describe the action that you took and, if possible, the result of your action. In responding to a hypothetical situation, try to give an example from your experience that illustrates how you would handle the situation. In order to effectively conduct a behavioral interview, it is very important to do your homework. Refer to the section on structured interviews earlier in this chapter.

Computer-Assisted Interviews

Computer-assisted job interviews are becoming more common, especially when screening large numbers of candidates. These "interviews" provide an opportunity for employers to obtain responses that are structured and can be easily quantified and analyzed. You will most likely encounter computer-assisted job interviews when you apply for entry-level jobs in fields that require a large number of workers. The process is normally used to screen out unqualified applicants.

You usually complete a computer-assisted interview at an employer's human resources office and it will probably consist of a number of short answer or multiple choice questions on your work experience, education, training, attitudes toward work, skills, and other related topics. Remember that this process will be used for screening and you will usually be interviewed in person if you survive the initial screening.

You should prepare for a computer-assisted interview as you would for an in-person interview. You need to articulate your experience and training, your goals, and what you can contribute to the organization. It is extremely important that you learn all that you can about the organization and the field before beginning any interview, but especially a computer-assisted interview.

Internet Interviews

This type of interview is very similar to a computer-assisted interview, except that you are asked to answer a series of questions via email rather than traveling to the organization's human resource office.

Telephone Interviews

If you apply for a position that is some distance away, you may be asked to participate in a telephone interview. The general guidelines for telephone interviews are the same as for in-person interviews, except that you must give special attention to demonstrating your enthusiasm about the position and engaging your interviewer(s) in a dialogue during the telephone interview. Avoid giving one-sentence answers simply because of the impersonality of the telephone conference. Take a very active role in structuring the interview so that you can showcase your skills, experience, and personality. If you are given a choice between a telephone and an in-person interview, you should always opt for the in-person interview, even if it is inconvenient. Remember that an effective job campaign involves expense of both time and money. The investment of your resources to travel to an in-person interview may be very worthwhile.

Negotiating a Salary

Congratulations! You have received a job offer. Now you must consider the proposed salary and related benefits. It is generally not a good idea to accept or reject a job offer on the spot. Express your appreciation to the employer, ask for any additional information that you might use in making your decision, and tell the employer specifically when you will respond, usually within a day or two. Remember that you now have an opportunity to negotiate, since the employer has made a decision that you are the person for the job. This is the point in the job-finding process when you have the most power, and this is especially true if your field is one with a shortage of qualified personnel.

While you have a good deal of power, it is important to avoid being arrogant. You may be working with these people. You may wish to negotiate salary and benefits, but must do so in a positive way. It also helps if you have some idea about the amount of flexibility that the employer has in the offer of salary and benefits.

The research that you have done during the job campaign should help you to know the salary range for this and comparable positions and if the employer has flexibility in determining your salary and benefits. While many organizations leave room for negotiations, others, especially public organizations such as school systems, may have a rigid salary scale that offers little room for negotiations. Use some of the Web sites described in Chapter 15 to obtain salary information. This can help as you enter the salary negotiation process.

By all means wait until you have a job offer before you attempt to negotiate a salary. When you do make a counter offer, try to do it in person. Avoid negotiating just for salary. Consider other benefits such as an earlier merit increase, tuition, flexible hours, telecommuting, relocation expenses, paid memberships, and additional vacation time. Often, an employer may have more flexibility in providing these benefits than with the salary that can be offered. This is not the time to haggle. Your negotiations need to be very deliberate and professional.

SUMMARY

SECTION *four*

Conduct an Effective Job Campaign

This section has provided practical information on planning a job campaign. One important factor to remember is to keep active and maintain control over the situation. You need to protect yourself from rejection shock and have support systems built into your job campaign. You should be thoroughly prepared for each step in your campaign. This is not an easy process, but you greatly increase your chances of success by organizing and controlling your job campaign. Once you have a job or change jobs, your need to make thoughtful career and life decisions continues. Issues of career and life transitions, job revitalization, and lifestyle planning are always part of your life.

ADDITIONAL RESOURCES

Job Hunting and Networking

Allen, J. (2001). *Successful job search strategies for the disabled: Understanding the ADA.* New York: John Wiley & Sons, Incorporated.

Bolles, R. (2008). *What color is your parachute? 2009: A practical manual for job-hunters and career-changers.* Berkeley, CA: Ten Speed Press.

Bolles, R. & Bolles, M. E. (2008). *Job Hunting Online: A Guide to Using Job Listings, Message Boards, Research Sites, the Underweb, Counseling, Networking Self-Assessment Tools, Niche Sites.* Berkeley, CA: Ten Speed Press.

Bolles, R. N & Brown, D. S. (2000). *Job-hunting for the so-called handicapped: Or people who have disabilities.* Berkeley, CA: Ten Speed Press.

Chope, R. (2000). *Dancing naked. Breaking through the emotional limits that keep you from the job you want.* Oakland, CA: New Harbinger Publishing.

Darling, D. (2003). *The networking survival guide: Get the success you want by tapping into the people you know.* New York: McGraw-Hill Companies.

DeCarlo, L. & Guarneri, S. (2008). *Job search bloopers: Every mistake you can make on the road to career suicide . . . and how to avoid them.* Franklin Lakes, NJ: Career Press.

Dikel, M. & Roehm, F. (2008). *The guide to Internet job searching 2008–2009 edition.* New York: McGraw-Hill.

Doyle, A. (2008). *Internet your way to a new job: How to really find a job online.* Cupertino, CA: HappyAbout.info.

Doyle, A. (2006). *The About.com guide to job searching: All you need to get the job you want.* Avon, MA: Adams Media Corporation.

Fisher, D. & Vilas, S. (2000). *Power networking: 55 secrets for personal and professional success.* Austin, TX: Bard Press.

Geary, G. (2004). *Over-40 job search guide: 10 strategies for making your age an advantage in your career.* Indianapolis, IN: JIST Works.

Hansen, K. (2008). *A foot in the door: Networking your way into the hidden job market.* Berkeley, CA: Ten Speed Press.

Hawkins, G. (2004). *How to find work that works.* London: Jessica Kingsley Publishers.

Henderson, D. G. (2004). *Job search: Marketing your military experience.* Mechanicsburg, PA: Stackpole Books.

Kallos, J. (2004). *Because netiquette matters: Your comprehensive reference guide to e-mail etiquette and proper technology use.* Philadelphia, PA: Xlibris Corporation.

Kehn, R. (2002). *Internet job hunting.* Avon, MA: Adams Media Corporation.

Krannich, R. L. & Krannich, C. R. (2005). *The ex-offender's job hunting guide: 10 steps to a new life in the work world.* Manassas, VA: Impact Publications.

Lauber, D. (2002). *International job finder: Where the jobs are worldwide.* River Forest, IL: Planning Communications.

Piotrowski, K. (2009). *Career coward's guide to job searching: Sensible strategies for overcoming job search fears.* Indianapolis, IN: JIST Works.

Ryan, D. J. (2004). *Job search handbook for people with disabilities.* Indianapolis, IN: JIST Works.

Sautter, E. & Crompton, D. (2008). *Seven days to online networking: Make connections to advance your career and business quickly.* Indianapolis, IN: JIST Works.

Strawbridge, M. (2006). *Netiquette: Internet etiquette in the age of the blog.* Ely, Cambridgeshire, UK: Software Reference Ltd.

Tullier, L. M. (2004). *Networking for job search and career success.* Indianapolis, IN: JIST Works.

Wall, J. E. (2006). *Job seeker's online goldmine: A step-by-step guidebook to government and no-cost web tools.* Indianapolis, IN: JIST Works.

Weir, M. (2008). *Confessions of an introvert: The shy girl's guide to career, networking and getting the most out of life.* Naperville, IL: Sphinx Publishing.

Woodward. J. (2007). *Finding a job after 50: Reinvent yourself for the 21st century.* Franklin Lakes, NJ: Career Press.

Yate, M. (2007). *Knock 'em dead 2008: The ultimate job seeker's guide.* Holbrook, MA: Adams Media.

Employment Interviewing/Salary Negotiation

Adams, B., Bob Adams Publishers. (2005). *Adams job interview almanac.* Holbrook, MA: Adams Media Corporation.

Beshara, T. (2008). *Acing the interview: How to ask and answer the questions that will get you the job.* New York: AMACOM.

Chapman, J. (2006). *Negotiating your salary: How to make $1000 a minute.* Berkeley, CA: Ten Speed Press.

Dawson, R. (2006). *Secrets of power salary negotiating: Inside secrets from a master negotiator.* Franklin Lakes, NJ: Career Press.

Deluca, M. J. & Deluca, N. F. (2006). *Perfect phrases for negotiating salary and job offers: Hundreds of ready-to-use phrases to help you get the best possible salary, perks or promotion.* NY: McGraw-Hill.

Deluca, M. J. & Deluca, N. F. (2004). *24 hours to the perfect interview: Quick steps for planning, organizing, and preparing for the interview that gets the job.* New York: McGraw-Hill.

Deluca, M. J., & Deluca, N. F. (2001). *More best answers to the 201 most frequently asked interview questions.* New York: McGraw-Hill.

Fry, R. (2006). *101 great answers to the toughest interview questions.* (4th ed.): Clifton Park, NY: Thomson Delmar Learning.

Fry, R. (2006). *101 smart questions to ask in your interview.* Clifton Park, NY: Delmar Cengage Learning.

Kador, J. (2002). *201 best questions to ask on your interview.* New York: McGraw-Hill.

Kessler, R. (2006). *Competency-based interviews: Master the tough new interview style and give them the answers that will win you the job.* Franklin Lakes, NJ: Career Press.

Mathias, L. (2007). *How to say it: Job interviews.* Paramus, NJ: Prentice-Hall Press.

Medley, H. A. (2005). *Sweaty palms—the neglected art of being interviewed.* New York: Time Warner Business.

Oliver, V. (2005). *301 smart answers to tough interview questions.* Naperville, IL: Sourcebooks, Inc.

Resumé and Cover Letter Writing

Block, J. & Betrus, M. (2002). *2500 keywords to get you hired.* New York: McGraw-Hill.

Enelow, W. (2003). *Best resumes for people without a four-year degree.* Manassas, VA: Impact Publications.

Enelow, W. & Krannich, R. (2006). *Best resumes and letters for ex-offenders.* Manassas, VA: Impact Publications.

Enelow, W. & Kursmark, L. (2005). *Expert resumes for military-to-civilian transitions.* Indianapolis, IN: JIST Works.

Greene, B. (2004). *Get the interview every time: Fortune 500 hiring professionals' tips for writing winning resumes and cover letters.* Chicago: Dearborn Trade Publishing.

Ireland, S. (2006). *The complete idiot's guide to the perfect resume.* Royersford, PA: Alpha Publishing.

Isaacs, K. & Hofferber, K. (2003). *The career change resume: How to reinvent your resume and land your dream job.* New York: McGraw-Hill Companies.

Jackson, T. (2004). *The perfect resume: Today's ultimate job search tool.* Portland, OR: Broadway Books.

Kennedy, J. L. (2007). *Resumes for dummies.* New York: Hungry Minds.

Krannich, R. L. (2005). *Nail the cover letter: Great tips for creating dynamite letters.* Manassas, VA: Impact Publications.

Krannich, R. L. (2005). *Nail the resume: Great Tips for creating dynamite resumes.* Manassas, VA: Impact Publications.

Krannich, R. L. & Enelow, W. (2002). *Best resumes and CVs for international jobs: Your passport to the global job market.* Manassas, VA: Impact Publications.

Parker, Y. (2002). *Damn good resume guide: A crash course in resume writing.* Berkeley, CA: Ten Speed Press.

Savino, C. & Krannich, R. (2007). *Military-to-civilian resumes and letters: How to best communicate your strengths to employers.* Manassas, VA: Impact Publications.

Schuman, N. (2007). *Everything resume book: Create a winning resume that stands out from the crowd.* Holbrook, MA: Adams Media.

Smith, M. H. (2006). *Bioblogs: Resumes for the 21st century.* Manassas, VA: Impact Publications.

Wallace, R. (2005). *Adams resume almanac.* Holbrook, MA: Adams Media Corporation.

Washington, T. (2003). *Resume power: Selling yourself on paper in the new millennium* Bellevue, WA: Mt. Vernon Press.

Whitcomb, S. B. (2007). *Cover letter magic.* Indianapolis, IN: JIST Works.

Yate, M. (2006). *Cover letters that knock 'em dead.* Holbrook, MA: Adams Media.

Yate, M. (2006). *Resumes that knock 'em dead.* Holbrook, MA: Adams Media.

Federal Employment Resources

Damp, D. (2005). *The book of U.S. government jobs: Where they are, what's available, and how to get one* (9th ed.). Moon Township, PA: Brookhaven Press.

Government Job News and Info Tech Employment, eds. (2008). *Government jobs in America: U.S., state, city & federal jobs & careers—with job titles, salaries & pension estimates: Why you want one, what jobs are available, how to get one.* Washington, DC: Government Job News.

Troutman, K. K. (2007). *Federal resume guidebook: Write a winning federal resume to get in, get promoted, and survive in a government career!* Indianapolis, IN: JIST Works.

Troutman, K. K. (2003). *10 steps to a federal job: Navigating the federal system, writing federal resumes, KSA's and cover letters with a mission.* Indianapolis, IN: JIST Works.

Troutman, K. K., Troutman, E. K. & Roscoe, E. (2006). *Military to Federal career guide: Ten steps to transforming your military experience into a competitive federal resume.* Baltimore, MD: The Resume Place.

Whiteman, L. (2008). *How to land a top-paying federal job: Your complete guide to opportunities, internships, resumes and cover letters, application essays (KSAs), interviews, salaries, promotions and more!* New York: AMACOM.

SECTION *five*

Enhance Work Performance and Satisfaction

When you make a commitment to a job, it is important to do your best and seek opportunities for growth. Because success breeds other successes, you can create new opportunities and increase your work satisfaction by concentrating on doing the best possible job. You will increase your opportunities for promotions and for assuming new responsibilities. You will also decrease the possibility of losing your job or of becoming dissatisfied with your work.

It is helpful to review your work periodically so that you can make necessary changes. This review will help you to maintain your effectiveness on the job. It will help you to seek new challenges and opportunities without having to look for a new job. You may be able to avoid that "locked in" feeling that comes when you think that you have no place to go with your work.

Is it worthwhile to take time once in a while to review your work? Certainly! Few things are more important than your career satisfaction. Various studies of human behavior have shown that work satisfaction is a possible predictor of longevity, while dissatisfaction with one's job have many negative effects on an individual. It is important to take charge of your career and your life by periodically evaluating where you have been, where you are, and where you are going. This section will help you to make the most of your work.

CHAPTER 23

How to Be an Effective Worker

WORK SUCCESS SKILLS

What action can you take to improve your overall work status? Prepare, plan, and develop yourself to meet the challenge of making the most of your work. There are certain skills that will help you to be effective on your job and assist you in reaching your career goals. Think about what skills would be most important to success in your work.

If you were the boss, what skills would you want your employees to have?

1. _____
2. _____
3. _____
4. _____
5. _____

6. _____
7. _____
8. _____
9. _____
10. _____

> *Leaders in learning organizations are responsible for building organizations where people are continually expanding their capabilities to shape their future.*
>
> —Frederic M. Hudson, *The Adult Years*

Compare your list with these 15 qualities derived from recent ACT employer research (*Managesmarter*, 2006). These attitudes were identified by employers because of their need for qualified employees and because of intense competition for profit and productivity in their businesses.

1. **Carefulness.** Avoid costly errors by tending to detail which enables a steady and consistent work flow . . . be judicious.

2. **Cooperation.** Interact effectively with colleagues in the work environment through teamwork, networking, and collaboration . . . be a listener and a learner.

3. **Creativity.** Provide innovative problem solving to address diverse challenges and infuse fresh and novel perspectives . . . be a right-brained thinker.

4. **Discipline.** Stay on task to accomplish the desired result with minimal digressions despite routine or tedium . . . be dedicated.

5. **Drive.** Aspire to higher personal and professional goals and work hard to accomplish short and long range objectives . . . be an achiever.

6. **Good attitude.** Develop strong work habits and attitudes such as initiative, dependability, reliability, and unselfishness . . . be a role model.

7. **Goodwill.** Assume the best intentions of others rather than presuming the negative . . . be a positive force.

8. **Influence.** Hone your leadership skills to positively impact the work environment through confident persuasion and negotiation . . . be a leader.

9. **Optimism.** Earn respect and admiration by demonstrating a positive and upbeat work ethic regardless of rank or job title . . . be ethical.

10. **Order.** Develop a system to eliminate chaos in your personal and professional life to expedite the important and eliminate the unimportant . . . be focused.

11. **Safe work behaviors.** Avoid accidents as well as self-injurious behavior patterns and maintain a healthy lifestyle to eliminate unnecessary risk-taking in work and home environments . . . be healthy.

12. **Savvy.** Focus on the big picture and remain attentive to political and social clues in the work environment . . . be astute about the work culture.

13. **Sociability.** Enjoy colleagues and build effective connections for a productive and satisfying work climate . . . be enthusiastic.

14. **Stability.** Remain composed and rational, especially in anxious or stressful times at work . . . be solid emotionally and mentally.

15. **Vigor.** Get the job done with an upbeat tempo and a can-do attitude . . . be a force of nature.

These are very worthwhile skills to develop, because they are highly valued by employers. If you enhance these skills, you are more likely to open new opportunities in your work. If you take the time and effort to develop these skills it is also much less likely that you will lose your job. **Remember that these are primarily self-management skills. You have control over them and they transfer from one job to another.**

What work success skills would you like to develop or improve? Try to list at least five.

1. _____

2. _____

3. _____

4. _____

5. _____

In the following spaces, give one example of how you can take action to develop or improve each of these five work success skills.

1. _____

2. _____

3. _____

4. _____

5. _____

FIFTEEN TACTICS FOR CAREER GROWTH

The last section focused on 15 qualities, or work success skills, that can enhance effectiveness in the workplace. These qualities are, by definition, considered self-management skills because you have control over how you demonstrate these qualities on a daily basis. Focusing on these qualities will assist you as an employee, an entrepreneur, or as a job seeker. The attitude that you bring to your current position will be enhanced, or these qualities could assist you in obtaining a new position. Now that you have identified an action plan to improve your work success skills, what can you do to grow in your position or as an entrepreneur?

The following tactics for career growth can help you develop your skills, expand your network of contacts, feel better about yourself, and enjoy your work. In addition to the work success skills that you identified, consider these career growth tactics. They can help you to keep your job *and* to grow in your career.

1. **Learn to read the management signs.** Be aware of new developments in your organization that may present opportunities for you. Keep informed about the organization's policies and priorities and look for danger signals of potential cutbacks, layoffs, and firings *before* they happen. In a time of retrenchment, you may be able to save your job or move to another one rather than hiding your head in the sand and saying "That would *never* happen to me!"

2. **Document your achievements.** A record of your accomplishments can be valuable for negotiating raises, promotions, and, in extreme cases, to help you to keep your job. Make significant contributions to the organization through your creativity, dedication, and hard work. Keep a log of these contributions.

3. **Get out of your box.** Become knowledgeable about other areas within your organization and develop skills that would transfer from one job to another. If someone is sick for the day, ask to fill in for that person so that you can broaden your base of knowledge about the organization. Whenever possible, visit someone in person rather than sending an e-mail message or telephoning. The more skills you possess and the more people you know, the more valuable you are to the organization.

4. **Think like management.** If you have to make a decision or solve a problem, try to assess how the management of your organization would like you to act. Ask yourself how your supervisor or your supervisor's supervisor would want you to respond, given their orientation and the goals of the organization. Take this into consideration before taking action.

5. **Concentrate on the things over which you have control.** Use your time at work effectively. Invest your effort in the activities and projects over which you have control. You, and others, will be able to see the direct result of your work. Avoid spending too much of your time and effort on general issues where there is little that you can do to affect the outcome.

6. **Prepare for your next job.** The emphasis on lifelong learning is here to stay. You will need more education and training, given the rapid changes in the world of work. Here are some ways to keep learning.

   - On-the-job professional development programs
   - Adult education programs
   - Apprenticeships and cooperative education
   - Community college programs
   - Weekend college and other specialized course offerings
   - Private, trade, or technical schools
   - Home study through correspondence courses
   - Industrial training programs
   - Government and military training programs
   - Four-year college or university programs

7. **Promote yourself.** This may be uncomfortable for you, but think of it as taking the initiative to inform others in your organization about your projects. Talk about your accomplishments with coworkers and supervisors to keep them up to date with your projects. Inform, but don't boast.

8. **Find a mentor.** A mentor can help you understand and possibly gain access to the inner structure of your organization. Select someone you admire, and attempt to establish a positive professional relationship. Ideally, your mentor should be in a position to help you to grow and provide you with valuable advice and support.

9. **Continue informational interviewing.** By continuing to develop your informational interviewing techniques, as described in Section 3, you can enlarge and enrich your circle of professional contacts, keep up to date in your field, and discover potential career growth opportunities.

10. **Think success.** What are your motivating skills? Certain activities give you a thrill of success. It could be organizing a baseball game or raising funds for your PTA. Identify these skills and use them in your everyday life. If organizing is a motivating skill, use it at work to reorganize outdated systems. If raising funds interests you, build this into your work or community service.

> *The greatest discovery in our generation is that human beings, by changing the inner attitudes of their minds, can change the outer aspects of their lives.*
>
> —William James

11. **Show a genuine interest in others.** Do your best to work cooperatively with others. Show an interest in their work and value what they do. Form support systems and be supportive of others.

12. **Always be willing to learn.** Learn as much as possible about your job and the organization in which you work. Take any opportunity to attend in-service seminars, classes, skill-building workshops, and other training programs. Many organizations highly value their training programs and the employees who choose to participate.

13. **Be willing to take on new challenges.** Seize opportunities to meet new challenges in your work. There may be some risk involved, but usually the risk is worth taking.

14. **Maintain a positive attitude.** Be willing to help others and be nice to others. People will stay away from someone who is always depressed or negative. A positive attitude will help you to feel better about your work and will cause others to be positive toward you.

15. **Be open to change.** Be willing to accept suggestions from others. Avoid being defensive if you are criticized. Encourage comments from others and show that you are open to new ideas and procedures.

These tactics will help you to:

- grow in your work
- keep your job
- enjoy your work and your life
- learn new skills
- be in position for promotions
- position yourself for organizational changes

Remember that you have a great deal of control over your work because you control your attitude, your skills, and, to a certain extent, how others respond to you.

PROFESSIONAL DEVELOPMENT

Professional development should be a part of everyone's work. Some organizations provide regular opportunities for professional development by encouraging training in new technologies, continuing education, attendance at conferences, and other activities designed to enhance an employee's career. Other organizations provide few or no incentives for professional growth. An organization's commitment to professional development should be a factor in making a decision whether to work for the organization.

Remember, whatever the organizational commitment is to professional development, you have the primary responsibility for your professional growth. Just as you must take charge of the direction of your life and career, you must take charge of your own professional development. Your coworkers may complain about the lack of promotion opportunities or professional development and use this as an excuse to do nothing about advancement or learning valuable skills. Even if your present employer does not support or encourage your professional development, there are many challenging and rewarding professional development activities that you can create. The following is a listing of the steps you can take to enhance your professional growth both on and off your job.

Professional Development Opportunities in the Workplace

1. Volunteer to take on new assignments, especially those in which you will be required to learn a new skill.

2. Challenge yourself by accepting new responsibilities for short or extended periods. Expand your outlook by taking on selected aspects of a colleague's job.

3. Train on the job in new technologies, new procedures, and new techniques. Take advantage of in-house training opportunities.

4. Create opportunities to solve old problems or to develop new systems with a team of colleagues. Develop yourself professionally by discovering new approaches to the organization's concerns.

5. Wage a campaign for self-improvement by participating in workshops that deal with topics such as stress and time management, communication skills, relaxation techniques, and health and exercise. Personal growth leads to professional enhancement by increasing creativity, energy, and productivity. Integrate health and balance into your daily routine.

6. Read professional literature that may be available through your human resources office, library, mail system, and the World Wide Web. Look for and attend seminars that offer new ideas.

7. Serve on committees or task forces charged with critical issues such as planning and evaluation.

8. Continue informational interviewing by meeting with colleagues and sharing ideas. Learn about your career and how your skills would be integrated into other organizations. Discuss new approaches to work responsibilities and to fulfilling the goals of your organization. Listen to how others have dealt with challenges similar to those that you face.

9. Represent your organization at local, state, and national conferences or conventions. Offer to present your unique ideas or to serve on planning committees.

10. Investigate tuition assistance opportunities, educational or professional leave, purchase of materials, or any other support for professional growth that your organization provides.

11. Write articles or promotion pieces for journals or newsletters. Contribute to your career and your organization by sharing personal research, innovative ideas, and your opinions.

12. Study with experts in your field. Identify individuals who have achieved distinction and read what they have written. Arrange to hear them speak. Take any opportunity to study with them.

13. Mentor students or interns of any age and at any educational level. Offering your expertise to students learning your profession can help you to clarify your own goals, to learn about new developments in your field, and to make a contribution to others.

Professional Development Opportunities Outside of Your Workplace

1. Register for courses and seminars. Work toward certificates and degrees that will give you credentials and enhance your professional growth.

2. Join professional associations, attend meetings, and volunteer to be an active member.

3. Become an officer or board member of a civic, neighborhood, religious, or professional organization.

4. Develop informal networks of colleagues. Arrange for regular meetings to discuss issues. Find a mentor.

5. Actively work to stay current in the developments in your field. Read professional literature. Write an article, book review, or commentary for a professional journal. Teach a course in which you share your knowledge and experience.

6. Consider all forms of enrichment opportunities sponsored by adult education programs, clubs, churches, community colleges, universities, and community agencies.

7. Give yourself time to reflect, relax, and renew. Some of your best, most creative, and most effective work may be sparked while you are taking a walk, sitting by the side of a stream, climbing a mountain, or traveling in the country. Listen to yourself.

8. Expand your interests. Too much time spent on work issues can negatively influence your ability to grow, to remain enthusiastic, and to be productive on the job. Develop a range of outlets for all seasons that you can enjoy alone or with family and friends. One of the best ways to develop professionally is to be able to concentrate completely on activities that have nothing to do with your career.

9. Maintain good eating habits and have a regular exercise program. Taking care of your body can have a profound influence on your work effectiveness, on your family relationships, and on your mental attitude.

10. Learn, learn, learn all that you can in as many ways as you can as quickly as you can.

EVOLVING INTO A PERSON OF INFLUENCE

While it is important to think about the influence of others in our lives, your own personal influence is also a consideration. When you think of persons of influence, what characteristics do they possess? Think about those you admire most. Include people who are related to you, people in your neighborhood, people you work with, people you have read about, and people who have achieved local, national, or world significance. What qualities do you admire in them?

Name at least five characteristics that you believe are critical attributes for a person of influence. Then, prioritize them from one as the most important to five as the least important.

1. _____

2. _____

3. _____

4. _____

5. _____

After you have listed and prioritized these characteristics, analyze your own growth related to each of the characteristics. In column one, rate your development in each characteristic, providing your perspective on where you are in relationship to where you want to be. In column two, identify your satisfaction with your development.

Characteristics	My Development low high	My Satisfaction low high
1. _____	1 2 3 4 5	1 2 3 4 5
2. _____	1 2 3 4 5	1 2 3 4 5
3. _____	1 2 3 4 5	1 2 3 4 5
4. _____	1 2 3 4 5	1 2 3 4 5
5. _____	1 2 3 4 5	1 2 3 4 5

Take a few minutes to focus on your rating of your development and satisfaction. What patterns do you observe? What characteristics would you like to improve? Is there something that you can do to enhance your own sphere of influence? How can you maximize your influence to contribute to the world? These are questions for you to consider as you evolve and become a person of influence.

Illiteracy refers not to the inability to read but to the failure to learn how to learn throughout the life cycle.

—Frederic M. Hudson, *The Adult Years*

CHAPTER 24

Make Time Your Friend

Time is a finite and precious resource, yet it is often taken for granted. Without conscious decision making, we allow busyness to take over while events swirl around us. Time can be either a blessing or a curse. Describe your relationship with time in one word.

My relationship with time is

_____.

This chapter will help you to analyze your relationship with time by taking you through an assessment of time and values. It will help you focus on the guiding principles directing the expenditure of your time. Traditional time management techniques, which focus on your commitments and schedule and offer concrete tips for streamlining work and personal habits, may be important for you to consider in addition to this chapter. A section on time management can be found in Chapter 26.

Everyone, regardless of income, social status, background, or profession has 24 hours in a day. How you choose to allocate this most precious resource is your very personal decision.

What challenges you about the allocation of time in your work and home life? Do you feel trapped or overwhelmed by time? Do you . . .

- have competing demands for your time?
- feel conflicted about how to allocate time?
- feel pressured by not having enough time?
- see the solution as packing more responsibilities into smaller amounts of time?
- feel guilty about time allocation decisions?
- feel out of balance with the time in your life?
- feel anxiety and stress due to tremendous time pressures?
- allow responding to crisis after crisis to shape your days?

- become satisfied with short-term solutions rather than long-term adjustments that would be necessary to address bigger issues?

If you have answered "yes" to three or more of these questions, it is now TIME to examine your decisions and consider alternatives.

YOUR TIME ANALYSIS

If time is a curse rather than a blessing, complete the following time analysis adapted from *First Things First* by Steven Covey (1995, pp. 32–102). It is strongly recommended that you read this book if you would like to further address the clarification of time and values.

Read through the following four categories and think about how you allocate your time in a typical week. In what category do you spend most of your time? Write a percentage of time for each category so that the numbers add up to 100 percent, and describe the major activities within each category. Be patient with yourself as you think through a typical week's responsibilities and activities.

Category I: Crisis—Time with the Important and Urgent

Examples: Immediate problems, imminent deadlines, overwhelming projects, anything with immediate response time required

Percentage of time spent in a typical week _____

Describe your weekly activities and responsibilities in this category.

_____

_____

_____

Category II: Planning—Time with the Important and Not Urgent

Examples: Preparation, relationships, thinking, reading, developing strategies

Percentage of time spent in a typical week _____

Describe your weekly activities and responsibilities in this category.

_____

_____

_____

Category III: Interruptions—Time with the Not Important and Urgent

Examples: Some mail, some phone calls, many activities, some reports

Percentage of time spent in a typical week _____

Describe your weekly activities and responsibilities in this category.

_____

_____

_____

Category IV: Time Wasters

Examples: Trivia/minutia, irrelevant mail and calls, daydreaming, extensive personal involvement

Percentage of time spent in a typical week _____

Describe your weekly activities and responsibilities in this category

_____

_____

_____

Now that you have completed the Time Analysis, which category occupies most of your week in your work and home life? Most of your month?

_____

_____

_____

What have you learned from your Time Analysis about how you allocate your most precious resource? How might you better spend your time?

_____

_____

_____

If most of your activities and responsibilities are located in _Category I: Crisis_

If most of your time is taken up by activities and responsibilities that are important and urgent, you may wear out, maybe not today, but tomorrow. You most likely will not have time to complete this workbook or take stock of your situation because you are in perpetual motion. You know that you operate from a place of exhaustion and pain due to fear and a sense of lack of control. Maybe you have never experienced life outside of Category I. If so, the critical question for you is: **Will you still be important if what you do is not always urgent and important?** Basing your self-esteem and value on what you do rather than who you are is one of the issues that you will need to address before you attempt to move from one category to another. A balance of activities and responsibilities throughout the Time Analysis is desirable. Only **you** can decide what is the right balance for you.

If most of your activities and responsibilities are located in *Category II: Planning*

If you are like many adults, the activities and responsibilities characterized as important and not urgent seem to represent time spent with meaning and significance. The lower stress and anxiety means you have the luxury to be creative, thoughtful, and deliberate in your expenditure of time. Why should this time be a luxury rather than an important part of every day, or at the very least, every week? Assessing your own performance, identifying the learning gaps, and taking steps to fill them is critical to your own professional development. This is the category that allows for that type of activity. It is your responsibility in any position to build your expertise and increase your skills. If you are not allocating any time to this category, you will not keep up with others who attend to these critical self-growth areas. Make an appointment with yourself and log it in as you would any other appointment with a dignitary! Taking time to complete the exercises in this workbook is a Category II activity since it is an investment in you and your career. It empowers you to move forward with confidence and some measure of assurance that you are on the "right" track. Allocate the time you need to plan, organize, learn, and create your own future!

If most of your activities and responsibilities are located in *Category III: Interruptions*

Most work involves responsibilities that are considered urgent by someone, but often not by you. It is easy to feel at the mercy of the urgent and not important! Telephone calls, e-mail, faxes, and office interlopers find you wherever you are and when you least expect them. What a colleague defines as important and urgent may not be as important and urgent to you. Try to expeditiously negotiate the interruptions in your life with grace and respect. Every position has some responsibilities that are routine and urgent, but unimportant in the grand scheme of things. What can you do to affect the system and change the culture so that most of your responsibilities are considered important? Shuffling job responsibilities among coworkers is a way to bring everyone's expertise level up to a certain standard and is helpful when change of personnel becomes inevitable. Another way to view this category is to handle the "not important" detail tasks as though each one were very important and urgent. This may earn you respect and help you build expertise for career mobility. Ignoring urgent tasks, no matter how unimportant, may prove to be counterproductive to your career and the welfare of your organization. Accomplish these tasks with dispatch so you have time to spend in the planning category.

If most of your activities and responsibilities are located in *Category IV: Time Wasters*

What are you afraid of? Pick yourself up and get yourself going. Your unfulfilled potential as a human being, a worker, a citizen, and a contributing member of society is a loss to the entire universe. You are not challenging yourself to grow and bloom because of perceived obstacles that stand in your way. Address obstacles by acknowledging that they exist and distinguish between the ones that are outside of your control and those that are a product of your own thinking. Work with someone you admire and respect to help you overcome your fear of evolving into a person of influence. Stretch a little bit at a time by taking on small challenges.

YOUR TIME ACTION PLAN

If you are now occupying a category that is not fulfilling and satisfying to you, make a conscious commitment to the important by moving part of your day to the category that would be more beneficial to you. How do you accomplish this when you have conflicting demands imposed upon you by colleagues and supervisors? You move from a less desirable category to a more desirable one by choice and design, not by remaining subject to other people's schedules. You accomplish this by changing your thinking and possibly by changing your life. Your time is your most precious resource.

Changing your life is an option you may choose to accept once you analyze and acknowledge the realities of your own life. Try to take hold and consider the overarching issue of the value of time in your life. You have 24 hours each day to make a difference, create your contribution, and leave a legacy. No one has more hours than that. Make each day count toward what is important to you. Decide on how you want to live your life and do not acquiesce to the factors that you may think are outside of your control. How do **you** choose to allocate your most precious resource?

> *More stability of purpose is necessary to deal with less stability in the environment.*
>
> —Tom Peters, *Thriving on Chaos*

Manage Your Time Effectively

One way that you can take care of yourself is to maintain control of your time. Effective time management helps you to excel at your job and to be able to devote time to your other life priorities. You can feel much more in control and much less stressed if you can manage your time effectively. The following are some suggestions for improving your time management skills.

- **Establish priorities.** Think about what parts of your job and your life are most important. Make sure that you allow time for the things that mean the most to you.

- **Set goals.** Establish goals at work and outside your work. Evaluate the time that you spend in relation to your goals.

- **Make a schedule.** Plan ahead how you will spend your time. Make sure that your schedule reflects time spent on your goals and priorities.

- **Know what time of day is best for you.** Some people do their best work early in the morning; others are most productive or creative late at night. Try to schedule your most important activities during the time of day that is best for you.

- **Leave time each day for planning.** Spend a few minutes each day thinking about what you have to do. Consider your goals and priorities. Make plans for what you want to do rather than just responding to others' demands.

- **Have a daily "to do" list.** Make a list of things to do and then do them. Cross things off when you complete them. You will be more organized, less likely to forget things, and more satisfied with your accomplishments when you can cross several things off your list.

- **Use waiting time.** Everyone ends up waiting at some point during the day. Have something to read or something you can do while you are waiting. You may be surprised at how much you can do with this "found time."

- **Don't try to do everything at once.** Break down major projects into smaller tasks that you can accomplish in specific time segments. Avoid putting off major tasks until you have a large block of time to work on them, because it may be quite a while before you can devote a large block of time.

- **Handle paperwork efficiently.** Keep your paperwork organized. Try to handle each piece of paper just once.

- **Eliminate time wasters.** Avoid being drawn into activities that take up your time with little to show for it in the end. Cut out unnecessary functions. Look for ways to streamline procedures to save time.

- **Make an appointment with yourself.** Block off time for activities or planning just for you on a daily or weekly basis.

Now think about how you are spending your time. What are three things that you can do in the next week to manage your time more effectively?

1. _____

2. _____

3. _____

This is just a brief outline of some time management techniques. You may wish to consider taking a course or workshop in time management. It could be time well spent.

CHAPTER 25

Don't Be Your Own Worst Enemy

Some people have problems with their work because of situations over which they have little or no control. However, in many cases of work dissatisfaction, the problems come from within the individual. In this section, you will learn how to avoid causing problems for yourself. Are you creating blocks to your work satisfaction? What can you do to overcome blocks that are put there by others or by situations? Internal blocks to work satisfaction originate from your own feelings, perceptions, and actions. External blocks to work satisfaction originate from outside factors.

INTERNAL BLOCKS TO WORK SATISFACTION

Many people cause problems for themselves in their work environment. Unreasonable expectations, a negative attitude, an unwillingness to compromise, and work habits inconsistent with the requirements of the job are all internal blocks to job satisfaction and job success. These internal blocks can result in the loss of a job or in a very negative work situation. The following are examples of internal blocks to success.

- Frequent absences
- Frequently coming to work late
- Too much attention to outside interests
- Being irresponsible
- Being negative, making trouble
- Laziness
- Misrepresenting the facts of a situation
- Not being adaptable

- Carelessness
- Lack of initiative
- Disloyalty
- Unwillingness to follow rules
- Fear of change
- Unwillingness to take a risk
- Reluctance to try something new

There are many more internal blocks to work success. The most important thing to remember about these internal blocks is that **they are within your control. You can change them if you choose to.** It is important to analyze your own work style and to determine how it fits with the expectations of your job. For example, if you do not work well under pressure, you may wish to avoid taking a job in which you would constantly be faced with deadlines. If you have family responsibilities that often take you away from work, you may want to find an employer who is willing to give you some flexibility with your work hours. One way to avoid internal blocks to work success is to match your work style with the organization. This matching works both ways, but when you begin a job, it is unreasonable to expect the organization to bend significantly to meet your needs. You have the control, however, of the initial choice of where you work, the specific job you take, and adjusting your work style accordingly.

Assessment of Your Internal Blocks to Work Satisfaction

If you are currently employed or can think back to a previous job, list five *internal* blocks that have interfered with your work satisfaction.

Internal blocks

1. _____

2. _____

3. _____

4. _____

5. _____

What can you do to overcome these blocks? Remember that they come from within you, so you do have control over them. Some examples might be to take a course in time management, concentrate on the things you enjoy at work, consciously develop a more positive attitude, and look at change as an opportunity rather than as a threat. Try to think of at least one possible way of dealing with each of the internal blocks that you listed and write your ideas in the spaces below. Be creative!

How to deal with my internal blocks

1. _____

2. _____

3. _____

4. _____

5. _____

EXTERNAL BLOCKS TO WORK SATISFACTION

At some point in your work life you may be faced with an organizational shift that results in the loss of your job or in your arbitrary reassignment to other work. This could be called an external block, because you have little or no control over the situation. You may work with an organization that has inflexible rules about salary, vacation time, promotion, hours, or your daily responsibilities. You *may* find that the factors over which you

DON'T LET THE BLOCKS GET YOU DOWN!

have no control create an unacceptable situation, and you will have to look for other work. However, before you give up on a job, concentrate on those things over which you *do* have control. You may be able to improve your work satisfaction simply by concentrating on the things you *can* change rather than feeling hopeless about the things you cannot change. Some examples of external blocks are:

- Office politics
- No upward mobility
- Financial limits
- No opportunity to try new things
- Lack of education or training
- Geographic location
- Organizational inconsistencies

Assessment of Your External Blocks to Work Satisfaction

Now try to think of five *external* blocks to work satisfaction that you face on your job or have faced in the past, and write them in the following spaces.

External blocks

1. _____

2. _____

3. _____

4. _____

5. _____

What can you do to overcome these blocks? These are blocks over which you may have little or no control, but think how you might be able to deal with them, perhaps in one small way. A few examples are to take an assertiveness training course to help you deal with office politics, to start an exercise program to relieve tension and stress, or to research another career to evaluate the amount of risk involved if you were to change careers. Try to think of at least one thing that you could do to deal with each of the external blocks that you listed. Use your imagination. Write your ideas in the following spaces.

How to deal with my external blocks

1. _____

2. _____

3. _____

4. _____

5. _____

GETTING STUCK ON A CAREER PLATEAU

At some point in your work life, you may encounter a career plateau. This term refers to a situation in which you find little or no opportunity for growth or advancement within your work environment. Instead of facing another mountain to climb, such as a new set of responsibilities or a promotion, you find that your career has leveled off. Many people face career plateaus at some point during their work lives. If you find yourself on a career plateau, ask yourself the following questions:

Do I like my plateau?

Even though you may have limited opportunity for change, you may like it where you are. Do an assessment of your job satisfaction. You may be on a plateau, but it could be an enjoyable place to spend some time.

Can I make changes?

You may feel blocked by limited opportunities for growth in your work. However, look carefully at the changes that you can make. Too often we measure career change in terms of major transitions, such as promotions, new jobs, and totally new responsibilities. Are there smaller changes that will enhance your work? Consider volunteering to help others, serving as a mentor to new employees, changing procedures, sharing your expertise with new colleagues, catching up on new developments in your field, adjusting the amount of time spent on certain activities, creating new approaches to work responsibilities, and other ways of enhancing your work.

Can I enhance my lifestyle?

Sometimes a career plateau will give you time to relax and consider all aspects of your life. Perhaps too much of your time has been consumed by work. Reduced pressure from your career can provide an opportunity to spend time on interests and hobbies, to make new friendships, to spend more time with family, and to pursue other life-enriching experiences.

Will the plateau change?

You may be at a plateau now, but what about the future? Are new opportunities likely to open up in a year or more? Is it worth waiting in order to assess new developments on your plateau? Perhaps patience will reap greater rewards.

Is there unexplored territory on my plateau?

Have you investigated all aspects of your career? Perhaps there are opportunities that you have not yet considered. Through informational interviewing, creatively exploring options, and keeping an open mind toward your job, you may find that there is a way to move on from your plateau to new heights.

Am I too limited by my plateau?

After answering the preceding questions, if you feel frustrated and limited by your plateau, go on to Chapter 27, Routine Maintenance—Your Two-Year Work Checkup. Complete the activities in that chapter. If you still feel that you have few options with your current job, it may be time to start the career and life planning process. Go back to Section 1 and begin the self-assessment that is so essential to the reevaluation of your career and life goals.

THE ULTIMATE BLOCK—LOSS OF YOUR WORK

Try to think of the worst external block to achieving job satisfaction and career success. Would it be the sudden loss of your work? As the world of work changes rapidly in the years to come, new jobs will arise and other jobs will be eliminated. Layoffs, reductions in force, organizational consolidations, and forced early retirements are to be expected. You may have some control if you keep aware of the trends and avoid taking a job in a declining field. However, if you do lose your job, here are some points to consider.

- Expect to feel angry, sad, depressed, and lost for a while. These emotions are normal after a loss.

- Don't expect to solve this problem right away. Relax and be good to yourself.

- Be constructive. You have options available. The job loss could even turn out to be positive in the long run.

- Involve your family and friends. Build a support system for yourself where you can "be yourself." Talk, cry, rant and rave, let it all out.

- Complete the exercises in this book along with someone else in transition. Compare your results, brainstorm alternatives, and support one another.

- Seek professional assistance, both in conducting a job campaign and in dealing with your personal concerns.

- Develop a daily and weekly schedule of activities so that you do not procrastinate.

- Maintain daily contact with people. Don't allow yourself to feel cut off from others. Use informational interviewing to expand your network.

- Avoid searching for the ideal job. If you are not working, your primary goal should be to return to work in an acceptable job.

- Use the job-hunting methods that work best. Keep actively involved in the process. Don't use the passive approach of just sitting at home and sending out resumés.

- Use all job-hunting resources, including private and public employment agencies and services.

- Although this is probably not the best time to do career and life planning, you may use this as an opportunity to change the direction of your career and perhaps to get some training to enhance your options.

- Join or start a job-hunting support group through professional organizations, churches, agencies, or other contacts in order to share job leads, improve interviewing skills, and build confidence. Encouraging and helping others can have a positive effect on your self-esteem.

Take Care of Yourself

Many factors influence your work satisfaction and success. Some have been addressed in the first two chapters of Section 5. Others may not be as directly related to your work but can have a major impact on how effective you are on the job. Consider carefully the following ways to take care of yourself so that you can be more effective in your work.

AVOID MAJOR VALUE CONFLICTS

If your work conflicts with your life priorities, as expressed by your values, you may need to make some changes. For example, if your work requires you to be away from your family more than you would like, it is very important to assess whether you can change this. If your work requires you to engage in activities that you find distasteful or even dishonest, this can be a real problem that needs action. If you can be committed to the overall purpose of the organization for which you work, you will probably experience less conflict. On the other hand, if the organization's philosophy conflicts with your personal values in significant ways, you can expect to have problems with job satisfaction. In the following spaces, list any value conflicts that you experience in your work.

Value conflicts

_____

_____

_____

_____

Can you tolerate these conflicts or are they serious enough to require action? Remember that to do nothing about a serious value conflict can cause stress and other problems over time.

DEAL EFFECTIVELY WITH STRESS

Take Care of Yourself

1. Avoid major value conflicts

2. Deal effectively with stress

3. Manage your time effectively

4. Pursue other interests

Stress is a by-product of some event or combination of events in your life. It is your body's reaction to what you see as a challenge or threat. You cannot escape stress because it is a part of your life that helps you to grow and to meet certain life demands. Most jobs and certainly everyday life pose stressful situations to you, such as these:

- You had to work overtime and you are late picking up your daughter from preschool when you get a flat tire.

- You have three projects that are due for the boss and your son develops the chicken pox.

- You have four sales appointments and your car develops transmission problems after your first appointment.

- You are getting ready for work and, in the middle of your shower, your hot water runs out.

- Your in-laws have just arrived for an extended stay. Meanwhile, your daughter announces that she is quitting high school to join a religious cult.

What are some stressful situations you've faced within the past week?

1. _____   4. _____

2. _____   5. _____

3. _____   6. _____

How do you normally react to stresses in your life? **Circle** those that apply to you.

chronic anxiety	depression
headache	worrying
nervousness	short attention span
backache	not eating/eating
insomnia	hyperactivity
perspiration	increased heartbeat
irritability	drinking
smoking	withdrawing from others
aggressive behavior	need for pills
hives	tenseness

Your perception of life's events can radically alter your reaction. For example, if you view standing before a group of colleagues as a threat, you may break out in a sweat, develop wobbly knees, and feel your heart race. Another person may consider this as an opportunity for attention and may not have any stress symptoms whatsoever. How you react to life's events varies according to your perceived level of stress.

Stress Management Analysis

Analyze your own stress patterns by completing the following sentences.

1. When I feel anxious or stressful, I usually _____

   _____

   _____

2. I can generally tell when I am under stress. When I am stressed . . .

   a. I think _____

      _____

   b. I feel _____

      _____

   c. I act _____

      _____

3. Presently, I am spending _____ percent of each day in stressful situations.

4. Although I realize **I am responsible for my own feelings**, the following people and situations contribute to my stress.

   Names   **Situations**

   a. _____   a. _____

   b. _____   b. _____

   c. _____   c. _____

5. I usually use the following strategies for coping (thoughts, feelings, and behaviors)

   _____

   _____

   _____

6. The most effective strategies are:

   a. _____

   b. _____

   c. _____

7. The least effective strategies are:

   a. _____

   b. _____

   c. _____

Stress Reduction Program

Your stress-reducing program might include all or some of the following techniques. Use those techniques that work for you and integrate them into your life now.

1. **Get physical.** Work off your tension by playing a sport or just walking. Exercise regularly. Play to relax.

2. **Share the load.** Develop an empathetic support system, including family and friends. Blow off steam and ask for suggestions.

3. **Set priorities.** Make lists and prioritize your tasks. Some things are not worth doing at all. You don't have to do everything. Delegate dinner or pay for house cleaning or painting.

4. **Attitude adjustment.** Accept what you cannot change. Take control of your reaction.

5. **Smell the roses.** Enjoy life's small pleasures. Treat yourself to something.

6. **Eat right.** Take care of your body by eating properly. A balanced diet can help you feel better.

7. **Rest and sleep.** Leave your worries out of the bedroom. Lack of rest can impair your ability to deal with stress.

8. **Go slow.** Adjusting and adapting takes time. Making too many changes all at once is not healthy. Don't initiate more changes when you are stressed.

9. **Trial and error.** Evaluate how you managed during stressful situations in the past and use your most successful strategies the next time you are under stress.

10. **Ask for help.** Consult professionals if you are withdrawing from life, depressed, overly anxious, or suffer from many stress-related symptoms.

PURSUE OTHER INTERESTS

A major problem that is often faced by people who are very dedicated to their work is that they become so committed to their work that the rest of their life suffers. This, in turn, can lead to problems at work when feelings of exhaustion and discouragement set in. It is very important to have interests that you pursue outside of your work and that you make time for these interests. These help you to relax, to be with other people, to reduce stress, and to just have fun. Are you allowing enough time to pursue your interests outside of work? In the following spaces, list five outside interests that give you a break from your work.

1. _____

2. _____

3. _____

4. _____

5. _____

Now look back at your list. Have you spent time on any of these interests in the past week? If not, you may want to manage your time so that you can pursue these interests.

You can be much more effective in your work if you take the time to think about your priorities, your values, your use of time, the enjoyable things that you do outside of work, and the need to control stress. Be a good friend to yourself. Give yourself a break once in a while. Make sure that you save time for the things that you like most, both on and off the job.

CHAPTER 27

Routine Maintenance—
Your Two-Year Checkup

Just as you need to take in your car (or train) for routine maintenance, your work deserves a checkup at least every other year. Take some time to sit back and look at your current situation. What are the positives and negatives in your work life? What, if anything, needs to be changed? This chapter will help you to examine your work in order to improve your satisfaction. Your routine maintenance has four major checkpoints.

1. Your work environment

2. Your people contacts

3. Your work itself

4. Your expectations

By looking closely at these four components of your work, you can isolate the areas which are less satisfying and work to improve them. This may be more practical and more rewarding than simply giving up on your job and looking for a new one. Your objective in this evaluation is to weigh what you do not like against what you do like about your work. Even if your negatives *outnumber* your positives, the positive aspects of your work may *outweigh* the negatives.

For example, a teacher's nine-month contract and benefits may outweigh the lack of flexibility of time during the workday. The challenge and excitement of work with a high degree of responsibility may outweigh the considerable time demands of the job. A total job-keeping and job-revitalization program demands that you undertake a careful analysis of your current work situation. It is not unusual to become disenchanted with your work as you fall into a routine and lose sight of some potential challenges. Often the unknown seems to be more attractive simply because it is unknown. This "grass is always greener" dream can cause further frustration and anxiety because the unknown is not always better; rather, it can be worse. Change for the sake of change can lead to a career blunder. In order to avoid this problem, you may wish to evaluate your present situation, identify possible options, and then make tentative plans to improve your situation.

This chapter will help you to examine your work environment and to consider changes that you can make.

YOUR WORK ENVIRONMENT

Your *work environment* is one component that you need to examine carefully as part of your checkup. Consider your present work and make a check (✓) in the column that best indicates your current level of satisfaction. Please feel free to add any other work environment characteristics that are unique to your situation.

Work Environment	Very Satisfied	Satisfied	Not Satisfied
Office location			
Pay			
Benefits			
Office policies			
Lunch arrangements and opportunities			
Time flexibility			
Vacations			
Sick leave			
Personal leave			
Promotion potential			
Travel opportunities			
Office arrangement			
Equipment quality			
Parking			
Surroundings outside			
Access to recreational facilities			
Air quality			
Cooling and heating systems			
Lighting			
Cafeteria and other on-site services			
Building security			
Supplies			
Maintenance			
Safety practices			
Commuting			
Decor and furnishings			
Restroom facilities			
A window in office			
Other:			

Now take a few minutes to assess what you can do to improve your work environment. Look at your checks in the Not Satisfied box and write those characteristics below. How can you creatively improve your work environment? Look for changes that you can make, either by taking action yourself or by working to change the system. If you can make even one or two changes, you will feel more in control of your environment.

I am not satisfied with	I could improve this by
_____	_____
_____	_____
_____	_____
_____	_____

YOUR PEOPLE CONTACTS

People contact is an integral part of most work. How much or how little people contact you have depends on you and what your work entails. Good interpersonal skills are important attributes in just about any career. Who are the people with whom you have contact throughout your workday (or night)? Are you satisfied with the **amount** and **quality** of the contacts you have with those people or would you like to see some changes made? Rate your people contacts on the following chart and feel free to add any other groups of people you contact in your work.

People Contacts	Satisfied with Amount and Quality of Contact	Dissatisfied with Amount of Contact	Dissatisfied with Quality of Contact
Dealings with the public			
Customers			
Supervisor			
Supervisor's boss			
Coworkers in your immediate vicinity			
Support staff			
Maintenance personnel			
Human resources staff			
Interns			
Colleagues in other organizations			
Sales people			
Your own staff			
Office staff			
Upper management			
President or CEO			
Committees			
Colleagues in your organization			
Team Interactions			
E-mail connections			
Telephone contacts			
Other:			

Now that you've checked those that apply to your work, list in the following spaces on the left the items that you've checked as "dissatisfied," either with the amount or quality of the contact. Think of ways that you can restructure your time in order to change the nature of these contacts, and write them in the spaces on the right. For example, if your supervisor always looks over your shoulder when you are working on a project, plan to discuss your current project and ask for her advice and opinions. If you are curious about how a peer in a similar organization deals with her job, structure time for an exchange of information that could give you new insights and perspective on your own position.

Dissatisfied with contact

_____

_____

_____

_____

I could improve this by

_____

_____

_____

_____

YOUR WORK ITSELF

The next step is to look at your work itself. What do you do when you are at work? What are your rewards? What are your frustrations? How do you spend your time? Complete the following chart. Check (✓) the response that *best* applies.

Your Work	Too Much	About Right	Not Enough
Independence			
Variety of tasks			
Challenge			
Tangible results			
Direction from supervisors			
Detailed job description			
Affirmations from supervisors			
Competition with colleagues			
Distractions			
Time at my desk			
Opportunity to interact with colleagues			
Meetings			
Ability to be creative			
Repetitive tasks			
Clear procedures			
Sense of purpose			
Opportunity to be helpful			
Opportunity to use my skills			
Feeling that the organization cares about me			
Team projects			
Cooperative environment			
Pressure to get the job done			
Feeling a sense of accomplishment			
Volume of work			
Deadlines			
Travel			
High morale			
Other:			

Now list in the following spaces the factors about your work that you checked "too much" or "not enough." Try to think of at least one thing that you might do to improve the situation.

Too much or not enough

_____

_____

_____

_____

_____

_____

I could improve this by

_____

_____

_____

_____

_____

_____

YOUR EXPECTATIONS

Your expectations of your work have a profound effect on you. Those with very low expectations tend to be more satisfied with their work because they never expected much in the first place. On the other hand, those with high expectations may need to reevaluate their expectations and feelings about success.

What did you dream of achieving in your career and life when you were a teenager? What did you dream of becoming in your childhood? What were your expectations of yourself?

I dreamed I would be . . .

_____

_____

_____

_____

The dream of youth can sometimes lead to an uncomfortable reality in adulthood if you haven't reevaluated your original career goals. By reevaluating your dream and by matching it more closely with your accomplishments, you will have successfully dealt with an important adult developmental task. In the process of reevaluating your dream you may need to redefine your idea of success.

Success means different things to different people. Your values determine what success is to you. If you are interested in assessing your values, you may wish to refer to Section One of this book. You may think success is managing a household, three children, and a part-time job; someone else may define success solely in terms of money, vacations, and luxury. In any career or life change, you may wish to examine more closely what your dream of accomplishment is, what your goals are, and how you would define success at this point in your life.

What expectations do you have for your work? What do you hope to accomplish? How important is your work to you? How much money do you hope to make? What position do you hope to reach?

My expectations

_____

_____

_____

_____

Look back at your expectations. Are they realistic, based on your present career, your education, your age, and the economy? If yes, go for it! If your expectations are not totally realistic, in what ways might you modify these expectations? Don't forget to look at your _total lifestyle_ for possible ways to fulfill your expectations.

Ways I might change my expectations

_____

_____

_____

EXPAND POSITIVES AND REDUCE NEGATIVES

Now think of the three **most positive** and the three **most negative** things about your present work. Write them in the following spaces. If you are not currently employed, think back to a previous job.

Positives

1. _____

2. _____

3. _____

Negatives

1. _____

2. _____

3. _____

How do your positives and negatives compare? Do your negatives overwhelm your positives, or do the positives make up for your negatives? Just how bad are your negatives? Are there any creative ways of dealing with your negatives? For example, if you dislike your supervisor, can you seek a transfer to a similar position within your organization? A change of scenery, coworkers, or supervisor may make a world of difference to your morale. What are some creative ways to deal with your negatives?

Try to think of at least two ways to **eliminate** or **reduce** each of your negatives.

Negative #1 _____

_____

_____

Negative #2 _____

_____

_____

Negative #3 _____

_____

_____

Now try to think of at least two ways that you can *expand* each of your positives.

Positive #1 _____

_____

_____

Positive #2 _____

_____

_____

Positive #3 _____

_____

_____

YOUR PERFECT WORK

Describe your perfect "dream" work. What would you do every day?

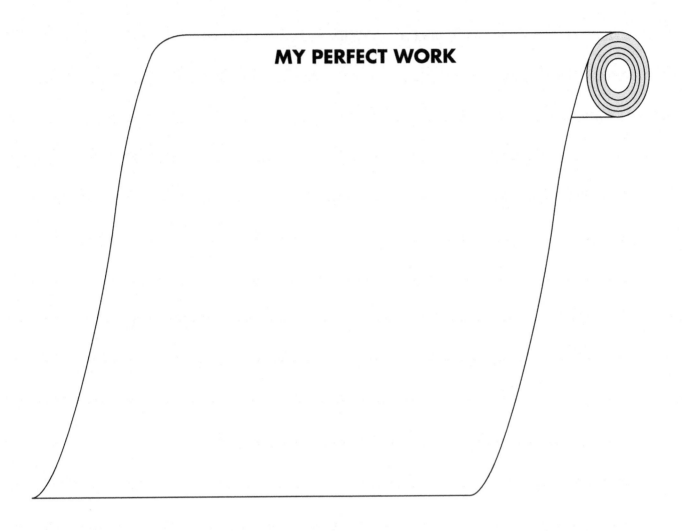

MY PERFECT WORK

Is there such a thing as a perfect job? a perfect life? What parts of your perfect dream work are most important to you? How can you integrate some elements of your dream work into your present work? Write some of your ideas in the following spaces.

I can integrate some elements of my perfect work into my present work by taking the following actions.

_____

_____

_____

_____

I can take the following actions to come closer in the future to having my perfect work.

_____

_____

_____

_____

> *It took me twenty years to become an overnight success.*
>
> —Eddie Cantor

CHAPTER 28

The Payoff—Who Decides Whether You've Done Good Work?

YOUR REWARD SYSTEM

Everyone works in order to achieve certain rewards. The need for rewards will vary from person to person, both in the type and amount of the reward. In order to assess your work satisfaction, it is important to consider what type of rewards you need for your work to be fulfilling. Generally, these rewards can be categorized as either extrinsic rewards or intrinsic rewards.

Extrinsic Rewards

Extrinsic rewards come from **other sources**. They involve someone giving you something as a result of your work. They come from sources that you do not control. They come from other people, from systems, from personnel policies, and from other external sources. The following are examples of extrinsic rewards.

- salary
- raises
- promotions
- praise/affirmation
- fringe benefits
- tangible results
- time off

- letters of commendation
- positive job evaluations
- bonuses
- paid leave
- thank yous
- awards for accomplishments
- stock options

Intrinsic Rewards

Intrinsic rewards come from within **you**. They are usually intangible and result from your own assessment of how well you have performed. While extrinsic rewards come from others, intrinsic rewards are dependent on your establishment of criteria for work success. The following are examples of intrinsic rewards.

- personal growth
- pride in your work
- feeling of accomplishment
- self-respect
- meeting a challenge
- setting and achieving goals

- solving a problem
- self-expression
- being creative
- using your skills and abilities
- developing new skills
- meaningful contribution

Most work involves rewards of both types. It is important for you to assess the types of rewards that are most important to you and then focus your work on achieving these rewards. Intrinsic rewards have the advantage of coming from within. You have more control over the rewards that you receive if you have established a good intrinsic reward system. However, everyone appreciates extrinsic rewards, and it is important that you know what you need. It may be possible to control some of the extrinsic rewards that are important to you by seeking feedback from others, by selecting work with tangible results, and by choosing a job with a large number of built-in reward systems.

The following questions are designed to help you assess what rewards are important to you. Try to be creative in exploring ways to increase both your extrinsic and intrinsic rewards.

Evaluating Your Extrinsic Rewards

1. Think about your present work and those jobs that you have had in the past. What type of extrinsic rewards—those rewards that come from others—are most important to you in order for you to feel that you've done a good job?

   _____

   _____

   _____

   _____

   _____

2. Now think again about your present work. (If you are not working at this time, think about your last job.) What kind of extrinsic rewards do you receive or have you received from others?

   _____

   _____

   _____

   _____

   _____

3. If certain extrinsic rewards are very important to you and these are missing, how could you change your work so that you can receive more of these rewards?

_____

_____

_____

_____

_____

_____

Evaluating Your Intrinsic Rewards

1. Think about your present work and the jobs that you have had in the past. What type of intrinsic rewards—those that come from within you—are most important to you in order to feel that you've done a good job?

_____

_____

_____

_____

_____

_____

2. What kind of intrinsic rewards do you receive from your present work, or did you receive from your last job?

_____

_____

_____

_____

_____

_____

3. What action can you take to increase the intrinsic rewards that you receive from your work?

_____

_____

_____

_____

_____

_____

> *When one door closes, another opens; but we often look so long and so regretfully upon the closed door that we do not see the one which has opened for us.*
>
> —Alexander Graham Bell

YOUR WORK SATISFACTION—IT'S YOUR DECISION

After looking at all aspects of your work life, the basic assessment of your satisfaction with your work is your responsibility. You can get help from others and explore alternatives, but you have to decide what **you need** to be satisfied with your work and whether your work can provide the satisfaction you want.

Some people never seem to be happy with their work. They look only at the negatives, and all work has some negatives. These people spend a lot of time and energy complaining about their work without doing anything about it. Some people are willing to accept whatever comes their way and to turn over control of their work to others. Some people expect too much from their work, so much that no job could meet all of the needs that they hope to fulfill. Others expect very little from their work, seeing a job as just another part of their total lifestyle.

For many people, moving from one job to another fulfills a need for change and for some it can enhance work satisfaction. However, this may not always be the best approach. Often, one can benefit greatly by growing with a job and by seeking ways to increase job responsibilities and enhance work satisfaction. The activities in this chapter have been designed to help you make the most of your current work. At some point, it may be necessary to change jobs entirely in order to fulfill your needs. However, look at what you can do now to make the most of your work. An investment of time and energy in what you are doing now can have the potential of significant rewards.

1. What actions can I take to make the most of my work?

_____

_____

_____

_____

_____

_____

2. What are the risks involved in these actions?

_____

_____

_____

_____

_____

_____

3. Are these risks worth the potential payoff?

_____

_____

_____

_____

_____

_____

They conquer who believe they can. He has not learned the lesson of life who does not each day surmount a fear.

—Ralph Waldo Emerson

Enhance Work Performance and Satisfaction

To make the most of my work, I need to take the following actions.

In the next week:

In the next month:

Within six months:

Within one year.

ADDITIONAL RESOURCES

Asher, D. (2007). *Who gets promoted, who doesn't, and why: 10 things you'd better do if you want to get ahead.* Berkeley, CA: Ten Speed Press.

Bakke, D. W. (2005). *Joy at work: A revolutionary approach to fun on the job.* Seattle, WA: PVG.

Berglas, S. (2001). *Reclaiming the fire: How successful people overcome burnout.* New York: Random House Publishing Group.

Bixler, S. (2000). *5 steps to professional presence: How to project confidence, competence, and credibility at work.* Holbrook, MA: Adams Media.

Bridges, W. (1998). *Creating you & company: Learn to think like the CEO of your own career.* Cambridge, MA: Perseus Books.

Brooks, R. (2004). *Your quick guide to self-employment.* Frederick, MD: Publish America, Inc.

Cohen, C. F. & Rabin, V. S. (2008). *Back on the career track: A guide for stay-at-home moms who want to return to work*. Lebanon, IN: Grand Central Publishing.

Covey, S. (2005). *The 8th habit: From effectiveness to greatness*. Mankato, MN: The Free Press.

Covey, S. (2004). *Seven habits of highly effective people*. New York: Simon & Schuster.

Covey S. (1996). *First things first*. New York: Simon & Schuster.

D'Alessandro, D. F. & Owens, M. (2004). *Career warfare: 10 rules for building a successful personal brand and fighting to keep it*. New York: McGraw-Hill Companies.

Darling, D. (2005). *Networking for career success*. New York: McGraw-Hill.

DuBrin, A. (2004). *Human relations for career and personal success*. Upper Saddle River, NJ: Prentice Hall.

Goleman, D. (2006). *Emotional intelligence: 10th anniversary edition; why it can matter more than IQ*. New York: Bantam Books.

Griffiths, B. (2003). *Do what you love for the rest of your life: A practical guide to career change and personal renewal*. New York: Ballantine Books.

Hoerr, T. (2001). *Thank God it's Monday! A tool kit for aligning your life vision and your work*. Fairfield, CT: Aslan Publishing.

Jensen, J. (2006). *You want me to work with who?: Eleven keys to a stress-free, satisfying, and successful work life . . . no matter who you work with*. New York: Penguin Group USA.

Kaye. B. & Jordan-Evans, S. (2003). *Love it, don't leave it: 26 ways to get what you want at work*. San Francisco: Berrett-Koehler Publishers, Inc.

Langford, B. (2005). *The etiquette edge: The unspoken rules for business success*. New York: AMACOM.

Leiter, M. P. & Maslash, C. (2005). *Banishing burnout: Six strategies for improving your relationship with work*. New York: John Wiley & Sons, Incorporated.

Lucht, J. (2005). *Executive job-changing workbook*. New York: Viceroy Press.

Ludden, L. (2002). *Job savvy: How to be to a success at work*. Indianapolis, IN: JIST Works.

Lyles, T. (2005). *Good stress: Unlocking the hidden power of stress to achieve lifelong success*. Deerfield Beach, FL: Healthful Communications Incorporated.

Parley, D., ed. (2007). *Managing stress in the workplace super series*, Fifth Ed. (Super). London: Institute of Leadership & Management (ILM).

Rath, T. & Clifton, D. O. (2004). *How full is your bucket? Positive strategies for work and life*. New York: Gallup Press.

Richardson, B. (2004). *Career comeback: Eight steps to getting back on your feet when you're fired, laid off, or your business ventures has failed—and finding more job satisfaction than ever before*. New York: Broadway Books.

Sabath, A. M. (2004). *Beyond business casual: What to wear to work if you want to get ahead*. Lincoln, NE: iUniverse, Incorporated.

Sapolsky, R. (2004). *Why zebras don't get ulcers*. New York: Henry Holt Company.

Schlossberg, N. (2007). *Overwhelmed: Coping with life's ups and downs*. Lanham, MD: Lexington Books.

Seitz, V. E. (2000). *Your executive image: How to look your best and project success for men and women*. Cincinnati, OH: Adams Media Corporation.

Shea, G. & Shea, G. F. (1999). *Making the most of being mentored*. Menlo Park, CA: Crisp Publications.

Violin, K. (2004). *Buff & polish: A practical guide to enhance your professional image and communication style.* Winter Haven, FL: Pentagon Publishing.

Weisinger, H. (2000). *Emotional intelligence at work.* San Francisco, CA: Jossey-Bass, Inc. Publishers.

Williams, Joan. (2001). *Unbending gender: Why family and work conflict and what to do about it.* New York: Oxford University Press.

Zander, R. S. & Zander, B. (2002). *The art of possibility: Transforming professional and personal life.* New York: Penguin Group (USA).

Zeigler, K. (2008). *Getting organized at work: 24 lessons for setting goals, establishing priorities, and managing your time.* New York: McGraw-Hill Companies.

Online Resource

Managesmarter: *15 Personal Skills You Need on the Job* (2006). www.presentations.com/msg/content_display/training/e3ied0764c52ea0c6b7a858277ba7f9e652?imw=Y

SECTION six

Create Quality and Balance in Your Life

No matter how old you are, what career you have, what your background may be, what your family situation is, or who you are, it is essential that you **actively plan** the lifestyle that you want to live. Your career will play a very important role in your lifestyle, but there are many other factors to consider. Some may be as important or even more important than your career. Your interests, family activities and responsibilities, recreation, religion, community activities, friendships, and many other parts of your life all contribute to the definition of your unique self and help to determine your happiness and satisfaction with life.

Many people depend too heavily on their careers for their identity. These people may have major problems when they are confronted by unforeseen career changes or retirement. It is vital to maintain a balanced lifestyle, one that involves a variety of activities and interests. The lifestyle that you develop **now** will tend to stay with you as you go through life. If you eventually choose to retire, a balanced lifestyle can help you to deal with this transition. In the 21st century workplace, many people may be faced with the necessity of choosing a less than totally fulfilling career. A balanced lifestyle can help to compensate for this. It is important to build a pattern of activities and interests that you can take with you through life.

This section will help you to look at the factors that make up a fulfilling lifestyle and a long, healthy life. It will help you to look at the actions that you can take now to develop a well-rounded lifestyle. As you read this section, keep one principle in mind: **Don't wait until retirement to do what you want to do**. The lifestyle you develop now will grow with you for the rest of your years.

Your lifestyle is unique. As you read this section, consider the following factors, which may play an important role in your life satisfaction.

- Your career
- Your attitude toward life
- Your interests
- Your health
- Your physical activity
- Your diet
- Your family
- Your friends and colleagues

- Your finances
- Your personal growth
- Your fun
- Your challenges
- Your spiritual life
- Your continuing opportunity to learn
- Your physical surroundings

> *The most important things you'll ever learn in life are the things you learn after you think you know it all.*
>
> —Harry Truman

CHAPTER 29

A Look into the Future

In this chapter we will consider the future. Try to project yourself years ahead and answer each of the following questions in the space provided below each question. Base your answers on what you **would like** to be doing in the future.

1. You are 68 years old and it is Thursday. You are just waking up.

   a. What will you do today?

   b. With whom, if anyone, will you have lunch?

   c. What will you do after six o'clock tonight?

   d. What will you do tomorrow (Friday)?

   e. What plans do you have for the weekend?

   f. With whom are you living?

g.   In what geographic area are you living?

h.   In what setting and in what kind of housing are you living?

i.   Are you working? If so, how does work fit into your life?

j.   If you are working, what kind of work do you do?

k.   What interests or hobbies do you have?

l.   What contacts do you have with other people?

m.   What are your major joys in life?

n.   What aspects of your life are most important to you?

o.   What are you receiving from others?

p.   What are you giving to others?

q.   What is your physical condition?

r.   What kind of family relationships do you have?

2. In the following spaces, summarize the answers you just wrote by asking yourself this question:

What do I want to be like at age 68?

_____

_____

_____

_____

_____

_____

3. Now ask yourself the following question.

What can I do now to start becoming the person I want to be at age 68?

_____

_____

_____

_____

_____

_____

It is important to start *now* to plan for the future, not only so that you have a better chance of becoming the person you would like to be, but also in order to begin doing some of the things that are most important to you now. Why wait? There is no time like the present. The activities and information in the following chapters will help you to plan for a personally satisfying lifestyle that can take you into the years ahead.

CHAPTER *30*

Think Positively

Each person's needs are unique. What may be good for one individual may not be appropriate for another. Your lifestyle can correspond to your own preferences and values if you energetically pursue the activities that are important to you. Positive thinking is your key to developing a lifestyle that meets your needs.

Have you ever met someone who is always looking at the world with a gloomy perspective? Some people prefer to dwell on the negative side of just about anything that happens in life. It is possible to find problems in almost anything. One can become reluctant to change because of the fear of potential problems. In order to appreciate life and to keep open to new relationships and experiences, think positively!

Try to get in the habit of looking at what you **can** do rather than what you cannot do. Look at what you **have** rather than at what you lack. When change takes place, concentrate on the gain that the change might bring rather than the loss. A positive attitude will help you to feel better about yourself and your choices. People will respond to you in a more positive way. You will probably be more successful on your job and you may well have a much better chance of staying healthy.

Erik Erikson (1959), a noted psychoanalyst, described eight stages of human development. Each stage was characterized by a major task. The last two stages that Erickson described were generativity versus self-absorption and integrity versus despair. In the task of generativity versus self-absorption, Erikson noted the importance of contributing to the growth and development of others, the community, the nation, and the world as opposed to being so wrapped up in one's self that there is little to give. In the last stage, integrity versus despair, Erikson described the importance of integrating one's life, including the rewards and disappointments, and moving on with a positive approach to life rather than despairing over lost opportunities.

There is significant research that indicates that happier people are healthier people. Those who are optimistic, less hostile, and more satisfied with life are less likely to develop chronic diseases later in life (*Consumer Reports on Health*, 2004). A Mayo Clinic study showed that people who scored highest on a scale of pessimism were approximately 20 percent more likely to die prematurely than were optimists. In another study, older adults who were hopeful about the future had a significantly lower death rate over a seven-year period. Other studies showed that people who are depressed, stressed, or angry had more physical and mental problems and were slower to heal after surgery. Some basic tactics for developing a more positive approach to life are:

1. Concentrate on those things over which you have some control.

2. Substitute positive thoughts for negative thoughts.

3. Focus on positive recent and long-term memories.

4. Look at the bright aspects of future events.

5. Take time to engage in activities that are satisfying and make you feel good.

6. Learn to manage negative experiences through counseling, meditation, and social support.

7. A good exercise program will help you to lower your level of stress and feel better about yourself.

A positive approach is critical in dealing successfully with these and other tasks that occur throughout life. Look at what can be accomplished rather than what cannot be accomplished. Is the glass of water half empty or half full? Consider the "half-full" side of life!

What parts of your life might benefit from a more positive approach right now? Write them in the box below.

CHAPTER *31*

Develop Interests

Interests and hobbies can contribute significantly to your enjoyment of life and to your self-esteem. They can also provide a very important balance to life and a valuable contrast to work. Those who take the time to develop and pursue interests outside of work generally have higher satisfaction with life as they grow older. Interests and hobbies fulfill a variety of individual needs and are a source of just plain fun. For example, if you play a musical instrument as a member of a jazz group, you will fulfill needs for creativity and interaction with others. In addition, you can fulfill a need to challenge yourself by improving your musical skills. Such an activity may even help to fulfill your financial needs if your jazz group gets paid for gigs. Collectors of items such as baseball cards, china, or stamps can fulfill needs in traveling to conventions, for excitement in discovering rare treasures, or for challenge and interaction in bargaining with other collectors.

As you take your train trip to the future, make time for your interests and take time to develop new ones. A variety of interests can add vitality and richness to your life by providing outlets for creativity, challenges, mental and physical activity, social opportunities, a sense of accomplishment, growth, and even income. Use the following table to assess your interests and hobbies.

PURSUING YOUR INTERESTS, HOBBIES, AND ACTIVITIES

Check (✓) the column that best represents your answer to each question.

	Yes	Somewhat	No
Do you have a variety of interests outside of work?			
Do you have hobbies?			
Do you actively pursue your interests or hobbies?			
Do you feel that you are able to spend the amount of time you want on your interests and hobbies?			
Do you feel that you have enough of a variety of interests and hobbies?			
Are many of the interests active (requiring your direct involvement) rather than passive (watching TV)?			
Do some of your interests involve other people?			
Do your interests and hobbies provide a good diversion from your work?			
If you are married, do you share interests and activities with your spouse?			
Do your interests and hobbies give you a sense of satisfaction and fulfillment?			
Do you have any interests or hobbies that could form the basis of a second career?			

If your answer was "somewhat" or "no" to any of the above questions, would you prefer your answers to be "yes"? If so, go back and place an X in the "yes" column. In the spaces below, write five actions that you can take to expand your interests, hobbies, and activities, or to spend more time on the activities that you enjoy.

1. _____

2. _____

3. _____

4. _____

5. _____

It is important to consider the type of lifestyle that you want to enjoy for the rest of your life. You can always continue to work, but it can be very helpful to think about the other things that you want to do that may or may not involve work. Consider making a "life list." Include activities, goals, accomplishments, experiences, travel, learning, and anything else that you want to make sure that you do in your life.

My Life List

1. _____	26. _____
2. _____	27. _____
3. _____	28. _____
4. _____	29. _____
5. _____	30. _____
6. _____	31. _____
7. _____	32. _____
8. _____	33. _____
9. _____	34. _____
10. _____	35. _____
11. _____	36. _____
12. _____	37. _____
13. _____	38. _____
14. _____	39. _____
15. _____	40. _____
16. _____	41. _____
17. _____	42. _____
18. _____	43. _____
19. _____	44. _____
20. _____	45. _____
21. _____	46. _____
22. _____	47. _____
23. _____	48. _____
24. _____	49. _____
25. _____	50. _____

If you have more than 50, continue your list on another page. Now go back over your list. It could form the foundation of a more fulfilling lifestyle. **Do not wait for a long time, such as until you retire, to do some of the things on your list.** Get started now!

CHAPTER 32

Take an Active Role in Staying Healthy

What could be more important to your quality of life than good health? A fatalistic attitude toward health stems from the belief that you have no control over your health. Nothing could be further from the truth. There are specific actions that you can take to increase your chances of staying in good health and of living longer. No matter what your age and lifestyle, you can become actively involved in giving yourself a better opportunity to be in good health. There are eight major factors over which you have control.

Factors in Staying Healthy

1. Physical Activity

2. Mental Activity

3. Involvement with Others

4. Diet and Nutrition

5. Managing Stress

6. Avoiding Self-Injurious Behavior

7. Getting Medical Care

8. Using Medicines Responsibly

THE IMPORTANCE OF PHYSICAL ACTIVITY

Regular physical activity of some type can have a profound effect on improving your health and it can also increase the length of your life. A landmark study of 17,000 Harvard alumni by Dr. Ralph Paffenbarger demonstrated beyond a reasonable doubt that regular exercise decreases the risk of mortality from all diseases (Higdon, 1986, p. 17). Many new studies have shown that even moderate exercise has great health benefits. Although exercise cannot halt the aging process, it can slow it significantly. There is also evidence that regular exercise causes the brain to release endorphins, the body's own form of painkiller. This causes a feeling of well-being and gives a psychological lift both during and after exercise.

The relationship between regular physical activity and health has been substantiated by many studies. The evidence is pervasive that being a couch potato is equated to being a smoker. Both activities are bad for your health. Here are some factors to consider in planning to have a more physically active life that are based on the recommendations in *Successful Aging* (1998) by John W. Rowe, M.D., and Robert L. Kahn, M.D:

1. Physical fitness is perhaps the single most important thing that you can do to remain healthy. Physical activity is integral to successful aging.

2. Unless we take action, the older we become, the less fit we become.

3. The most fit people, even if they have high blood pressure or smoke, are still at lower risk of death than nonsmokers with normal blood pressure who are couch potatoes.

4. Most people, even those of advancing age, still have the capacity to increase their muscle strength, balance, walking ability, and overall condition.

5. The benefits of physical activity have little to do with how old you are and what shape you are in at the beginning. The key is to exercise regularly.

6. Resistance (weight) training can be very beneficial, especially as people get older.

7. Beyond a doubt, physical activity cuts the risk of coronary heart disease. Exercise also decreases hypertension and helps to lower blood pressure. Exercise protects against colon cancer, can relieve arthritis pain and disability, can help those with osteoporosis, and has many other benefits.

8. The benefits of exercise appear to be cumulative. You should set a goal of burning about 150 calories a day, or about 1000 calories a week.

The type of exercise seems to be less important than the fact that you do exercise. It is not essential that everyone jog, swim, bike ride, or skate. Simple walking can be an excellent source of exercise. The important factor is that you do exercise regularly, that it becomes a part of your regular routine, and that you look for ways to increase the amount of physical activity that you gain in your normal daily activities. To help you to evaluate the effects of various types of exercise, the following chart is provided:

Activity	Calories Used per Hour*
Walking (4 mph)	320
Tennis (singles)	440
Running (6 mph)	700
Bicycling (5 1/2 mph)	240
Swimming (freestyle—slow)	540
Dancing (medium speed)	250
Golf (walking briskly, carrying clubs)	300

*These are estimates for a person of medium weight (about 150 pounds) and are given primarily to illustrate the differences between various types of exercise. For more specific information, consult one of the resources listed later in this chapter. Keep in mind that these figures can vary depending on an individual's weight and metabolism.

It is important to find the activity or combination of activities that you can incorporate into your routine, and do them. In addition, there are other actions that you can take to alter your normal lifestyle to get more exercise. Here are a few:

Ten Ways to Increase Your Physical Activity

1. Wake up a half hour early and walk, cycle, jog, or swim before breakfast.

2. When you drive, park some distance away from your destination and walk briskly from your car.

3. Replace a big lunch with a light lunch and spend the extra time in physical activity, such as walking.

4. Walk up stairs instead of taking the elevator.

5. Walk up and down several flights of stairs after each hour of work.

6. Replace coffee breaks with exercise breaks.

7. If you are going a short distance, walk instead of drive.

8. When you sit for long periods of time, take a break, get some fresh air, and walk.

9. Instead of paying to have housework done, do it yourself, if it is a potential source of exercise.

10. Replace power tools and appliances with manually operated ones.

THE IMPORTANCE OF MENTAL ACTIVITY

It is very important to keep your mind active as well as your body. Studies have shown that a person's mental ability is related to a person's physical status (Rowe and Kahn, pp. 125–142). Only two mental functions have been found to naturally decline over time: the speed of information processing, and explicit memory, which involves the intention to remember, and recall a specific name, number, or location on demand. Many studies have shown that people can improve their memory and mental capabilities by keeping involved in complex activities, such as working, reading, playing games such as bridge and chess, staying involved in continuing education, volunteering, and any other activity that provides a mental challenge. Staying mentally active is important to staying healthy. There is also a growing body of evidence that physical exercise is good for the brain. Aranti, Lori. RX for the Brain: Move. *The Washington Post*. December 4, 2007. p. F1.

INVOLVEMENT WITH OTHERS

A very significant amount of research has shown that people who have strong connectedness with others through family, friendships, and organizational memberships live longer (Rowe and Kahn, pp. 152–166). Part of a healthy lifestyle is to maintain positive relationships with family members and friends and to take the initiative to reach out to people. Through your work and other activities it is important to make connections with others and invest time in relationships. This is especially important if you find yourself in a job or in a new location where you have limited contact with others. In addition, the more meaningful your involvement is in an activity in which you interact with others, the greater is its impact on your health. This topic will be covered more fully in the next chapter.

DIET AND NUTRITION

You are what you eat, and you age by what you eat. Overeating is a problem in American society, and it can affect your lifespan. Extra fat puts a tremendous burden on the heart. As you get older, your body requires fewer calories. A man who weighs 150 pounds at age 30 and maintains a regular exercise program will weigh

200 pounds at age 60 if he does not reduce his calorie intake. The following table from the *American Medical Association Encyclopedia of Medicine* has been used as a standard guideline for ideal size-weight distribution (Clayman, 1989, p. 1073).

Men's Height (without shoes)	Normal Weight Ranges (without clothes)	Women's Height (without shoes)	Normal Weight Ranges (without clothes)
5'2"	113–143	4'10"	92–121
5'3"	116–146	4'11"	95–123
5'4"	119–149	5'0"	98–126
5'5"	122–153	5'1"	100–129
5'6"	125–157	5'2"	103–133
5'7"	128–161	5'3"	106–136
5'8"	131–165	5'4"	109–139
5'9"	134–170	5'5"	112–143
5'10"	137–175	5'6"	115–147
5'11"	141–180	5'7"	119–151
6'0"	145–184	5'8"	123–155
6'1"	149–189	5'9"	127–160
6'2"	153–194	5'10"	132–165
6'3"	158–200	5'11"	137–170
6'4"	163–206	6'0"	142–175

In addition to reducing excess calories, selection of the types of foods that you eat can enhance your health. There are many books and other resources on this subject and there are numerous studies underway that are designed to assess the effects of diet on health and longevity. It is important for you to remain current on the developments in this rapidly growing area. The following list of the seven healthiest changes that one can make in ones diet is based on the recommendations in *Eat, Drink and Be Healthy: The Harvard Medical School Guide to Healthy Eating* by Walter C. Willett, M.D. (2005).

1. Watch your weight. Keeping your weight from creeping up is more important than the ratio of fats to carbohydrates or the types and amounts of antioxidants in your food. The lower and more stable your weight, the greater your chances of staying healthy and living longer.

2. Eat fewer bad fats and more good fats. Fats from nuts, seeds, grains, fish, and liquid oils (olive, canola, soybean, corn sunflower, peanut, and other vegetable oils) are good for you, especially when you eat them in place of saturated fat and trans fat.

3. Eat fewer refined grain carbohydrates and more whole grain carbohydrates from grains, fruits, and vegetables.

4. Choose healthier sources of proteins, such as beans, nuts, fish, poultry, and eggs. The particular combination of saturated fats in red meat, or the potentially cancer-causing compounds that form when red meat is grilled or fried, is connected with a variety of diseases.

5. Eat plenty of vegetables and fruits. A diet rich in fruits and vegetables lowers blood pressure, decreases chances of having a heart attack or stroke, helps to protect you against a variety of cancers, and has other benefits. However, eating too many potatoes can raise levels of blood sugar and insulin.

6. Use alcohol in moderation. One drink a day for women and one or two drinks a day for men cuts the chances of having a heart attack or dying from heart disease by about a third and also decreases the risk of stroke.

7. Take a multivitamin for insurance. Several of the ingredients in a multivitamin, especially vitamins B6 and B12, folic acid, and vitamin D, help to prevent heart disease, cancer, osteoporosis, and other chronic diseases.

MANAGING STRESS

Stress comes from a variety of sources, and what is stressful for one person may not be stressful for another. It is well known that too much stress or the inability to deal with it can have a negative impact on your health. It is important to be prepared for stress that may come from some unexpected sources, such as the loss of colleagues at work, the loss of a sense of purpose, and others. The following are some general guidelines for avoiding stress.

- Have a support system. Maintain contact with others. Participate in activities with others.

- Develop goals, both daily and long term. Have a reason to get up in the morning. Continue to challenge yourself.

- Have a variety of activities that give you a feeling of satisfaction and accomplishment.

- Continue to grow mentally. Read, take courses, join discussion groups.

- If confronted with a major stressing event, such as the loss of a spouse, seek help from others and from community support services.

- Try to look at the positive side of any change. Focus on what you can do, not on what you cannot do.

- Develop an optimistic approach to life. There is some evidence to indicate that people who look at the future from a positive point of view actually are healthier and live longer.

AVOIDING SELF-INJURIOUS BEHAVIOR

We have seen that through exercise, good diet, and positive lifestyle, it is possible to gain some control over your health and to develop the potential for a longer life. It is also possible to undermine your chances for good health and a long life. The following are examples of actions that work against the goal of a long and healthy life. These are self-destructive and should be avoided.

- Smoking

- Excessive drinking or use of drugs

- Failing to wear a seat belt

- Reckless driving

- Sudden intense exercise without proper preparation (shoveling snow or running before getting in shape)

- Neglect of a physical problem or the failure to have regular checkups

GETTING MEDICAL CARE

It is very important to obtain prompt medical assistance for health problems that emerge and to have regular checkups. Untreated medical problems can get worse, but problems found early can usually be corrected. It is essential to find a doctor in whom you have confidence. However, you cannot simply defer your medical concerns to a doctor. You have certain responsibilities. Among them are:

- Make a list of all your medical problems with appropriate details. Do not keep information from your doctor and be honest with her.

- Don't limit a visit to immediate problems. For example, if you have not had a routine checkup for some time, make arrangements to get one.

- Your relationship with your doctor is a partnership and you should work together to develop a health maintenance program that is right for you. You have primary responsibility for the success of this program.

- Do not avoid examinations or tests that may be necessary but unpleasant.

- Feel free to get a second opinion before surgery or other major medical interventions.

- If you don't understand something your doctor is doing or telling you, ask for an explanation or clarification. As a partner in your own health care, it is essential to get this information in order to make decisions or take action. You should know your condition and the treatment that will be required.

USING MEDICINE RESPONSIBLY

Before using any medicine on a regular basis, you should check with your doctor. Certain nonprescription medicines can cause problems if misused. The following are some precautions.

- Do not assume that all commercial nonprescription medicines are safe to take just because the label indicates dosage and contents or if they are recommended by a pharmacist.

- Inform your doctor of all prescription and nonprescription medications you are taking. This may prevent one drug from harmfully combining with another.

- Do not accept without question the claims made for medicines in various types of advertising.

- The use of mood-altering pills or sleeping pills should be monitored by your doctor.

- Although drugs must be screened and tested before they are available to the public, do not assume that all drugs are totally reliable.

- Many commercially available medications that deal with problems such as constipation and sleeplessness may not be as effective as a good diet and exercise program.

- Do not "try out" a prescription written for a friend or family member. Check with your doctor.

The following resource provides useful information on prescription drugs.

Consumer Drug Reference 2008. Consumer Reports Books. Check www.consumerreports.org.

Chapter *33*

Maintain Good Interpersonal Relationships

In Section Two you identified your personal board of directors, your support groups, and your network of contacts. As you go through life, it is very important to maintain healthy interpersonal relationships by reaching out to others. Evaluating existing support and developing new sources of support are part of your lifestyle checkup. It is not necessary for you to have a wide variety of relationships. Usually the quality of the relationships is more important than the quantity. As described in Chapter 32, those who are "joiners," who participate regularly in activities with others, are generally more satisfied with their lives and actually live longer.

Invest time and energy in your interpersonal relationships. If you are married or have a significant other, your relationship with your partner requires time, thought, adaptability, and flexibility. Maximize your positive relationships with family members and friends. If you find this difficult, seek help in order to build on your existing family relationships.

Look for activities and organizations that provide opportunities for interaction with others. Develop an accepting attitude as you deal with others. Be tolerant of your own and others' shortcomings and learn to be a good listener. The following table is provided so that you can evaluate your interpersonal relationships.

IMPROVING YOUR INTERPERSONAL RELATIONSHIPS

Please check the column that best represents your answer to each question.

	Yes	Somewhat	No
Do you participate with others in community or recreational activities?			
Do you interact with others at work?			
Do you have friends that you see regularly?			
Do you have regular contact with family?			
Do you have people that you can share your concerns with?			
Do you have people you can turn to for help?			
Are you able to spend as much time with your family as you wish?			
If you are married or have a partner, do you communicate well with your spouse or partner?			
If you are married or have a partner, are you satisfied with your relationship with your spouse or partner?			
Do you initiate contacts with others?			
Are you satisfied with the quality of the time you spend with family and friends?			
Do you feel lonely?			

If your answer was "somewhat" or "no" to any of the above questions, would you prefer your answer to be "yes"? If so, go back and place an "X in the "yes" column.

In the following spaces, list what you can do now or in the near future to turn your "somewhat" or "no" answers into "yes" answers.

_____

_____

_____

_____

_____

_____

_____

_____

_____

_____

CHAPTER 34

Make the Most of Your Financial Resources

One key to a satisfying lifestyle is to feel in control of your finances. Money, as an extrinsic reward, is a primary value for many people and may be their main motivation for working. To others, intrinsic rewards, such as satisfaction and contribution, remain more important motivating factors. For those who seek intrinsic and extrinsic rewards for work, it is essential to have sufficient financial resources to meet basic physical needs and to provide a certain degree of independence and security. No matter what your values may be and the role that money plays in your life, it can be helpful to follow some basic guidelines for maintaining financial stability.

GUIDELINES FOR FINANCIAL STABILITY

1. **Define your financial goals.** Take some time to determine what is important to you and what you wish to accomplish with your resources. Do you want to own a home? Do you want a nest egg for retirement? Do you want to save for your own education or your children's education? Are there recreation or career-related activities that will strain your resources? Consider the kind of lifestyle that you want and set financial goals that will help you to attain that lifestyle.

2. **Make saving a regular way of life.** Most financial planning experts agree that it is important to save between 5 percent and 10 percent of your monthly paycheck. They advise you to pay yourself first, before paying the bills. Putting something—anything—aside on a regular basis establishes a pattern of saving. The more that you can save early in life, the better. You can establish the habit of saving and can benefit from long-term compounding of interest. Consider saving methods that are automatic, such as payroll deductions to credit union accounts, savings bonds, and other automatic investments.

3. **Take advantage of long-term compounding.** Most investments, when left to grow over time, can provide significant long-term rewards. Consider an investment of $1,000 that is left to compound at the modest level of 7 percent.

$1000 @ 7% =	$1403	after	5 years
	$1907	after	10 years
	$2759	after	15 years
	$3870	after	20 years
	$5427	after	25 years

Different investment opportunities provide varying rates of risk and of return. The most important fact is that early savings reap very significant long-term rewards. However, it is never too late to start a regular savings plan.

4. **Plan ahead to meet financial goals.** If you have a young child and start early in the child's life to set aside funds for college, the money will grow and you will probably be ready to help your child with a variety of options when the time comes for college. If you value travel and plan to develop this interest in later years, it would be prudent to save regularly for a travel fund. It is often easier to save when the money is designated to meet a specific goal.

5. **Take advantage of company savings plans.** Some organizations provide you with the opportunity to make tax-deferred contributions to retirement savings plans. Others provide programs that allow you to buy company stock at reduced rates. Many of these plans offer significant opportunities for long-term savings that are highly favorable compared with other types of investments. The convenience of automatic payroll deductions also encourages regular contributions. Consider these opportunities carefully as you evaluate your present job and before you change jobs.

6. **Maintain an emergency fund.** Try to have a savings account that you can depend on for unforeseen expenses. These funds should be easily accessible and immediately available. Some financial planners suggest that this rainy-day fund should be approximately equal to six months' salary.

7. **Carry adequate insurance.** The amount of insurance that you carry depends on your family commitments, your age, and other responsibilities. There are resources on financial planning that can give guidelines on the amount of insurance for your specific situation. Take advantage of company-sponsored insurance programs, because life and health insurance are usually offered at lower rates. If you are the primary wage earner, consider the purchase of long-term disability insurance. This type of insurance, which is overlooked by many, guarantees income should you be unable to work. Carefully examine and choose insurance products that are available on the open market. Become informed about the relative merits of different types of insurance.

8. **Take advantage of your company's pension plan or 401K plan.** While an increasing number of companies are eliminating traditional pension plans, those that do offer these plans normally require contributions, but some give you different options for contributions and even the type of plan to which your contributions would go. Increasingly, organizations will provide 401K plans to which you can contribute and to which the organization may also contribute. If you have a choice, consider issues such as time required for vesting, investment of funds, and transferability of the plan to another work setting. Too many people passively accept a plan without investigating it. Do research and stay informed about your pension plan options. If you do not have a pension plan available through your place of employment, establish your own. The trend is for organizations to give more responsibility for retirement saving to individual employees. Company pension plans, 401K savings plans, and other similar programs provide good opportunities for long-term savings. Consider your options carefully.

9. **Take responsibility for your own long-term financial needs.** Do not assume that Social Security will fulfill your financial needs as you approach retirement. Plan to supplement these earnings with

your own savings. A variety of savings plans are available and some, such as individual retirement accounts (IRAs) or Keogh plans for the self-employed, provide significant tax benefits.

10. **Live within your means.** Periodically evaluate your financial situation. Where does your money go? Does the way you spend your money reflect your values? Could you spend less in one area to provide more resources for another more important area? Have you developed a budget? If not, would a budget help you to regulate your monthly expenses? Do you tend to overspend by credit card use? It is easy to fall into patterns of spending money without having the resources available. Take time on a regular basis to analyze your finances.

These are ten simple suggestions for making the most of your financial resources. There are many books, magazines, and other resources on financial planning, investment strategies, and budgeting. Use available print resources, workshops, classes, and professional consultants as you develop your financial plan and take control of your financial destiny.

CHAPTER 35

Continue to Learn

No matter what your age or life stage, it is important to continue to learn. The opportunities for continuing education for adults are growing daily. College is no longer the exclusive realm of the 18- to 21-year-old age group; adults by the millions return to college for a variety of reasons. Adults of all ages, ethnic origins, cultural heritage, and socioeconomic levels are back in the classroom learning a wide variety of subjects. Learning opportunities are found not only within colleges, but in organizations, on videotape, through the mail, online, in informal groups, and through professional associations. Continued learning is important for success for a variety of reasons.

ADVANTAGES OF CONTINUED LEARNING

Lifelong learning helps you to:

- Change careers or jobs
- Learn or update skills
- Pursue interests
- Meet people
- Develop support systems
- Teach and mentor others
- Use existing skills and knowledge
- Create balance in your life
- Keep involved with the changing world

- Keep mentally and physically active
- Expand your knowledge
- Take a study trip
- Exchange ideas
- Meet challenges
- Take a risk
- Increase self-esteem
- Earn a degree or another degree
- Enjoy life

BARRIERS TO CONTINUED LEARNING

Although continued learning provides so many opportunities for growth, many people do not take advantage of them. Barriers seem to block the way to continued learning. These barriers include believing the following myths.

- Intelligence declines with aging.

- Adults cannot compete in the classroom with younger students.

- Institutions are not interested in the adult student.

- Learning is for others, not yourself.

- Having a degree already exempts you from learning.

- Brain cells are dead and cannot be revived.

- Anxiety will prevent learning.

- There is no time to learn.

- Learning is too much work and too difficult when you work full time.

These myths are internal barriers that can distract you from your next step on your career path or avocational pursuits. The barriers are in your mind and can be overcome if you are motivated to keep learning. Stretching your mind can pay off in a big way. Given the technologies of today and the pace of changing technologies for tomorrow, continuing to learn is the only way to meet future challenges.

OPPORTUNITIES FOR CONTINUED LEARNING

As you go through life, consider a variety of ways to continue to learn for career and lifestyle purposes. The following are some continuing education options:

- College and university courses
- Online and other home-study programs
- Adult education programs
- Corporate training programs
- Hobby groups
- Musical groups
- Technical certification programs
- Study-travel groups

- Learning with a friend
- Teaching
- Tutoring
- Elderhostel programs
- Workshops
- Reading
- Writing

How can you take advantage of opportunities for continued learning? What are some ideas that you have for continuing your learning? In the following spaces, list the ten areas that you would like to expand through learning in the next five years. Put a check mark (✓) next to the ones that are job or career related. If your answers are all job related, then add one or two that are specifically for fun.

1. _____

2. _____

3. _____

4. _____

5. _____

6. _____

7. _____

8. _____

9. _____

10. _____

CHAPTER 36

Your Lifestyle Checkup

The following pages contain a guide for a lifestyle checkup. Every so often, it is important to evaluate how things are going in your life. This book contains many checklists and exercises designed to help you assess a variety of factors. This lifestyle checkup summarizes this section and ends the book. Review this checkup periodically. If you wish to make some changes, go to the appropriate chapter in this book for detailed assistance in reviewing your options.

YOUR WORK

It is important to periodically assess the evolution of your career. To do this, turn back to Section 5 and complete Chapter 27, Routine Maintenance—Your Two-Year Work Checkup. When you are finished with your checkup, answer the following questions:

1. Do you want to change your work? _____

   If yes, what are your alternatives? _____

   _____

   _____

2. Do you want to stay in your career but change jobs? _____

   If yes, what are some alternatives? _____

   _____

   _____

3. Do you want to change the setting in which you work? _____

   If yes, what are some alternatives? _____

   _____

   _____

4. Do you want to change the type of people you work with? _____

   If yes, what kind of people do you want to work with? _____

   _____

   _____

5. Do you want to keep your job but change your duties? _____

   If yes, what are some alternatives? _____

   _____

   _____

YOUR FAMILY

Evaluate your family life. Consider the possibility of enhancing relationships, time spent, communication, and the support that you give and receive. Family relationships are dynamic and ever changing. Include your extended family as you answer the following questions.

1. What are the sources of satisfaction in your family life?

   _____   _____

   _____   _____

   _____   _____

   _____   _____

2. What are the sources of frustration in your family life?

   _____   _____

   _____   _____

   _____   _____

   _____   _____

3. Would you like to change your family life? If so, in what ways?

_____   _____

_____   _____

_____   _____

_____   _____

4. How many of these changes can you actually make? When and how will you make these changes?

_____   _____

_____   _____

_____   _____

_____   _____

5. Is there anything about your extended relationships, including your friends, that you would like to change? If yes, what changes would you like to make?

_____

_____

_____

_____

YOUR VALUES

What are your life priorities at the present time? Is your career of primary importance? How about the time you spend with your family? Do you have outside interests, community activities, or creative outlets? Do you spend time in volunteer work, have a second job, or go to school? There are many factors in your life that compete for your time and attention. What you value most often determines how you will spend your time. You are always making value decisions, and an awareness of what values are most important to you can help you to live a more harmonious and less stressful life. When you know which values have a higher priority, you can more easily make life's major and minor decisions. Your values do change as you go through the various life stages. If you are currently seeking some change in your career or lifestyle, it may be due in part to the fact that some of your values may have changed. What was important to you in the past may be less important now. You may want to devote greater attention in your life to new activities or to some of the things you did not have as much time for in the past.

1. What aspects of your life are most important to you at the present time?

_____   _____

_____   _____

_____   _____

2.   Now place them in order, with the most important first.

_____   _____

_____   _____

_____   _____

3.   Have your values changed over the past five to ten years? Are things that were important then less important now? Have other things taken on greater importance? In what ways have your values changed? List those things that have become more important and those that have become less important to you.

More important   **Less important**

_____   _____

_____   _____

_____   _____

4.   Are you spending your time in the way that reflects your values and priorities? In the spaces below, write several changes that you can make to give more time to the activities and relationships that you value most.

_____   _____

_____   _____

_____   _____

YOUR PHYSICAL CHARACTERISTICS

Studies have shown that men are healthiest from ages 15 to 25 and women from ages 15 to 30. The more serious physical problems associated with aging, such as arthritis, rheumatism, heart ailments, and the like do not normally begin until around age 65 for women and 60 for men. However, physical changes that take place earlier can have an effect on your daily life. Vision peaks in the late teens, declines slightly in the twenties, remains stable through the mid-forties, and then declines steadily. Hearing peaks around age 10, remains high through the forties, and often declines rapidly after age 60. Taste, smell, and touch remain relatively stable, although there may be a slight decline in later life. Contrary to common belief, mental faculties do not generally deteriorate with age unless there is illness. Although individuals ages 18 to 25 do best on IQ tests, the wisdom and experience that comes with increasing age compensate for reduced speed in learning. Physical strength and stamina decrease with age, although physical activity can play an important role in slowing this process.

It is important for you to evaluate whether any physical changes you may be undergoing have a bearing on your current experience. A physically demanding job may become difficult to maintain. A high-paced job with long hours may cause you to have physical problems. You may have to adjust some of your leisure activities to reflect your changing physical capabilities. If so, it is important to replace these activities and not to simply give them up. If you have been experiencing any physical problems, it is important to have them evaluated by qualified personnel. Consider the influence on your physical health as you make any decision to change your lifestyle or career.

1. What physical changes have you experienced that may have an effect on your job or your leisure activities?

   _____   _____

   _____   _____

2. What physical problems may be related to your work or lifestyle?

   _____   _____

   _____   _____

3. How would you resolve a conflict between what you want to do and what you are physically able to do?

Want to do	Able to do	Resolution
_____	_____	_____
_____	_____	_____

4. What kind of action is necessary to accommodate your physical condition?

   Medical assistance_____

   Job change_____

   Lifestyle change_____

YOUR PSYCHOLOGICAL CHARACTERISTICS

What is your outlook on life? Are you bored with your work or lifestyle? This can happen after you have worked for a number of years. Do you find yourself generally frustrated and feel that you are not worth as much as you once were? If your work seems to leave you dead-ended, this can have a negative effect on your self-confidence. If you previously devoted most of your efforts to your job, you may now need to branch out in different directions.

Do you feel that you have lost time when you compare yourself with someone else your age? This is a common concern, because it is based on our societal values, which tend to indicate that certain things are done at certain ages. Feeling that you are out of step with where you should be at your age can lead to a lack of self-worth and a sense of hopelessness. It is important to remember that you need to evaluate your own lifestyle and what you yourself want to do. Comparisons with others, unless you derive support and inspiration from them, can be self-defeating. There is a distinct danger in approaching life changes with a negative, apprehensive, or defeatist outlook. If you can prepare yourself to approach these changes as opportunities for growth, your happiness and self-worth can increase.

1. What are some of the things that you often find yourself worrying about?

_____   _____

_____   _____

_____   _____

_____   _____

2. How would you describe your outlook on life? Positive? Negative? In what ways?

Some positive approaches I take   **Some negative approaches I take**

_____   _____

_____   _____

_____   _____

_____   _____

3. What concerns can you actually change or do something about?

Concern   **Solution**

_____   _____

_____   _____

_____   _____

_____   _____

YOUR LEISURE

Do you have much leisure time? How do you spend your leisure time? Many of the hours that you have for leisure are actually taken up by household chores, eating, sleeping, personal care, and other programmed activities that you must do. Leisure time is time available to you to do what you wish. You are free to schedule it or not schedule it, depending on your own preferences. If you are unhappy with your current lifestyle, look at how you are spending your time. Do you have time available to pursue your own interests independent of your job and the demands of others? It may help to assume greater control of your nonwork time and make sure that you block out time for yourself. In addition, evaluate the type of activity that you normally do in your leisure time. Sewing, for example, can be a good leisure time activity if you truly enjoy it and derive satisfaction from it. To others, sewing may simply be work and must be done out of necessity. If you enjoy working on your car and find it relaxing, it is a valuable leisure activity. However, if you feel you must do it to save on repair bills, this activity takes on quite a different meaning.

It is important for people to have some balance in their lives, and fulfilling leisure activities can be very valuable. This is especially true as you progress through the developmental life stages and begin to look for other areas of fulfillment besides work and family. Interests that you enjoy pursuing for their own sake can play a significant role in your ability to lead a satisfying life. These interests can take many forms, can be done alone or with people, can be active or passive, and can be expensive or of little or no cost. What is important is that you enjoy doing them for their own sake.

1. Write in the spaces below four of your most satisfying leisure activities at this point in your life.

_____   _____

_____   _____

_____   _____

_____   _____

2. Next to each item just listed, indicate approximately when you last did this activity.

3. How might you change the way you spend your time so that you can more often do the things you like to do?

4. What are some other things that you would like to do in your leisure time, but do not do now?

_____   _____

_____   _____

_____   _____

_____   _____

YOUR PHYSICAL SURROUNDINGS

One possibility for change is the physical environment in which you work and live. Do you basically like the type of work you do but find yourself unhappy with the people with whom you work, the place where you work, or the distance you travel to work? If so, you may wish to consider looking for a job where you would be doing the same type of work but in a different setting. Compared with other job changes, this would be an easier change to make because it would not involve obtaining new job skills. Another source of dissatisfaction can be the home or neighborhood in which you live. If your values conflict with those of your neighbors, if you feel isolated, or if the apartment or house in which you live is not appropriate to your needs, this can have a distinctly negative effect on your general life satisfaction. Consider your options for making a change.

The third source of dissatisfaction can be the geographic area in which you live. Consider your interests and the lifestyle you want. Would you be happier in a warmer climate, in a more rural environment, in a small town, in a large city? If you have the option of moving, is this something you would like to consider? How important is closeness to family and friends? At times people tend to place too much emphasis on their residence or area they live as a source of dissatisfaction when there are really other problems that must be dealt with, but your physical environment *can* be a major factor in considering any change. A change in your environment could have positive effects on your lifestyle satisfaction.

1. What do you like about the setting where you work, your home, and the geographic area where you live?

Work	Home	Geographic area
_____	_____	_____
_____	_____	_____
_____	_____	_____
_____	_____	_____

2. What don't you like about the setting where you work, your home, and the geographic area where you live?

Work	Home	Geographic area
_____	_____	_____
_____	_____	_____
_____	_____	_____
_____	_____	_____

3. What changes in these three aspects of your physical environment can you realistically consider?

Work	Home	Geographic area
_____	_____	_____
_____	_____	_____
_____	_____	_____
_____	_____	_____

INFLUENCE OF OTHERS

What influence do others have over how you live your life or whether you can change your career? There are some legitimate concerns when you consider the influence of others. Family financial responsibilities are a reality, although too often these are used as an excuse to not even consider a major change. If you are unhappy with your career, talk it over with your spouse and family. Your happiness may be more important than stability, and they may be willing to make some sacrifices to help you achieve greater happiness. It is also important, if you have a partner, to make major decisions with your partner. Friends and other family members can also provide excellent support, if their primary concern is your satisfaction and happiness.

Too often, however, the influence of others can be a negative factor in making a change. You may find yourself comparing where you are in your life and what you have with others your age. This can be a needless source of anxiety. You may be too willing to let friends tell you what they think would be best for you. Some help can be useful, but you **must** make the decisions. Members of your extended family may like to have you around, but your own life fulfillment may be increased by moving from the area. Some people may value stability and, even though they are well-meaning, may attempt to impose those values on you. It is important that you not allow direct influence or perceived influence to be imposed on you when it comes to finally making a decision. Consider the advice of others who have your best interests at heart, but also consider their reference points. Then make your decision.

1. Who **has** influence over you, and in what ways?

Who	In what ways?
_____	_____
_____	_____
_____	_____
_____	_____

2. Who **should** have influence over you, and in what ways?

Who	In what ways?
_____	_____
_____	_____
_____	_____
_____	_____

3. Do you want to change the influence that other people have over you, either by becoming less dependent on some or by gaining new sources of support from friends or family? If yes, what changes would you like to make?

_____

_____

_____

SUMMARIZE YOUR LIFESTYLE CHECKUP

If you have identified some changes that you want to make, now is the time to plan your action. Look back at your options and write them on the following chart.

1. Complete the following chart, indicating what changes you want to make and when you want to make them.

Changes I Want to Make	Now	Within the Next Month	Within the Next Year	In Five Years
a.				
b.				
c.				
d.				
e.				
Others:				

2. Rank these changes.

   Priority #1 _____

   Priority #2 _____

   Priority #3 _____

   Priority #4 _____

   Priority #5 _____

3. Now develop a plan of action. How will you go about making your top priority change?

   #1 _____

   _____

How will you go about making your other priority changes?

#2 _____

_____

#3 _____

_____

#4 _____

_____

#5 _____

_____

What Kind of Help Do You Need in Making These Changes?

- **Self-Evaluation.** If, for example, you want to change your career but are unsure about alternatives, you might want to consider Sections One through Three of this book. You might also want to enroll in a career exploration course, or seek individual counseling. Both are available at the counseling service of your local community or four-year college, at community agencies, or at private counseling services.

- **Information.** You will need information in order to make changes. At the end of this chapter is a bibliography of written resources that may help you. The career resources center in your local library or college can be a good source of information on careers, educational opportunities, and leisure activities.

- **Support from Others.** You should use family and friends as sources of support. Test ideas and share your decision-making process with those whom your decision will affect. Get help from those whose opinions you value. Remember that you will make the final choice, but the involvement of others can be of great help.

- **Identify Realistic Options.** Some changes may be very difficult to achieve because they conflict with your responsibilities. They may involve major adjustments in your life and in the lives of your family members. Determine which changes can be realistically made and work on them. If you can first make some changes that seem minor, these may make quite a difference in your life so that you do not have to make a major change that would cause a great deal of upheaval for yourself and your family.

- **Decision Making.** You can deal effectively with change and make decisions. See Section Two of this book. Remember that even if, after considering a change, you decide not to change, it is still a decision that you reached. You will be better off for having considered your alternatives.

- **Nothing Is Forever.** Have confidence in your ability to make decisions and to make changes. Do not become overly concerned about making the right change. Remember that change can bring about growth. Even though one change may not work out, you can simply change again. By knowing yourself better and by knowing how to make decisions, you can gain greater control over your life.

SECTION
six

Create Quality and Balance in Your Life

As you go through life, set aside the time to evaluate where you are and where you want to go. Think about charting new directions, laying some new track, and taking your train down that track. These new directions may be career related or may involve other parts of your life. Avoid just going along the tracks without making any decisions and without pulling over to think about where you have been, where you are right now, and where you want to be. Keep control of your train trip throughout life. Make sure that your trip reflects your priorities. Be willing to consider and implement changes and even chart a new course. Appreciate all the aspects of your trip, not just your career, as you take charge of the direction and quality of your journey.

ADDITIONAL RESOURCES

Work/Life Balance

Alboher, A. (2007). *One person/multiple careers: A new model for work/life success.* New York: Warner Brothers Publications.

Berger, L. (2006). *The savvy part time professional: How to land, create, or negotiate the part-time job of your dreams.* Herndon, VA: Capital Books.

Cumming, B. (2005). *How to find a job after 50: From part-time to full-time, from career moves to new careers.* New York: Warner Business.

Drago, R. (2007). *Striking a balance: Work, family, life.* Boston: Dollars & Sense, The Economic Affairs Bureau.

Edwards, P. & Edwards, S. (2004). *Best home businesses for people 50+.* New York: Penguin Group USA.

Edwards, P. & Edwards, S. (2001). *The practical dreamer's handbook.* New York: Penguin Putnam.

Gahrmann, N. R. (2002). *Succeeding as a super busy parent: 75 practical tips for life, love, kids, and career.* West Conshohocken, PA: Infinity Publishing.

Gambles, R., Rapoport, R. & Le, S. (2006). *The myth of work-life balance: The challenge of our time for men, women and societies.* New York: John Wiley & Sons, Incorporated.

Greene, B. (2003). *Get with the program.* New York: Simon & Schuster.

Griffiths, B. (2002). *Do what you love for the rest of your life.* New York: Ballantine Books.

Jeffers, S. (2006). *Feel the fear and do it anyway.* New York: Columbine Books.

Kossek, E. E., Lautsch, B. & Lautsch, B. A. (2007). *CEO of me: Creating a life that works in the flexible job age.* Philadelphia, PA: Wharton School Publishing.

Kraar, J. (2005). *Breakthrough: The hate my job, need a life, got laid off, can't get no satisfaction solution.* Lincoln, NE: iUniverse, Inc.

Lewis-Hall, J. (2004). *Life's a journey—not a sprint.* Carlsbad, CA: Hay House, Inc.

Lloyd, C. (1997). *Creating a life worth living.* New York: HarperCollins.

Marston, S. (2002). *If not now, when? Reclaiming ourselves at midlife.* New York: Warner Books.

Molloy, A. (2005). *Stop living your job, start living your life: 85 simple strategies to achieve work/life balance.* New York: Ulysses Press.

Morganstern, J. (2004). *Time management from the inside out: The foolproof plan for taking control of your schedule and your life.* New York: Henry Holt & Company, Inc.

Nelson, D. B. & Low, G. R. (2002). *Emotional intelligence: Achieving academic and career success.* Upper Saddle River, NJ: Prentice Hall.

Pattakos, A. (2004). *Prisoners of our thoughts: Viktor Frankl's principles at work.* San Francisco: Berrett-Koehler Publishers, Inc.

Pipher, M. (2000). *Another country: Navigating the emotional terrain of our elders.* New York: Riverhead Books.

Prafder, E. W. & Sovocool. C. (2005). *Keep your paycheck, live your passion: How to fulfill your dreams without having to quit your day job.* Avon, MA: Adams Media.

Savageau, D. (2007). *Places rated almanac.* Foster City, CA: Ten Speed Press.

Schlossberg, N. & Robinson, S. (1996). *Going to plan B: How you can cope, regroup, and start your life on a new path.* New York: Fireside.

Too, L. (2003). *Discover yourself.* Carlsbad, CA: Hay House, Inc.

Waitley, D. (1992). *The psychology of winning.* New York: Berkley.

Lifelong Learning

Bruno, F. J. (2001). *Going back to school: Survival strategies for adult students.* Lawrenceville, NJ: Thomson Learning, Inc.

Doolin, M. (2006). *The Success manual for adult college students.* Bangor, ME: Booklocker.com.

Phillips, V. (2000). *Never too late to learn: An adult student's guide to college.* New York: Princeton Review Publishing.

Siebert, A. (2008). *The adult student's guide to survival and success.* Portland, OR: Practical Psychology Press, Inc.

Mental and Physical Wellness

American Society of Health System Pharmacists and the Editors of Consumer Reports (2008). *Consumer drug reference 2008.* Yonkers, NY: Consumer Reports Books.

Casey, A., Benson, H. & MacDonald, A. (2004). *Mind your heart: A mind/body approach to stress management, exercise, and nutrition for heart health.* New York: Simon & Schuster Trade.

Cooper, C. L. & Cartwright, S. (1998). *Managing workplace stress.* Thousand Oaks, CA: Sage Publications.

Hay, L. & Gross. S. (2001). *Heal your body A-Z: The mental causes for physical illness and the way to overcome them.* Carlsbad, CA: Hay House, Inc.

McKhann, G. & Albert, M. (2002). *Keep your brain young.* New York: John Wiley & Sons.

Nichol, D. & Birchard, B. (2001). *The one-minute meditator: Relieving stress and finding meaning in everyday life.* Cambridge, MA: Perseus Publishing.

Oz, M. & Roisen, M. F. (2005). *You, the owner's manual: An insider's guide to the body that will make you healthier and younger.* New York: HarperCollins Publishers.

Reicher, G. & Burke, N. (1999). *Active wellness: 10 step program for a healthy body, mind & spirit.* New York: Time Life Custom Publishers.

Reichman, J. (2004). *Slow your clock down: The complete guide to a healthy, younger you.* New York: HarperCollins Publishers.

Rich, P., Copans, S. & Copans, K. (1999). *The healing journey through job loss: Your journal for reflection and revitalization.* New York: John Wiley & Sons.

Ryan, R. & Travis, J. (2004). *The wellness workbook.* Berkeley, CA: Ten Speed Press.

Sapolsky, R. M. (2004). *Why zebras don't get ulcers.* New York: Henry Holt & Company.

Tate, M. L. (2004). *"Sit and get" won't grow dendrites: 20 professional learning strategies that engage the adult brain.* Thousand Oaks, CA: Sage Publications.

Taub, E. A. (2000). *Balance your body, balance your life.* New York: Kensington Publishing.

Vaillant, G. E. (2002). *Aging Well.* Boston: Little, Brown and Company.

Weil, A. (2005). *Healthy aging: A lifelong guide to your physical and spiritual well-being.* New York: Knopf Publishing Group.

Whileman, T, Werghese, S. & Peterson, R. (1996). *The complete stress management workbook.* Grand Rapids, MI: Zondervan Publishing.

Willet, W. C. (2005). *Eat, drink and be healthy: The Harvard Medical School guide to healthy eating.* New York: Dell Publishing.

Financial Management

Bach, D. (2002) *Smart couples finish rich: 9 steps to creating a rich future for you and your partner.* New York: Broadway Books.

Chadzky, J. (2006). *Make money, not excuses: Wake up, take charge, and overcome your financial fears forever.* New York: Crown Publishing Group.

Chadzky, J. (2001). *Talking money.* NY: Warner Books.

Edelman, R. (2003). *Discover the wealth within you: A financial plan for creating a rich and fulfilling life.* New York: HarperCollins.

Orman, S. (2006). *Suze Orman's financial guidebook: Putting the 9 steps to work.* New York: Crown Publishing Group.

Orman, S. (2002). *The courage to be rich.* New York: Riverhead Books.

Retirement

Cullinane, J. & Fitzgerald, C. (2007). *The new retirement: The ultimate guide to the rest of your life.* New York: Rodale, Inc.

Egan, H. & Wagner, B. (2001). *I'm retiring, now what?* New York: Silver Lining Books.

Marston, S. (2002). *If not now, when? Reclaiming ourselves at midlife.* New York: Warner Books.

Schlossberg, N. (2004). *Retire smart, retire happy: Finding your true path in life.* Washington, DC: American Psychological Association.

Smith, M. H. & Smith, S. (2000). *101 secrets for a great retirement.* Chicago: Lowell House.

Trafford, A. (2004). *My time: Making the most of the rest of your life.* New York: Basic Books.

Waxman, B. & Mendelson, B. (2006). *How to love your retirement: Advice from hundreds of retirees.* Atlanta, GA: Hundreds of Heads Survival Guides.

Zelinski, E. J. (2004). *How to retire happy, wild, and free.* Berkeley, CA: Ten Speed Press.

Zelinski, E. J. (2003). *The joy of not working.* Berkeley, CA: Ten Speed Press.

Continuous Career
Options Listing

Add and delete career possibilities as you continue to do your research and informational interviewing. Keep track of your progress by reviewing this master list of careers. Happy career planning, now and in the future.

_____   _____

_____   _____

_____   _____

_____   _____

_____   _____

_____   _____

_____   _____

_____   _____

_____   _____

_____   _____

_____   _____

_____   _____

REFERENCES

American Society of Health System Pharmacists and the Editors of Consumer Reports (2008). *Consumer drug reference*. Yonkers, NY: Consumer Reports Books.

Aratani, L. RX for the brain: Move. In *The Washington Post*, December 4, 2007, p. F1.

Bloomfield, H. et al. (1977). *How to survive the loss of a love*. New York: Bantam Press.

Bolles, R. N. (2008). *What color is your parachute?* Berkeley, CA: Ten Speed Press.

Bolles, R. N. (1981). *The three boxes of life*. Berkeley, CA: Ten Speed Press.

Bolles, M. E. & Bolles, R. N. (2008). *Job hunting online: A guide to using job listings, message boards, research sites, the underweb, counseling, networking, self assessment tools, niche sites*. Berkeley, CA: Ten Speed Press.

Bridges, W. (2004). *Transitions: Making sense of life's changes* (2nd ed.). Cambridge, MA: Perseus Books.

Bridges, W. (2001). *The way of transition: Embracing life's most difficult moments*. Cambridge, MA: Perseus Books.

Bridges, W. (1994). *Job shift: How to prosper in a workplace without jobs*. Reading, MA: Addison-Wesley Publishing Co.

Brown, D & Brooks, L. (eds.). (1990). *Career choice and development* (2nd ed., pp. 308–337). San Francisco: Jossey-Bass.

Clayman, C. B. (ed.). (1989). *The American Medical Association encyclopedia of medicine*. New York: Random House.

Coles, R. (1993). *Call of service: Witness to idealism*. New York: Houghton Mifflin.

Covey, S. (1995). *First Things First*. New York: Simon and Schuster.

Dickel, M. R. & Roehm, F. E. (2008). *Guide to Internet job searching: 2008–2009 edition*. New York: McGraw-Hill.

Doyle, A. (2008). *Internet your way to a new job: How to really find a job online*. Cupertino, CA: HappyAbout.info.

Erikson, E. (1959). Identity and the life cycle. *Psychological Issues*, vol. 1, pp 1–171.

Fine, S. (1991). *Dictionary of cccupational titles* (4th ed.). Washington, DC: U.S. Department of Labor, Employment and Training Administration.

Frankl, V. (1946). *Man's search for meaning*. New York: Simon and Schuster.

Friedman, T. (2007). *The world is flat 3.0: A brief history of the 21st century*. New York: Picador.

Gilligan, C. (1983). *In a different voice*. Cambridge, MA: Harvard University Press.

Goleman, D. (2006). *Emotional intelligence: 10th anniversary edition*. New York: Bantam Press.

Gorman, T. (1996). *Multipreneuring: How to prosper in the emerging freelance economy*. New York: Fireside Publishing.

Happier and Healthier? *Consumer Reports on Health*, vol. 16, no. 3: 1–6. Yonkers, NY: Consumer Reports.

Herr, E. L., and Cramer, S. H. (1988). *Career guidance and counseling through the lifespan*. Boston: Scott Foresman.

Higdon, H. (1986). Newest research tells us: If you want long life, exercise. *50 Plus*, August, p. 17.

Holland, J. L. (1997). *Making vocational choices: A theory of vocational personalities and work environments* (3rd ed.). Odessa, FL: Psychological Assessment Resources.

Hudson, F. M. (1997). *The Adult Years: Mastering the art of self-renewal*. San Francisco: Jossey-Bass.

Krannich, R. L. and Krannich, C. R. (1998). *Best jobs for the 21st century*. Manassas Park, VA: Impact Publications.

Krumboltz, J. D. & Levin, A. S. (2004). *Luck is no accident: Making the most of happenstance in your life and career*. Atascadero, CA: Impact Publishers.

Lathrop, R. (1981). *Who's hiring who*. Berkeley, CA: Ten Speed Press.

Levinson, D. J. (1986). *The seasons of a man's life*. New York: Ballantine Books.

Maslow, A. (1970). *Motivation and personality* (2nd ed.). New York: Harper & Row.

Myers, I. B. with Myers, P. B. (1995). *Gifts differing: Understanding personality type*. Palo Alto, CA: Davies-Black.

Osipow, S. H. (1983). *Theories of career development*. Englewood Cliffs, NJ: Prentice-Hall.

Pausch, R. (2008). *The last lecture*. CA: Hyperion Publishing.

Perun, P. J. & Bielby, D. D. (1980). Structure and dynamics of the individual life course. In K.W. Black (ed.). *Life course: Integrative theories and exemplary populations* (pp. 97–120). Boulder, CO: Westview Press.

Pink, D. (2006). *A whole new mind: Why right-brainers will rule the future*. NJ: Penguin Group USA.

Rifkin, J. (1995). *The end of work*. New York: G.P. Putnam & Sons.

Rowe, J. W. & Kahn, R. L. (1998). *Successful aging*. New York: Dell Publishing.

Satir, V. (1975). *Self-esteem*. Palo Alto, CA: Celestial Arts.

Schlossberg, N. (1981). A model for analyzing human adaptation to transition. *The Counseling Psychologist*, vol. 9, no. 2.

Schlossberg, N., Troll, L. & Leibowitz, Z. (1978). *Perspectives on counseling adults: Issues and skills*. Monterey, CA: Brooks/Cole.

Sheehy, G. (1977). *Passages: Predictable crises of adult life*. New York: Bantam-Doubleday.

Simon, S. B. (1989). *Getting unstuck: Breaking through the barriers to change*. New York: Warner.

Super, D. E. (1957). *The psychology of careers*. New York: Harper-Collins.

Super, D. E., Savickas, M. L. & Super, C. M. (1996). The lifespan, lifespace approach to careers. In D. Brown and L. Brooks (eds.) *Career choice and development* (3rd ed., pp 121–178). San Francisco: Jossey-Bass.

Swanson, J. L. & Fouad, N. A. (1999). *Career theory and practice: Learning through case studies*. Thousand Oaks, CA: Sage Publications.

Tiedeman, D. V. & Miller-Tiedeman, A. (1990). Career decision-making: An individualistic perspective. In D. Brown and L. Brooks (eds.) *Career choice and development* (2nd ed., pp. 308–337). San Francisco: Jossey-Bass.

Troutman, K. K. (2007). *Federal resume guidebook* (4th ed.). Indianapolis, IN: JIST Works.

Van Gennep, A. (1960). *The rites of passage*. Chicago: University of Chicago Press.

Online resource:

Managesmarter: *15 Personal Skills You Need on the Job* (2006). www.presentations.com/msg/content_display/training/e3ied0764c52ea0c6b7a858277ba7f9e652?imw=Y

INDEX

resources for, 72–73
self-esteem tree analysis, 57–58
sources of, 53–55
Self-evaluation, 36–41
Self-management skills, 32–34, 236–237
Self-renewal qualities, 87–89
Self-satisfaction, 16
Senge, P., 107
SIGI software, 22
Simon, S., 60
Skills and abilities analysis, 24–25
communication skills and abilities, 36–37
functional skills, 34–36
physical skills and abilities, 39–41
self-evaluation of, 36–38
self-management skills, 32–34
successes, analysis of, 27–31
successes, listing of, 25–26
technical skills and abilities, 39
work content skills, 41
work success skills, 235–237
Social personality type, 19
Special-needs support groups, 102–103
Spengler, O., 118
Spielberg, S., 80
State-level resources, 22–23
Sternberg, R., 80
Stress, 255
management of, 256–257
perceptions of/reactions to, 255–256
reduction of, 257–258
Strong Interest Inventory (SII), 21, 129, 144
Successful Aging, 288
Suddarth, B., 223
Support systems
institutional/community networks, 91
interpersonal networks, 103–104, 293–294
mentors, 105–107
support elements, making changes, 311
support groups, 102–103
transitions management, 91–92
See also Influence of others
Surviving Corporate Transition, 77

Technical skills, 39
Technology in the workplace, 78, 193, 194, 202
Telecommuting, 83, 228
Telephone-based job interviews, 227
Thorson, J., 80
Time factor, 14–16, 178, 190
action planning and, 246–247

allocation challenges, 244
crisis activities and, 244
interruptions and, 244
job campaigns, 189–190
job satisfaction, consciousness of time and, 243–246
planning activities and, 246–247
self-care, time management techniques and, 254–256
time analysis, 244–246
time wasters and, 245, 246
Training requirements, 151
Transition process, 84
change *vs.* transition, phases of, 84–85
defined, 84, 89
individual perception of transition and, 89–90
negotiating effectively, 89
oncoming change, clues to, 84
personal characteristics and, 90–91
process framework for, 84
response to change and, 85
self-renewing adults, qualities of, 87–89
support systems and, 91
worksheet for, 86
See also Change processes; Risk-taking
Transitions: Making Sense of Life's Changes, 77, 84
Truman, H. S., 79, 278

Values. *See* Personal values; Work values
Van Gennep, A., 84
Vocational Information and Occupational Coordinating Committees (VOICC), 22
Volunteer work, 134, 151, 179, 199, 215

Washington, B. T., 112
The Way of Transition, 77
Web sites. *See* Internet resources
Well being. *See* Balanced lifestyle; Lifestyle checkup
What Color is Your Parachute, 24–25
A Whole New Mind, 77
Willett, W., 290
Work checkup, 259
expectations analysis, 263–264
ideal work goal, reassessment of, 266–267
people contacts checklist, 261–262
positives/negatives, listing of, 264–265
work activities checklist, 262–263
work environment checklist, 260–261
See also Job satisfaction; Lifestyle checkup
Work content skills, 41

CPSIA information can be obtained
at www.ICGtesting.com
Printed in the USA
LVOW05s1038060118

562053LV00004B/11/P

9 780757 560484